McKinley Park Branch
1915 West 35th Street
Chicago, Illinois 60609

P9-CRA-058

TESTING! TESTING!

WHAT EVERY PARENT SHOULD KNOW ABOUT SCHOOL TESTS

W. JAMES POPHAM

UNIVERSITY OF CALIFORNIA, LOS ANGELES

ALLYN AND BACON

BOSTON • LONDON • TORONTO • SYDNEY • TOKYO • SINGAPORE

Vice President: *Paul A. Smith*
Editorial Assistant: *Shannon Morrow*
Marketing Manager: *Jeff Lasser*
Editorial Production Service: *Chestnut Hill Enterprises, Inc.*
Manufacturing Buyer: *Julie McNeill*
Cover Administrator: *Linda Knowles*

Copyright © 2000 by Allyn & Bacon
A Pearson Education Company
160 Gould Street
Needham Heights, MA 02494

Internet: www.abacon.com

All rights reserved. No part of the material protected by this copyright notice may be reproduced or utilized in any form or by any means, electronic or mechanical, including photocopying, recording, or by any information storage and retrieval system, without written permission from the copyright holder.

Between the time Website information is gathered and published, some sites may have closed. Also, the transcription of URLs can result in typographical errors. The publisher would appreciate notification where these occur so that they may be corrected in subsequent editions.

Library of Congress Cataloging-in-Publication Data

Popham, W. James.
    Testing! Testing! : what every parent should know about school
tests / W. James Popham.
        p.   cm.
    ISBN 0-205-30595-4
    1. Educational tests and measurements–United States Handbooks,
manuals, etc.   I. Title.
    LB3051.p6144   2000
    371.26'0973–dc21   99-37785
                                                                CIP

Printed in the United States of America

10 9 8 7 6 5 4 3 2 1   04 03 02 01 00 99

Cartoons: Joan Orme

CONTENTS

PREFACE

*T*his is a book written for parents who want to improve their children's educational experiences. It's a book about school testing. I've tried to keep the book's content as simple as I can, but even I am reluctant to characterize the book as a "fun read." It has neither a plot nor a story line. And the book's main character is *you*.

Even though the book deals with an important topic, I've tried to maintain a light writing style, tossing in an occasional bit of whimsy to keep you alert. You'll also find a number of test-related cartoons to make the book somewhat more parent-palatable. If you read only the cartoons, however, you may miss much of the book's content.

Let me be clear about one thing. I want parents to read this book. School testing has, in recent decades, become really significant stuff. School testing now influences what teachers teach, how educators are evaluated, and whether children are successful in school. Parents should be playing pivotal roles regarding the use of school tests. But parents can't really participate as they should in dealing with school tests if they are uninformed about school testing.

Informed parents, however, can make an enormous difference in the way that educational tests are used. If you finish this book, you'll be in a position to make a genuine contribution to your own child's education—and to the education of your child's classmates.

I've been wanting to write this book for a number of years now. I think both the topic (school testing) and the audience (parents) are as important as they come.

During three decades as a faculty member in the UCLA Graduate School of Education, I've written a good many books. (Professors are supposed to do that.) But I've never tried to write a more potentially useful book than this.

I hope you'll read this book about school tests from cover to cover. If you do, you'll not immediately move to a higher tax bracket, but it will help your child get a better education.

W. J. P.

R06066 06915

Testing! Testing!

1

SCHOOL TESTS—WHY SHOULD PARENTS CARE?

*T*his book is intended to help parents understand more about the tests their children must take in school. If you've just started to read the book, it's likely that you're a parent—and that you have one or more school-age children. Moreover, you've sensed that you probably ought to know something about school testing. If you have, you've passed *your* first test about testing!

In this opening chapter, I'm going to identify the reasons that parents really *do* need to know about the different kinds of tests their children are required to take in school. As you'll discover, parents who are more familiar with school tests, given to students almost on a daily basis these days, will be parents who can help their children get the most out of school. And that's not a bad outcome.

I'm really pleased that you've decided to learn about school testing. It's an especially important topic these days. That's because, in the past decade or so, both the frequency and the *significance* of educational testing have risen dramatically. Go back a generation or two, and you'll find that even then there were a fair number of school tests dished out by teachers. But the results of those tests played a much less important role in determining a child's future. Now, all sorts of pivotal decisions hinge on how well children perform on school tests. And that, in general, is why parents need to understand what takes place when their children take a test in school. Today's educational testing has become a major determiner of your child's school success.

A Parent-to-Parent Pledge

I have four children. Fortunately, they've all finished their schooling, so I now need less anxiety-reduction medication. But I still have the scars to prove that I hovered and worried while one daughter and three sons trudged through educationland. I vividly recall those father–son and father–daughter talks about school. (Daughters are, in my experience, infinitely easier to work with than sons—not only in school-related matters, but in all realms of life.) There was frequently a fair amount of tension as I tried to be a helpful parent, especially about school-related issues. Being a helpful parent, as you already know, can be tough duty.

Accordingly, I'm going to offer you a parent-to-parent pledge. (Grandparents and guardians are also covered by this warranty.) Here it is: *I'll keep the book's content as simple as possible.* There's no reason that testing needs to be made all that technical or all that numerical. Actually, as you'll see, the basis of school testing is really just plain common sense, but common sense that all too often gets shrouded in unnecessary complexity. It needn't be.

I've been working in the field of school testing for more than thirty years, most of that time as a professor in the UCLA Graduate School of Education. I've taught hundreds of teachers and teachers-in-training how to build and use educational tests. But in recent years, because of the increased importance given to school testing, I've been spending much more time providing parents with the key information they need to know about educational testing. It was those conversations with parents that stimulated me to write a book for parents about school testing.

In this book, then, I promise to keep the concepts as nontechnical and as number-free as I can. I also pledge not to shovel more information about testing at you than you, as a busy parent, really need to know. The book is intended to transform you into a test-knowledgeable parent, *not* a testing expert. Besides that, if you regard the book as too off-putting, you'll be likely to set it aside. The book's publisher won't like that. Neither will I.

Why Learn about Testing

Later on in this first chapter, I'll describe several ways you can actually use the knowledge about school tests you'll be acquiring from this book. But before that, let me supply a few answers to the important question, "Why does a parent need to know *anything* about school testing?" There are four appropriate responses to that question, the first of which flows from the value of parental involvement.

Parental Involvement That Pays Off

During the past decade or so, educational researchers have concluded that one of the most important factors determining a child's success in school is the amount of *parental involvement* in that child's education. Simply put, a substantial set of research studies makes it clear that if children's parents display meaningful concern about their child's school experiences, children will be far more successful in school and, most likely, in life.

Parental involvement that pays off, however, must be genuine. Parents who are not genuinely involved sometimes ask their children, almost ritualistically, "How did it go at school today?" If that's the extent of a parent's involvement, then it's really pretty superficial involvement. *Genuine* parental involvement means that you really need to spend enough time with your child to acquire a reasonably accurate picture of what your child is experiencing in school. Ideally, you need to be involved in your child's education on a day-to-day basis, or as close to that as you can manage.

The message an involved parent communicates to a child is enormously powerful: "What you are going through at school is important stuff—it's so important that it's worth my time to find out about what's happening to you at school." That message almost always supplies solid educational motivation for students. Children typically conclude that if their parents think what's taking place at school is worthwhile, then school must surely be worthwhile. And if children think school is worthwhile, then those children will be more likely to put out meaningful effort at school. And effort, educational researchers tell us, is the most important determiner of how well children will do in school. That includes your child.

Parental involvement with school needs to take place as soon as a child scurries off to kindergarten or preschool. The parent's signal to the child must be unmistakably clear: *What you are experiencing at school is significant.* It is so significant that I want you to keep me up-to-date on what's happening to you in school.

As a parent, you are almost certainly a busy person. I've known few parents who suffered significant boredom induced by excessive leisure hours. So you might be wondering, "Where is the time coming from that I'm supposed to devote to this parent involvement?" The answer is simple: you must get cunning. (Parents, because they are much older than their children, have the potential to be far more cunning.)

You need to use what is otherwise downtime to get *efficiently* involved in your child's schooling. For example, when you're waiting in line with your child at a grocery store, you could ask, "What's happening with that group project you're doing in social studies?" or "Tell me what you're up to in science these days?" Then, on the way home, follow up by asking, "How are you feeling about your part in the social studies project," or "Are you satisfied with your level of effort in science?"

Surely, there'll be other opportunities for school involvement at home, some of which may actually involve sitting down for several minutes to explore your child's understanding of what's happening in mathematics or language arts. Your interest always must be authentic. Remember, you're trying to communicate the *honest* perception that you care about what's going on in school. Children are remarkably skilled in spotting parental insincerity.

You need to *listen, understand,* and *remember.* Your child will be genuinely impressed if you *listen,* then ask clarifying questions until you *understand,* and *remember* what you've learned. The next time you talk about school, you won't need to start from scratch. Suppose a child hears you ask questions such as, "Wasn't today the first day of your group reports in geography; how did they go?" That child will correctly conclude that *My parent really is on top of what's happening to me in school.* If there's one, single thing you can do to improve the likelihood of your child's educational success, it will be to become genuinely involved in the child's school experiences.

Especially these days, with educational tests playing an increasingly significant role in what your child is going through at school, to be *fully* involved in your child's schooling, you simply can't leave out educational testing. There are, of course, teacher-made tests that influence the grades your child will receive. In addition, however, the results of those classroom

tests will typically be used by teachers to determine the kinds of instructional activities your child receives. This means the nature of the instruction your child experiences often can be directly traced to classroom tests and the way your child performs on them.

Then there are the nationally standardized achievement tests being used so often these days to measure a school's effectiveness, and sometimes even a teacher's effectiveness. These tests, and the preparation your child receives to get ready for such tests, also play an important role in shaping what goes on at school.

You'll find that educators these days often refer to *high-stakes tests.* A high-stakes educational test is one for which students' performances have important consequences, either for students or for the educators who taught them.

One common type of high-stakes test is a high school graduation exam that must be passed before a student receives a high-school diploma. A number of states currently use such examinations. Any test whose results can significantly influence a student's educational career, such as a grade-to-grade promotion test, is a high-stakes test.

But tests can also be high-stakes if their results are used to arrive at conclusions about the quality of teachers or school administrators. Suppose a state's education officials have constructed a basic skills test that is administered to students in every grade starting at grade three. If results of this annual test are released in the state's newspapers so that school-by-school rankings are possible, it's definitely a high-stakes test.

What parents need to recognize is the enormous *instructional* impact that high-stakes tests can have. This is illustrated in Figure 1.1, where you can see that the content of an important, high-stakes test serves as an instructional magnet. Whatever content is tested in a high-stakes test gets taught by teachers. It will get taught in your child's classroom as well.

There are other sorts of tests your child is likely to be given while in school, for example, *attitude inventories* that measure children's attitudes toward specific subjects such as math and science. There also may be *confidence inventories* that gauge children's personal confidence as writers or speakers. You'll learn about such tests in this book.

My point is this: You can't be adequately involved in your child's education if the topic of school testing is off-limits. And school testing *will* be off-limits to you if you don't know anything more about such testing than what you recall from your own school days. Educational testing has become not only more important in recent years, but it is almost certainly different from what you recall when you were a student. In short, there are new things to be learned about educational testing. You need to know those things.

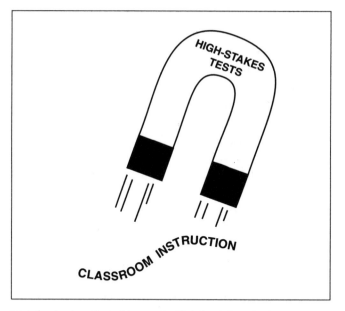

1.1 The instructional impact of high-stakes tests

If your involvement in your child's education is ongoing, you'll en-counter many instances in which your child's education hinges on how the child performed on a test. For you to fully understand what's involved in those situations, you need to have a reasonable understanding of the kind of testing that's going on.

So, if you're going to provide "full-service" parental involvement in your child's schooling, such involvement definitely depends on your fa-miliarity with the nature of the school tests your child is required to take. Therefore, the first reason you need to learn about school testing is that it will allow you to become more fully involved with your child's educa-tional experiences.

Two-Way Communication with Teachers and Administrators

One-way communication isn't all that wonderful. Parents don't like to be lectured to by educators. Educators don't like to be lectured to by parents. There will be frequent times when you may want to discuss your child's progress with the child's teacher or even with the school's principal. In those parent–educator exchanges, what's needed is genuine two-way com-munication.

There is nothing more likely to stifle an effective parent–teacher communication than when one communicator is talking about something that's a total mystery to the other communicator. So, when parent–educator conversations take place, those conversations should remain two-way throughout, and not be transformed into one-way educator monologue whenever the topic of educational testing comes up.

Parents should not be intimidated when teachers talk about results of the tests children take in schools. No topic of educational significance to a child should be excluded merely because the teacher knows things that the parent doesn't. The topic of educational testing is all too often a prohibited topic for parents. It shouldn't be.

As you'll see in this book, there's nothing all that technical about educational testing. Basic common sense is all that a parent requires in order to converse meaningfully with educators about testing, but that common sense will need to be bolstered by the parent's familiarity with (1) a handful of fundamental measurement concepts, and (2) a modest amount of testing terminology. You'll learn about both of these in the chapters to follow.

So, the second reason that parents should become conversant with the "mysteries" of educational testing is that parents need to be able to carry on meaningful two-directional communications with the teachers and administrators who educate their children.

A parent needs to be able to address important test-related issues using concepts and terms that educators understand. For instance, a test-knowledgeable parent will, with understanding, be able to ask a teacher, "Why is my daughter's percentile rank on the district norms so much higher than her percentile rank on the national norms?"

A parent also needs to be able to comprehend what educators are saying when they engage in any sort of testing talk. For instance, suppose a teacher tells you that, "Your son's year-to-year progress on the district mathematics test, although variable, is well within the test's standard error of measurement." You need to understand what the teacher is talking about. If you knew what is meant by a test's "standard error of measurement," you'd readily understand. Productive two-way communications between parents and educators are likely to occur only if both parties understand what's being said.

Let me pause for a moment to provide you with an important tip: *Do not assume that your child's teacher, or even your child's principal, understands all that much about educational testing.* In many locales, teachers-in-training or administrators-in-training are not required to take *any* coursework in educational testing. Sometimes the graduate programs for educators devote only a few weeks to the study of school testing. It's possible that when you finish this book, you'll know *considerably* more about educational testing than the educator with whom you're communicating.

It has been said that, "A little knowledge is a dangerous thing." That little knowledge can be even more dangerous if a *somewhat* knowledgeable parent is working with an educator who has *no* knowledge. Along the way, I'll supply you with suggestions about how to deal tactfully with educators who know less than you do about testing.

To restate this second reason why you need to learn about educational testing: You really can't be *an effective advocate* for your child if you know little about school tests and how they work. If you want your two-way communications with educators to turn out well for your child, you need to know what makes educational tests tick.

Avoiding the Misuse of Standardized Test Scores

A third reason you need to understand more about educational testing is that there's a widespread misapplication of standardized test results these days, and some of those misapplications may bear directly on your own judgments about the effectiveness of your child's school, and even your child's teachers.

In most communities, it is now a common practice to rank schools according to each school's scores on some sort of nationally standardized test. These rankings are typically published in local newspapers. The high-ranked schools are regarded as effective; the low-ranked schools are regarded as ineffective. In recent years, in fact, the lowest ranked schools are being routinely designated as "failing," "weak," or "poor" schools. The teachers and administrators who operate those schools, as a consequence, are often regarded as "failing," " weak," or "poor."

This is an altogether *inappropriate* use of students' scores on standardized tests. You need to understand why it is so wrong-headed when people evaluate a school's instructional effectiveness based on its students' standardized test scores. If your child goes to a school where the school's standardized tests scores are super, this does not *necessarily* signify that good instruction is taking place in that school. And, on the flip side, if the students in your child's school aren't scoring all that well on standardized achievement tests, this does not *necessarily* mean that the school's educators are ineffective.

Almost all parents, and most educational policymakers (such as members of local or state school boards) assume that students' scores on standardized tests reflect the quality of the instruction being provided to students. That assumption is dead wrong. Parents need to understand why. You need to understand why so that you don't get sucked into this common, but nonetheless incorrect interpretation of students' scores on standardized tests.

If you recognize the appropriate and inappropriate uses of students' standardized test scores, you'll then be in a position to employ the results of these tests to make more defensible decisions about your child's education. In Chapter 3, you'll learn why standardized test scores should not be used to evaluate instructional quality. In Chapter 11, you'll learn how teachers, placed in an untenable situation where they are pressured to boost students' standardized test scores, sometimes resort to score-boosting practices that will have a negative effect on your child's education.

If you understand why it is that standardized test scores provide a distorted picture of educators' effectiveness, then you can help teachers avoid the test-score-trap in which they now find themselves. If you do, then teachers can discard the educationally unsound score-boosting practices now seen with such increased frequency.

As you'll find out in Chapter 11, teachers are not villains who choose to engage in wrongful test-preparation practices. On the contrary, *classroom teachers are the victims* of a flawed framework for evaluating schools. To the extent that you learn why it is that standardized tests are unsound indicators of educational quality, you can supply badly needed support for teachers—including those who teach your child. You can help educate other parents about the misuse of standardized test scores as indicators of educational quality.

Interpreting Your Child's Performance on Standardized Tests

I just pointed out that students' standardized test scores should not be used to make judgments about the quality of schools or teachers. But there *is* an appropriate role for standardized tests, and that role deals specifically with your child's relative strengths and weaknesses.

With few exceptions, after a child completes a standardized test, the child's parents receive a report of the child's test performance. Even though the publishers of standardized tests try to make these reports readily interpretable, the reports often remain mystifying for many parents. As a consequence, some parents regard their children's standardized test-reports with the same glee they'd display if asked to decipher Egyptian hieroglyphics.

If a test-report informs you that your child "scored in the first *stanine* on a standardized test," is that good or bad? If a test-report informs you that your child earned "a grade-equivalent score of 6.4," should you be happy or sad? Clearly, if you find your child's standardized test score reports to be so complex that you can't make sense out of them, you'll be unable to secure the insights that, like undiscovered treasures, are sometimes hidden in those reports. In Chapter 4, you'll learn how to make sense out of your child's standardized test-reports.

To review, then, I've trotted out four reasons why parents need to learn more about educational testing. Those four reasons are represented graphically in Figure 1.2. As you can see, the four reasons are so that you can (1) engage in more complete educational involvement with your child, (2) take part in more meaningful two-way communication with teachers and administrators, (3) avoid misusing standardized test results to evaluate the quality of your child's education, and (4) accurately interpret your own child's performances on standardized tests.

This Book's Objectives

It's fairly common practice these days for teachers to plan their lessons only after first identifying the student outcomes that they intend the

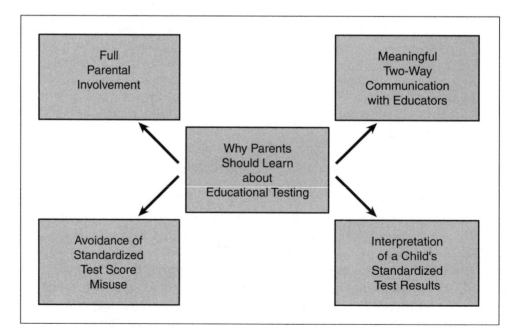

1.2 Four reasons why parents should become more knowledgeable regarding educational tests

lessons to accomplish. Typically, these intended outcomes are referred to as the "instructional objectives" that it is hoped students will achieve. Quite frequently, teachers inform their students of the nature of these instructional objectives before teaching gets underway. This is done so that students can then focus their attention on what, in the teacher's view, is most instructionally important.

Well, because we're dealing in this book with an educational topic, it seems only appropriate for me to spell out what my objectives are for the book. I'll conclude this first chapter by informing you of what I hope will be accomplished by your reading this book. I'll also provide a brief preview of how I hope those objectives will be attained.

Objective 1: An Increase in Test-Related Knowledge

The book's first objective is to expand your knowledge about educational testing—the kind of educational testing that bears directly on your child's success in school. "Knowledge" refers to your acquisition of key information regarding educational testing. To help promote this increased knowledge, the next chapter will describe the most fundamental concepts underlying educational testing. Then there will be other chapters that describe the nuts and bolts of educational testing, not only of the traditional sort, but also several innovations in educational testing. After finishing those chapters, you'll know a good deal about the most likely types of tests your child is apt to encounter in school.

Along the way, I'll be introducing you to certain terms that you'll need to understand if you're going to be a test-knowledgeable parent. Whenever a word or phrase is really significant to your understanding of educational testing, I'll put it in the margin with the label, *Testing Terms,* plus a brief definition. I'll also define those terms in the text itself, but as a reminder of the really significant terminology to master, you'll find an in-margin glossary provided throughout the book.

If you don't really care to become familiar with the kinds of testing terms I've placed in the in-margin definitions, that's fine. Just read on without giving those terms a second glance. If, however, you want to possess a working knowledge of educational testing's truly important terms, then you should find the in-margin *Testing Terms* helpful.

Let me be frank. I want you to learn enough about testing so that you can be an effective advocate for your child, especially when you interact with your child's teachers or school administrators. I've been selective, but I've tried to identify the key testing terms you'll need so that you won't become intimidated if some teacher or administrator tosses a few technical testing terms your way. If you know what those terms mean, you'll be sur-

prised at how the level of the dialogue will get raised. And that's what you want, a high-level dialogue focused on what's educationally best for your child.

Do you have to learn all of the content you'll read about in this book? Absolutely not! So, to help you identify the truly significant content in each chapter, starting with Chapter 2, I'll close out each chapter with a brief summary of *What Do You Really Need to Know about This Chapter's Content?"* In these end-of-chapter summaries, I'll isolate what you really *need to know.* Hopefully, you'll acquire some other *nice-to-know* information about testing as you read the book. However, what you truly need to take away from a chapter will be staked out at the end of each chapter. If you combine these end-of-chapter summaries and the in-margin *Testing Terms,* you'll be able to accomplish Objective 1 with little difficulty.

And, after you've read the book, if you simply keep it on the shelf as a reference, you can use the index at the book's conclusion if you ever need to look up particular topics.

Objective 2: Acquisition of Test-Related Skills

In addition to your acquisition of key knowledge regarding educational testing, there are several important test-related *skills* you need to master.

The first of these skills is to be able to communicate about educational testing to the educators who are responsible for your child's progress in school. You'll find that, on occasion, you'll also need to communicate with other parents who, like you, are concerned about their children's education.

To increase your *test-related communication skill,* in many chapters I'll provide *A Parent Puzzle* for you to solve. Each puzzle is an exercise consisting of a partially completed fictitious dialogue either between (1) an educator and parent, such as might take place at a back-to-school night for parents, (2) a parent and other parents, such as might take place over a morning cup of coffee as parents discuss their children's school or teachers, or (3) a parent and a child. I'll chop off the dialogue *before* it ends, then ask you to decide what you'd say next if *you* were taking part in the dialogue.

There will be many ways for a parent to say something appropriate, and usually an equal number of ways for a parent to say something inappropriate. *After* you've tried to think of what you might say, you can look at the bottom of the *A Parent Puzzle* and see what I'd recommend that a parent should (and shouldn't) say. In all *A Parent Puzzle*s, I've used student names that would fit either a boy or girl. I hope this will make it easier for you to project yourself into the role of the parent in these practice dialogues.

A second skill I hope you'll acquire is the ability to explain to others (parents or educators) why standardized tests should *not* be used to judge instructional quality. After learning (in Chapter 3) about why students' performances on such tests are not an appropriate indication of educational quality, you can try your hand at *A Parent Puzzle* that deals with this misuse of standardized tests.

A third skill you'll need is the ability to interpret your child's standardized-test-score reports. In Chapter 4, I'll explain how these reports work and describe the ways that test publishers try to let parents know how their children have performed. After looking over Chapter 4's examples, you should be able to apply your newly acquired interpretive skills to reports from any standardized test that's used with your child.

There are several other test-related skills that you are likely to acquire as you read the book, but these three are the most pertinent for parents who wish to help their children make appropriate progress in school.

Objective 3: Increased Confidence regarding Educational Testing

The third and final objective for the book really hinges on the first two, that is, your acquisition of test-related knowledge and skills. As a consequence of enhancing your knowledge and skills about educational tests, you should find that your confidence regarding educational testing should increase sharply. As a consequence, you'll be more likely to carry out some important test-related activities regarding your child's education because you'll be more self-assured in your own test-related knowledge and skills. There's a strong relationship between people's confidence and their willingness to act. With greater confidence about educational testing, you'll be more likely to get suitably involved in the testing side of your child's schooling.

Starting with Chapter 2, you'll find *Possible Parent Action–Options* at the close of each chapter. What I try to do is lay out a few things you might care to do based on the chapter you've just finished reading. Many readers, of course, will choose to take no action whatsoever. Quite properly, they'll simply be in a better position to deal with educational testing if the chapter's topic ever comes up in connection with their child's education.

However, if you do want to undertake one or more activities based on a particular chapter, there'll be several options from which you can make selections. Obviously, the more confidence about educational testing that you have, the more likely it is you'll care to undertake any of the *Possible Parent Action–Options* set forth at the close of each chapter.

One choice that will routinely be included in each chapter's *Possible Parent Action–Options* is for you to refer your child's teacher or, more frequently, the principal in your child's school to one or more of the items cited in each subsequent chapter's *Suggested Resources for Your Child's Teacher or Principal.*

Each chapter's short list of books, articles, and videotapes is intended to supply you with an easily followed action–option if you want the educators who work with your child to know more about the topic treated in the chapter. Clearly, it would be inappropriate for you to try to teach such educators about the content of the chapters you'll soon be reading. School administrators and teachers are quite understandably reluctant to be lectured to by a "layperson" who's had no special training in education. But if you really believe that your child's educators should learn more about a given topic, then one *nonconfrontational* option you might employ is to simply bring their attention to a given book, article, or videotape. You can point out you've been reading about school tests in a book written for parents, and wondered if they'd be interested in the same topic, but in a resource more relevant to the concerns of professional educators than parents.

I'll offer some suggestions later in the book about how to encourage educators to consult these resources without offending them. You do not want to "get in the face " of an educator who works with your child. However, *tactful* isolation of relevant resources can sometimes work well.

In many instances, it will make more sense to bring some of a chapter's resources to the attention of your child's school principal or assistant principal who can, if it seems appropriate, then relay those resources to your child's teacher.

Your confidence about educational testing should increase as you read on in the book. However, you might want to see whether your test-related confidence actually has been enhanced after you complete the book. At the end of this chapter on page 18, you'll find an *Educational Testing Preliminary Confidence Inventory.* At the book's close, on page 279, you'll find an *Educational Testing Final Confidence Inventory.* There are no right or wrong answers for these inventories. Instead, the inventories simply try to find out how confident you would be if you were called on to carry out certain activities regarding educational testing.

If you wish to do so, you might complete the preliminary inventory immediately, score it, then complete the final inventory after you've finished the book. You can see if there was, in fact, a meaningful boost in your personal confidence about engaging in the activities related to educational testing that are identified in the inventories. Because only *you* will complete the two confidence inventories, no one except you even needs to know how your scores turned out. If you're really somewhat paranoid, complete both inventories behind locked doors.

To repeat, the three major instructional objectives that I hope this book will accomplish are portrayed in Figure 1.3. I hope you'll achieve those three objectives because, if you do, you can participate more effectively in your child's education. When you interact with educators or other parents about school-related testing, you'll really know what you're talking about. And, as a result, some better educational decisions will be made about children.

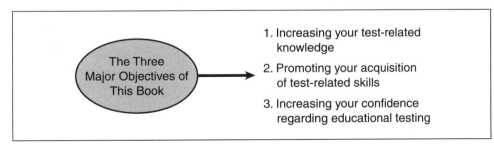

1.3 The chief instructional objectives of *Testing! Testing!*

Review

In this first chapter, four reasons were given for parents to learn more about educational testing. They were, briefly, to (1) provide more complete parental involvement in your child's education, (2) carry out meaningful two-way communication with educators, (3) avoid misusing standardized tests to evaluate educational quality, and (4) interpret your child's standardized test results.

The book's three major objectives are focused on your increased knowledge, skills, and confidence regarding educational testing. A preview was provided of how these objectives would be promoted. In all subsequent chapters, each chapter will be concluded with a brief summary, that is, *What Do You Really Need to Know about This Chapter's Content?* Each chapter will also contain follow-up activities in which you might engage *(Possible Parent Action–Options)* and a set of relevant resources that might be of interest to your child's teacher or school administrator *(Suggested Resources for Your Child's Teacher or Principal)*.

At the chapter's close, you'll find the previously described *Educational Testing Preliminary Confidence Inventory.* If you want to complete the inventory at this point, to help evaluate your potentially increasing confidence as you read the book, please do so. Remember, a final version of this confidence inventory is provided at the end of the book.

Whether or not you complete the confidence inventory, you're ready to move on to Chapter 2 and begin learning about the nature of educational testing. Remember, the more you learn about school testing, the more you'll be able to help with your child's education. That's a goal worth accomplishing.

SUGGESTED RESOURCES FOR YOUR CHILD'S TEACHER OR PRINCIPAL

Printed Materials

McMillan, James H. *Classroom Assessment: Principles and Practice for Effective Instruction.* Boston: Allyn and Bacon, 1997. *Chapter 1 of this introductory volume about classroom assessment raises a series of important assessment-related issues for educators to consider.*

Popham, W. James. "School-Site Assessment: What Principals Need to Know." *Principal*, 75, no. 2 (November 1995): 38–40. *This brief article identifies the assessment competencies that school principals really ought to possess.*

Rothman, Robert. *Measuring Up: Standards, Assessment, and School Reform.* San Francisco: Jossey-Bass Publishers, 1995. *In this book one of the nation's most perceptive educational reporters describes, with clarity and objectivity, how a reconceptualization of educational assessment could dramatically transform education.*

Weber, Ellen. *Student Assessment That Works: A Practical Approach.* Boston: Allyn and Bacon, 1999. *In Chapter 1 of this practical guidebook about student assessment, the author describes a model for student assessment based on a collaboration among parents, students, and teachers.*

Videotape Programs

IOX Assessment Associates. *Title I Assessment: What Educators Need to Know.* (5301 Beethoven St., Ste. 190, Los Angeles, CA 90066). *This video is of interest only to educators who staff a Title I school. The federal assessment requirements linked to Title I programs are described.*

National Council on Measurement in Education. *The ABCs of School Testing.* Washington, DC (1230 17th St., NW, Washington, DC 20036). *Although intended to assist parents in understanding the many uses of testing in schools today, this introductory video also provides educators with a succinct overview of the role of assessment in schools.*

Northwest Regional Educational Laboratory. *Facing the Challenges of a New Era of Educational Assessment.* IOX Assessment Associates (5301 Beethoven St., Ste. 190, Los Angeles, CA 90066). *Viewers learn how the nature of educational assessment has changed over the years. Suggestions are given about the ways educators can best allocate their limited assessment dollars and energies.*

Northwest Regional Educational Laboratory. *Understanding the Meaning and Importance of Quality Classroom Assessment.* IOX Assessment Associates (5301 Beethoven St., Ste. 190, Los Angeles, CA 90066). *Educators learn how to decide what should be assessed and how to avoid assessment problems.*

Educational Testing: Preliminary Confidence Inventory

Directions: This inventory is designed to measure the confidence you would have in carrying out certain activities related to educational testing. There are no right or wrong answers, so please answer honestly. Below, at the left, are 10 things a parent might be called on to do. If *you* were required to carry out each activity, indicate how confident you would be by circling the appropriate response for that activity using the following scheme:

VC =	FC =	LC =	NC =
Very Confident	Fairly Confident	A Little Confident	Not Confident at All

If *you* were asked to: How confident could you be?

1. explain to a friend why standardized   VC   FC   LC   NC
    achievement tests shouldn't be used
    to evaluate instruction.

2. discuss with a friend the most common   VC   FC   LC   NC
    ways that teachers give grades to
    students.

3. help other parents to draft a set of   VC   FC   LC   NC
    guidelines about "how *not* to prepare
    students for major tests."

4. describe to a friend the chief strengths   VC   FC   LC   NC
    and weaknesses of two-choice test items.

5. lead a parent study group's discussion   VC   FC   LC   NC
    of "Portfolio Assessment: Should Our
    School Use It?"

6. explain to another parent what is meant   VC   FC   LC   NC
    by the expression "assessment validity."

7. describe to a friend how teachers could   VC   FC   LC   NC
    collect convincing test-based evidence
    of their instructional effectiveness.

8. explain to a parent–teacher meeting what   VC   FC   LC   NC
    is meant by a performance test and how
    such tests can guide instruction.

9. tell a school principal what kinds of   VC   FC   LC   NC
    affective assessment instruments should
    be used in your child's school.

10. show parents what a rubric is and how it   VC   FC   LC   NC
    should be built if it is going to help
    instructional decision making.

Scoring Guide: Score each item using the following key: VC = 4, FC = 3, LC = 2, NC = 1; then add the scores for all 10 items. Scores of 30–40 = substantial confidence; 20–29 = moderate confidence; 10–19 = weak confidence.

2

CORE CONCEPTS OF EDUCATIONAL TESTING

*I*n this chapter, you'll learn about a set of fundamental concepts that underlie all educational testing. Think of the chapter as *Educational Testing 101,* a minicourse in the basics of school tests.

"Why," you might ask, "do I need to know about the basics of school testing?" That's a reasonable question and, as you might guess, I have prepared an altogether compelling answer. As a parent, you need to know about certain concepts of testing because, if you don't possess that knowledge, then educators can too easily overwhelm you with a ton of "testing talk" that you simply won't understand. As a result, like so many parents before you, you'll be obliged to acquiesce to those educators' views. They'll be referring to key ideas with which you're not familiar.

The core concepts of testing aren't terrifying. And they aren't all that numerous. In this chapter, after considering what's meant by the expression, "an educational test," you're going to learn about *five* central testing ideas. (That's less than a half-dozen!) First, you'll consider the fundamental reason that educational testing occurs at all, namely, how such tests are used to make *interpretations* about students. Second, you'll learn about *the kinds of things educators test,* that is, how educators actually decide what to cover in a test. Third, you'll take a look at *validity,* perhaps the single most important concept in educational testing. Fourth, you'll consider *reliability,* an important attribute of any good educational test. Finally, you'll be learning about the ways that educators think about *test bias* because, to the extent that a test is biased, it is unlikely to yield accurate results. After you've learned about these five core concepts of testing, you'll be well equipped to tackle most issues regarding testing topics that might have an impact on your child.

I promise not to deal with these five concepts in so much detail that your brain cells soon seek sanctuary, thus leading to a book-induced form of parental paralysis. I'll only describe the essence of each concept, and those descriptions will be based on the level of understanding needed by a parent, not a testing expert. You see, all five of these core testing concepts are really quite simple, and they're based on nothing more than common sense.

What's in a Name?

Not all educators refer to a test as a *test*. Two widely used synonyms for an *educational test* are an *educational assessment* and an *educational measurement*. The most fashionable descriptor these days is probably *educational assessment*. For many people, the name *test* conjures up images of a traditional paper-and-pencil measurement instrument. In contrast, *assessment* seems like a more appropriate label for some of the recently devised approaches to educational measurement that you'll be learning about later in the book. In Chapters 8 and 9, for example, you'll learn about the uses of "performance tests" and the role of "portfolio" measurement. Most educators these days refer to such tests as forms of assessment. So, at least for the next few years, *assessment* appears to be the preferred way of describing educational tests. Teachers talk about "classroom assessment," and measurement specialists refer to state-level and national-level "large-scale assessment."

Don't be surprised, however, if you find yourself talking to teachers and the phrases they use to describe educational testing shift from "measurement" to "assessment" to "testing." The three descriptors are essentially interchangeable. In this book, I'll use all three, typically just for variety, but also to make it clear that although "test" is a four-letter word, there are lengthier descriptors waiting on the sidelines.

Testing Terms:

Curriculum

The educational *ends* sought for students, usually described as goals or objectives

To make the most sense out of this chapter, here are a couple of other terms you're going to need, *curriculum* and *instruction*. *Curriculum* refers to the educational *ends* that teachers are supposed to promote, for example, the skills or knowledge that teachers might want their students to achieve. *Instruction*, on the other hand, refers to educational *means*, that is, the activities a teacher has students engage in so that the curricular ends are achieved. To illustrate, if a goal of the *curriculum* is to have students become skilled in writing narrative essays, then the teacher's *instruction* might consist of providing students with plenty of in-class practice in writing such essays. *Curriculum* describes what students are supposed to learn. *Instruction* describes how students are supposed to learn it.

Most often these days, the curriculum guidelines that teachers are supposed to follow consist of a set of *educational objectives,* that is, the knowledge and skills it is hoped children will achieve during school. To be honest with you (dishonesty does not induce confidence in a reader), most sets of district-level or state-level content standards are so general that teachers have great freedom to carry out a wide variety of instructional activities that they believe are relevant to the prescribed curriculum. You'll be taking a closer look at curricular selections later in the chapter.

All right, let's look at the first of our five core concepts of educational testing.

Testing Terms:
Instruction
The educational *means,* that is, the activities employed to promote students' attainment of curricular goals

Educational Measurement as Interpretation-Making

Children are tested in school so that educators can make accurate judgments about children's knowledge, skills, or attitudes. Once the teacher makes a test-based *interpretation* about a student, then that interpretation can be used in a variety of ways. For example, the teacher can decide the child needs more instruction so that a particular skill can be mastered. Or, in contrast, the teacher might determine the child has already comprehended a set of information, so that it's time to move on to another topic. Then, too, test results are often used by teachers to help them assign grades to students.

When I was a high school teacher in Oregon (so long ago that I'm not sure Oregon was, at that time, a state or a territory), I confess that the *only* reason I gave tests was to help determine which students should be given which grades. Today's teachers typically use test results in many more ways, especially to guide the teacher's instructional decisions. Test results help teachers decide how long to keep teaching about something, whether to change their teaching activities, and so on. And, of course, teachers still use tests to assign grades.

Measuring what can't be seen. Here's the way that educational testing works. Generally speaking, teachers need to get a fix on a student's ability level with respect to a specific skill or body of knowledge, for example, the student's ability to spell words correctly. Now there is no way that a teacher can *look* at a student, even using a magnifying glass, and determine what the student's *spelling ability* is. A child's spelling ability, just like the child's skill in mathematics or the child's knowledge of geography, is covert. That is, it can't be seen.

Curricular Selections

To solve the problem of assessing the unseeable, teachers set up situations that call on students to display their covert abilities. More often than not, these situations require students to take tests. Those tests are typically based on the curriculum the teacher is supposed to cover. But, in reality, most curricular goals prescribed by state or district authorities constitute far more than can possibly be taught in the available instructional time. Many of these curricular documents are actually "wish lists" describing a galaxy of outcomes that curricular specialists would like to see accomplished. But most of the folks who draft these lengthy curricular documents really understand that there's insufficient time to teach *all* the knowledge and skills those documents contain.

As a consequence, teachers must typically make *curricular selections.* In other words, teachers must choose from official curricular documents the set of skills and knowledge they're going to try to *teach* and the skills and knowledge that they're going to *test.* An example of a teacher's curricular selection might be, for example, a student's "knowledge of key events in the colonization of the Americas" or a student's "ability to compose a persuasive written essay." Generally speaking, the most important of a teacher's curricular selections will be the basis of a teacher's classroom tests. Teachers will often try to teach students things that aren't assessed, but the teacher's truly significant curricular selections will usually be assessed.

The curricular content from which teachers can select, especially as their students grow older, is often extremely large. Think, for example, about the amount of mathematical content that a child ought to learn in the seventh grade. For that matter, think of all the spelling words that you'd want a child in the sixth grade to be able to spell accurately. Those are large bodies of curricular content.

Tests to Represent Curricular Selections

As a practical matter, teachers can't assess students with respect to *all* the content in a teacher's curricular selections. That's because kids would devote so much time to being tested that there'd be no time left over for teaching. Accordingly, teachers typically *sample* from their curricular selections when they build a test. To illustrate, if there are 500 spelling words that a teacher would like students to be able to spell correctly, the teacher might construct a test containing only 25 of the 500 words. The student's performance on this sample of spelling words is then used by the teacher to arrive at a judgment regarding the student's ability to spell the full set of 500 words.

Test-Based Interpretations

In Figure 2.1 you'll find a graphic representation of this central notion in educational measurement. First, at the left, there is a curricular selection, for instance, a skill or set of knowledge the teacher wants students to achieve. Then, there's a test that represents that curricular selection. Finally, based on the student's test performance, the teacher makes an *interpretation* about the student's status with respect to the knowledge or skill embodied in the curricular selection.

In Figure 2.2, I've used the earlier example about a student's spelling ability to illustrate how teachers arrive at test-based interpretations (or, if you prefer, test-based *inferences*) regarding whatever curricular selection the test represents. Notice that the teacher uses a student's response to only a 25-word spelling test to arrive at an interpretation regarding the student's mastery of the full 500 spelling words.

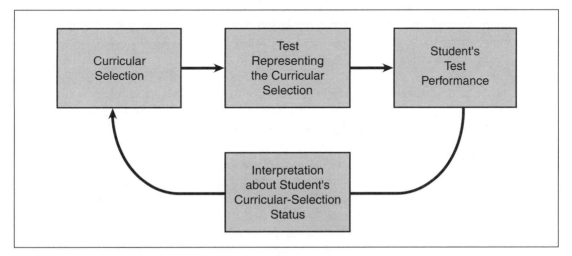

2.1 The process by which educators use a student's performance on a test to arrive at an interpretation regarding the student's curricular-selection status

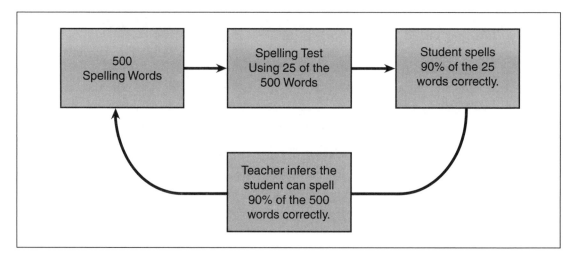

2.2 An illustration of how an interpretation based on a 25-word spelling test is made regarding a student's ability to spell 500 words

The essence of educational measurement is the deriving of interpretations about students regarding what a test *represents.* Teachers should not be preoccupied with the student's test responses themselves. Rather, students' test responses should be used to help teachers make interpretations about the knowledge, skills, or attitudes that were identified when curricular selections were originally made.

Whether a teacher is measuring your child's knowledge, skills, or attitudes, the role of an educational measurement device is to permit the teacher to make an accurate interpretation about your child's status with regard to whatever the test is measuring. That's because, in all instances, what's really at issue when teachers test children is the child's status with respect to the unseen attribute that's represented by the test.

This allows me to define with greater accuracy just what an educational test really is. It is *a measuring device that allows educators to arrive at interpretations regarding students' status with respect to the curricular selections represented by the test.*

I don't want to give the impression that whenever teachers decide to give a test, they spell out with great precision exactly what their curricular selection is, then set about to build a test that represents it. Most of the time, teachers simply create a test that they believe, in some fairly general way, "represents the things students will have been taught." (Those "things," in reality, constitute the curricular selections that the test represents.)

Testing Terms:

Educational Test

A measuring device whose use yields a score-based interpretation about a student's curricular-selection status (Synonyms: *Assessment, Measurement*)

Now that you know what the central role of educational measurement is, let's turn to the second of our five core concepts of educational assessment. That second concept deals with the sorts of things educational tests are intended to measure.

What Educational Tests Measure

As a parent, you've almost certainly gone to school. And you've doubtlessly been tested. Therefore, you already have an idea about what sorts of things teachers test because you've already been on the receiving end of many of their tests. In a nutshell, you probably think that "educational tests are supposed to measure what students are supposed to learn." You'd be correct. But if you're going to communicate effectively with teachers and administrators, you need to become familiar with the terminology they use when they talk about what their tests are supposedly measuring. You'll be surprised at the payoff you'll get by accurately using a few of the terms that most educators take for granted themselves. But educators also take it for granted that parents won't know such assessment terms.

If you recall the first core concept of "educational testing as interpretation-making," you'll remember that tests are intended to represent educators' most important *curricular selections*. And that's what you need to consider next, namely, the sorts of curricular selections that educational tests are supposed to be measuring.

Synonyms Aplenty

For the most part, teachers organize their classroom tests around the things they hope to teach their students. These "things" are usually referred to as *instructional objectives,* but the teacher might also use synonymous phrases such as educational *goals, aims,* or *outcomes.* In the past few years, many educators are using phrases such as *content standards* to refer to the things that students are supposed to learn.

There are, as you can see, all sorts of terms that educators might use to describe what they're supposed to be teaching and, therefore, what curricular selections are used to guide the creation of educational tests. Although it's tempting to conclude that educators are trying to confuse parents with such a pile of interchangeable terms, the diversity of descriptors for educators' curricular intentions simply reflects whatever was, when teachers began their careers, the most popular way to describe an educational intent. As newer teachers come onto the scene, they tend to use the currently fashionable curricular terminology; older teachers tend to stick with the curricular terminology they learned first. The result is a terminological jungle in which it's often necessary for parents to say, ever so gently, "Please tell me what you mean by that expression."

Bloom's Taxonomy

Many educators, but not all, describe their instructional objectives (and, therefore, the curricular selections on which their tests are based) according to the *Taxonomies of Educational Objectives* developed in the mid-fifties by the University of Chicago's Benjamin Bloom and his associates. A "taxonomy" is simply a ritzy name for a classification system. But, because it's quite likely your child's teacher may actually refer to Bloom's Taxonomy when speaking with parents, I want you to know what it is. In brief, Bloom's Taxonomy divides instructional objectives into the following three types:

- *Cognitive Objective:* the kinds of intellectual skills and knowledge that teachers want children to learn.
- *Affective Objectives:* the kinds of attitudes, values, or interests that teachers want children to acquire.
- *Psychomotor Objectives:* the small-muscle or large-muscle physical skills that children are supposed to learn in such fields as physical education.

Because cognitive instructional objectives dominate what teachers teach, Bloom's Taxonomy further divides those objectives into six levels starting at the lowest level with *knowledge* and ending at the highest level with *evaluation*. At the knowledge level, the student is merely asked to *memorize* information, for example, to memorize a set of historical facts or to memorize the rules of punctuation. Knowledge, as defined in Bloom's Taxonomy, is limited to *rote recall*. At any of the higher cognitive levels, the student must at least *use* knowledge so that, for example, students show they can (at the Taxonomy's upper five levels) *comprehend, apply, analyze, synthesize,* or *evaluate*. The upper levels of Bloom's Taxonomy call for the student to engage in very high-level thinking indeed.

So, when a teacher considers the intended outcomes of an instructional activity, it is very common for the teacher to identify those outcomes as cognitive, affective, or psychomotor in nature. What you, as a parent, have to be on watch for is a teacher's instructional objectives dominantly or exclusively at the knowledge level, that is, at the lowest level of Bloom's cognitive classification system. It's not that knowledge is a bad thing.

Clearly, students need to possess memorized information to cope with all sorts of situations. But if the *only* thing your child is learning consists of memorized facts, then the child is not being sufficiently challenged. Teachers who only test at the knowledge level of Bloom's cognitive taxonomy are seriously shortchanging their students.

Remember, what the teacher *tests* is typically what the teacher regards as most important. There's an expression that "educators measure what they treasure." That expression sums it up nicely. If teachers are only testing students for memorized information, then the teacher appears to believe memorized information (knowledge, according to Bloom's Taxonomy) is the teacher's most important curricular aim. It shouldn't be.

In Chapter 10, you'll take a look at affective objectives and how to assess student affect accurately, but let me preview that discussion a bit by suggesting that, in many cases, sensible *affective* outcomes are among the most important things a teacher can teach. If a child learns to *hate* mathematics, quite obviously, the long-term impact of such an affective outcome can be detrimental to the student's future mastery of mathematics. In contrast, if a child learns to *love* reading, then that affective outcome can be profoundly beneficial to the child's educational future. But if your child's teacher is not pursuing *and measuring* one or more significant affective outcomes, such as increasing students' positive attitudes toward learning, then you ought to be concerned. You'll learn much more about the kinds of affective assessments that are *and aren't* appropriate in Chapter 10.

Because *psychomotor* objectives are only encountered in a limited number of school subjects, such as when technology teachers promote keyboarding skills in a computer class, I'll not spend all that much time on psychomotor outcomes. But if your child is in a class where such small-muscle or large-muscle skills are to be promoted, then those skills will also form the basis of the potential curricular selections on which tests of students' psychomotor skills should be based.

Excessively Specific Objectives

In the 1960s and 1970s there was much advocacy of *behavioral* objectives, that is, instructional objectives that attempted to spell out—in very explicit terms—the nature of the postinstruction behavior desired from learners. Educators became so caught up with a quest for specific behavioral objectives that they'd sometimes attempt to promote students' mastery of hundreds and hundreds of tiny, explicit behavioral objectives. What was learned from that love affair with behavioral objectives is that too many hyperspecific objectives quite literally overwhelm teachers. They become so concerned about achieving a laundry list of bite-size objectives that, after a time, they pay little if any attention to those objectives.

If you find your child's teacher or school district has organized a curriculum about a seemingly endless array of hyperspecific educational objectives, you can be almost certain that those objectives are having no impact on the instructional process.

Ideally, a teacher will pursue an *intellectually manageable* set of instructional objectives, perhaps a half-dozen or so per subject area. If your child is being pushed to master hundreds of specific objectives, then a key lesson from the 1960s and 1970s has been missed by the educators who are advocating such objectives.

Curricular Constraints

Most teachers are limited in the kinds of instructional objectives they are supposed to pursue. These constraints usually take the form of some kind of official curriculum guidelines that have been adopted by a district school board or a state school board. As I pointed out earlier, however, these curricular documents are often so loaded with lofty goals so that teachers have a substantial amount of curricular choice when they actually decide what instructional activities to provide for their students.

For a parent, the implication of any teacher's curricular latitude is that you really need to be attentive to what your child's teacher is emphasizing

in class. There's typically so much "give" in prescribed curricular documents that different teachers' actual instructional objectives can range all over the place. *The very best way for parents to get an accurate fix on what a child's teacher is emphasizing instructionally is to review the teacher's classroom tests.*

Remember, classroom tests are supposed to represent the teacher's most significant curricular selections. A teacher's tests, therefore, are the key to understanding the teacher's curricular intentions. If the tests deal with trivial, unimportant content, it's pretty difficult for a teacher to argue that "although my tests assess puny content, what goes on in class is really profound."

Assessment Validity

Let's turn, now, to the third core concept of educational testing. If you were to ask measurement specialists what the single, most significant concept in educational testing is, almost all of them would give the same answer: *validity*. That nearly uniform reaction probably means you ought to know just a bit about what assessment validity is.

How Assessment Validity Works

Do you recall that the first of this chapter's core concepts described how a test was supposed to represent educators' curricular selections? In that way, a student's test performance could be used to make interpretations about the student's curricular-selection status? Well, just to remind you, I'm going to dish up Figure 2.1 again and add a sentence that shows you where assessment validity comes in. I'll call it Figure 2.3 so you think you're getting an extra figure, but it's really only a warmed-over and slightly altered Figure 2.1.

Notice in the figure that it is the validity of the interpretation, not the test, that's at issue. So, if you prefer, you might use the synonym *accuracy* to describe assessment validity. What educators are looking for is accurate test-based interpretations.

The Validity of Interpretations, Not Tests

If you spend any substantial amount of time talking to educators about educational testing, you'll almost certainly hear some teacher or school administrator referring to *a valid test*. Actually, *tests* do not possess validity. Instead, it is the *interpretation* based on the student's test performance that is valid or invalid.

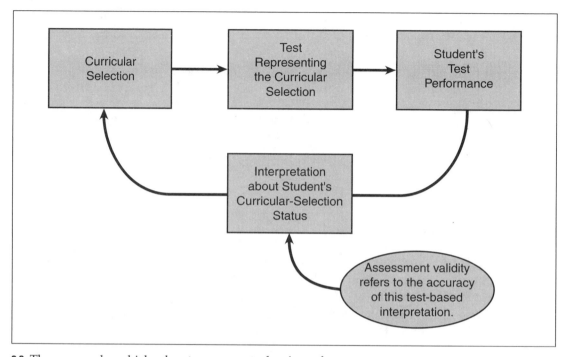

2.3 The process by which educators use a student's performance on a test to arrive at an interpretation regarding the student's curricular-selection status, and the point at which assessment validity enters that process

Now that you know that assessment validity refers to interpretations, not tests, you possess some potentially dangerous information. You could easily describe those educators who refer to "valid tests" as educators who really "don't understand the fundamental nature of assessment validity." Although you might be correct, and although such an educator put-down might be momentarily gratifying, it's not a shrewd move. You're out to win the long-term educational war for your child, not pick up any short-term battle trophies by embarrassing educators.

Perhaps the educator really knows better, but is assuming that valid score-based inferences will only be produced by good tests, and is simply employing a bit of labeling license. Whatever the educator's reason for such technical inaccuracy, or any others that you'll encounter, be careful about how you use what you're learning about educational testing in this book. It's intended to help you and your child's teachers make better educational decisions. It's *not* intended to serve as ammunition in a round of "nail-the-teacher" target practice.

Notice in Figure 2.3 that it is the accuracy of an educator's test-based interpretation that constitutes validity as it's used in a measurement sense.

A Parent Puzzle

Presented below is a fictional interchange between a teacher and a parent. Read the setting and the dialogue, then decide what you would say next if you were the parent in the interchange. After you've decided how you might respond, you can see how I might have responded and why. Remember, read the dialogue, then figure out what you'd say next. After having done so, take a peek at my response and the reasons for it. Because there will be several of these parent puzzles in the book, I'll refer to all parents as Mr. or Mrs. Smith. In a quest for gender equity, when only one parent is involved, I'll alternate between Mr. Smith and Mrs. Smith. (That's the best thing about fictional dialogues, you can alter them any way you want.)

(Setting: Pat Smith, a fifth-grade student, has been bringing weekly tests home since school began. Generally, Pat gets good grades on these tests. Pat's parents have been reviewing the tests as they come home, however, and have concluded that Pat's teacher is only testing Pat's memorization of low-level, factual information. At a back-to-school night, one of Pat's parents seeks out Pat's teacher to discuss the weekly tests.)

Teacher: "Good evening, Mr. Smith. I was told you'd like to talk with me about Pat's progress."

Parent: "That's right. Pat's mother and I have been pleased with Pat's grades and with the interest Pat seems to have in your class. But, frankly, we're a bit concerned about the nature of the weekly quizzes Pat's been bringing home. Could we talk about them?"

Teacher: "Of course. What I've been trying to do in class is to provide weekly opportunities for students to pull together what they've learned during the week. You'll see that some of the quizzes are 10 items in length and some are 20 items long. That depends on what we've covered during a particular week."

Parent: "But we notice that all of the quizzes contain True–False items. And, as far as we can tell, they seem to only be testing Pat's memory of facts, such as places, names, and dates. Are we misinterpreting what the quizzes set out to measure?"

Teacher: "Absolutely not! In my class, students acquire the basic knowledge they'll need in all subsequent classes. I'm sure you and Mrs. Smith will agree that Pat would be awash in those later classes without a solid foundation of knowledge. You do agree, don't you?"

Parent: (If you were Pat's parent, what would you say next?)

My Response: If I were Pat's father, I'd probably say something like this: "I definitely agree that knowledge is the cornerstone of learning, but Pat's mother and I are worried that Pat will be so caught up in the memorizing of information that there'll not be any opportunity to apply that information. I know you said that Pat would be able to use the knowledge in subsequent classes, but wouldn't there be some advantage if at least some of your tests assessed cognitive objectives that were at a higher level in Bloom's Taxonomy?"

My Reason: I'd first try to find something to agree with based on what the teacher said. I did so when I concurred that "knowledge is the cornerstone of learning." It is imperative that any conversation with your child's teacher be constructive, not

continued

A Parent Puzzle (continued)

confrontational. Then I'd continue to express my concerns about the test, and softly suggest a redirection in the content of "at least some" of the weekly tests. Finally, I'd frame my concerns according to the cognitive levels in Bloom's Taxonomy. I can assure you that your use of this technical language will definitely grab the teacher's attention. If the teacher is familiar with the Taxonomy, the teacher will realize you and Pat's mother are reviewing Pat's tests from a more sophisticated perspective than is typical. If the teacher is unfamiliar with Bloom's Taxonomy, you can bet the teacher will find out about the Taxonomy before the next back-to-school night.

If evidence can be assembled that the test yields valid interpretations, then the test can help educators make better decisions about students. If the test yields invalid interpretations, then educational decisions based on the test's results will obviously be flawed.

Here's a straightforward example of how you might think about assessment validity. Suppose a mathematics teacher has staked out a pretty clear picture of the mathematical computation skills she would like her students to master. That set of computation skills is one of the teacher's curricular selections. The teacher then constructs a final exam of forty items to represent her curricular selection. If students who get high scores on the exam have, in fact, mastered the teacher's computation objectives, while students who get low scores on the exam haven't mastered the teacher's computation objectives, then the teacher's score-based interpretations will be valid. Assessment validity is just that simple.

Testing Terms:
Validity
The accuracy of test-based interpretations about children's knowledge, skills, or affect

What you need to recognize regarding assessment validity is that the conclusion about what your child's test performance actually signifies is based on the *interpretation* that an educator makes about the meaning of your child's test performance. *There's no such thing as a valid test that yields unerringly accurate interpretations, all by itself, about a child.* Score-based interpretations are what teachers make, and those score-based interpretations may or may not be valid.

Validity Evidence

In order for educators to have confidence that their score-based interpretations are valid, evidence is assembled to support the idea that a test is measuring what it's supposed to measure. For high-stakes tests such as most nationally standardized tests, the collection of evidence bearing on assessment validity is usually quite an elaborate process. For classroom tests, because most teachers are busy people, there is usually little or no attention given to the gathering of validity evidence.

However, if teachers actually were to collect evidence bearing on the validity of their test-based interpretations, it would be referred to as *content-related evidence of validity* or, simply, as *content validity*. As that descriptive title suggests, what classroom tests must do if they are going to help teachers make valid interpretations about students is to adequately represent the content embodied in the teacher's curricular selections.

So, for example, if one of a teacher's curricular selections is "students' mastery of twenty-five pivotal punctuation rules," then that content should be well *represented* by any test that's supposed to permit valid interpretations about students' status with respect to the twenty-five punctuation rules. The test does *not* have to measure *all* twenty-five rules, but it must represent those rules. For instance, a test that included items dealing with only ten of the rules might be sufficient for the teacher to come up with a valid interpretation about students' abilities to use the full set of twenty-five rules.

Similarly, if a teacher is trying to promote students' mastery of one hundred vocabulary words, those words need only be *represented* by a test that could yield a valid score-based interpretation about students' mastery of the entire one hundred vocabulary words.

So, for classroom tests, the kind of evidence that one would like to have would deal with the question of whether the teacher's tests do, in fact, adequately represent the full range of content in the curricular selections that the test is supposed to represent.

To be frank, you'll rarely find that your child's teacher has such evidence on hand. But if you were talking with a teacher and had some doubts about the quality of the teacher's tests, you might ask, (oozing tact, of course), "whether this test represents a broader set of content or is this the entire content that the test is intended to assess?" If the teacher is curious about the reason for your interest, you might follow up with a comment such as, "I understand that content validity is the most crucial kind of validity evidence for teachers' classroom tests, and I was considering the test with that kind of assessment validity in mind."

By raising these sorts of questions with your child's teachers, you are not trying to put teachers on the defensive. Rather, you are letting them know that you're a parent who has taken the time to do some test-related homework on your own. If I were still a high school teacher and one of my parents made comments about the content validity of my classroom tests, you can bet that I would be giving my tests much more careful attention.

For one thing, I'd race to find out what "content validity" was. When I was a high school teacher, I'd never heard of it.

Let's turn, now, to the fourth of the core concepts in educational testimony, a concept that some measurement specialists believe is almost as important as validity.

Reliability

The *reliability* of an educational test refers to the consistency with which the test measures what it's measuring. If a test is unreliable, that is, inconsistent, there's little likelihood that an educator is going to make a valid score-based interpretation by using that test. *Reliability,* therefore, can be thought of as a necessary, but not sufficient condition for validity.

Three Varieties of Evidence

What parents should know about reliability, however, is that there are *three different* types of reliability that educators use when they're referring to a test's consistency.

- *Stability Reliability:* Also referred to as test–retest reliability, this kind of reliability refers to the similarity in the performances of students who have taken the same test on two different occasions (for example, several weeks apart).
- *Alternate-Form Reliability:* This kind of reliability describes the degree to which different forms of a test yield similar results. Classroom teachers rarely have alternate forms of a test, but multiple forms are available for most high-stakes tests.
- *Internal Consistency:* This kind of reliability describes the degree to which the items in a test function in a similar manner, that is, are measuring the same thing.

Testing Terms:
Reliability
The consistency with which a test measures whatever it is measuring

As a practical matter, teachers almost never collect evidence regarding the reliability of their tests. It's simply too much trouble for the payoff. However, for high-stakes tests, such as state-level tests or nationally standardized tests, reliability evidence is almost always collected. What you need to understand is that there are definite differences among the three kinds of reliability evidence. Even if a test developer collects evidence showing a test has high *internal consistency* reliability, this does *not* indicate that the test possesses *stability* reliability or *alternate-form* reliability. Though related, the three kinds of reliability evidence are really different.

The Standard Error of Measurement

The three kinds of reliability just described refer to *groups* of students. The better the reliability of a test, then the more consistency there will be when students are tested and, as a consequence, the more likely it will be that valid score-based interpretations will be made. But there's also one kind of reliability that bears directly on the consistency of the test result for an individual child. That reliability index is known as the *standard error of measurement*. The standard error of measurement for a test indicates how accurate a particular child's score is likely to be. As a parent, the standard error of measurement on a test will help inform you about the reliability of *your* child's performance on a test.

Testing Terms:

Standard Error of Measurement

An index of the accuracy of an individual's test score, expressed as a plus-or-minus error estimate around the score

The standard error of measurement works in the same way as the plus-or-minus error estimates you've encountered numerous times in media opinion polls. Suppose you see a TV news program reporting results of a poll about "How many parents favor a tuition-free college program, even if it requires a tax boost?" What you'll usually see at the bottom of the TV screen is a small-print statement that says "±3% margin of error." That's exactly how a standard error of measurement functions.

What these plus-or-minus error margins really signify is that if you were to carry out the opinion poll over and over until you'd done so one hundred times, then at least 90 percent of the time the results would be within plus or minus three percentage points of the TV-reported results. Clearly, the smaller the margins of error, the more confidence that someone can have in the accuracy of a particular poll results. An error margin ±10 percentage points, therefore, is less confidence-inducing than an error margin of ±2 percentage points.

Typically, the size of the error margins for these media-reported opinion polls depends on the number of people polled *and the quality of the questions asked.* The more people polled, the smaller the error margin. The better the questions asked, the smaller the error margin.

You'll not be getting any information about the standard error of measurement for your child's *classroom* tests. As I pointed out earlier, classroom teachers rarely conduct reliability analyses of their tests. But you *are* likely to find standard errors of measurement supplied whenever you receive a report of your child's performance on a major national- or state-level standardized examination. You'll see how standard errors of measurement are used in Chapter 4 when you consider how to interpret your child's standardized test-score reports.

Hopefully, you'll see that when your child earns a score on a particular test, that score is not terribly precise. There's a plus-or-minus error margin associated with *every* test score your child will ever receive. Contrary to many people's opinions, the scores yielded by educational tests are not all that accurate or not all that consistent. The standard error of measurement should make that clear to you. And, as you might suspect, if standard errors of measurement were calculated for teacher-made classroom tests, they would most likely be much larger than those found for standardized tests (the kind produced by measurement specialists).

What you need to be wary of is that not all test publishers use the same plus-or-minus error margins with their standard errors of measurement. Some may use a plus-or-minus 90 percent; some may use a plus-or-minus 95 percent. The lower the plus-or-minus percentage, the smaller will be the standard error of measurement.

Test Bias

It's time to take a brief look at the fifth and final core concept of educational testing, namely, *test bias*. Put simply, a test is biased to the extent that its items *offend* or *unfairly penalize* children because of children's personal characteristics such as their ethnicity, religion, gender, or geographic locale.

Offensiveness

One form of test bias stems from an item's *offensiveness*. An illustration of a test item that would *offend* a child because of personal characteristics would be an item depicting members of an ethnic group in a negative, stereotypic fashion. For instance, imagine in a standardized test that there was a brief story serving as the basis for several items designed to measure students' reading skills. Suppose that the story described an African-American person as a "watermelon man" and an Hispanic-American person as a "bean-eater." Because each of these descriptions relies on negative representations of the ethnic group involved, an African-American child or an Hispanic-American child who encountered that story might, quite naturally, become upset, so upset as to distort the child's responses to the test items based on the offensive story (not to mention the child's responses to all subsequent items on the test).

Such offensiveness, even if *unintended* by the test-makers, will usually have a negative effect on the offended child's test performance. And that negative effect will, in turn, decrease the validity of any interpretation about the child's ability to do whatever the test was supposed to be assessing.

Unfair Penalties

A second form of test bias occurs when there are parts of an item that *unfairly penalize* a test-taker. Think about a test item dealing with content that's less likely to be known by girls than boys. For instance, the item might be based on some kind of professional sport with which girls are less familiar than boys, such as the National Football League (NFL). Suppose the test item required the test-taker to be familiar with recent changes in NFL rules. Without that NFL familiarity, a child would be less likely to answer the item correctly.

Given such an item, girls would clearly be *unfairly* penalized. Although there would surely be some girls who know a great deal about the NFL, *on average* girls would do worse on the item simply because of their unfamiliarity with the NFL. That's unfair.

Similarly, it would be unfair to use test items containing content that only children from affluent families would be likely to know. For instance, suppose a mathematical item was based on symphonic music more likely to be known by children whose families could afford to buy tickets to the local symphony than by children whose families were just scraping by financially. The more affluent child would be likely to perform better on the symphonic-music item merely because of the child's exposure to classical music. The less affluent child would be unfairly penalized.

Disparate Impact versus Bias

Sometimes students from a minority group will perform less well on a test than students from the majority group. Sometimes the opposite is true. For example, Asian-American students (a minority) often outperform Caucasian students (the majority) on mathematics tests. When the average test performance of one group is meaningfully different from the average test performance of another group, this constitutes a *disparate impact*, that is, a test that produces different effects on students from two groups (such as girls and boys). It is sometimes thought by parents that any such disparate impact automatically signifies test bias. That's not so.

It is certainly possible that when a test yields a disparate impact, the test *may* be biased. Often, however, there's no bias at all. What the test may be picking up is inadequate prior instruction provided for the group of students scoring lower on the test. In other words, the test may be unbiased, but the students in the low-performing group had previously not been well taught. To find out whether disparate impact arises from test bias or from

prior instructional shortcomings, the items in the test need to be reviewed—one at a time—to see if they contain elements that might offend or unfairly penalize students because of students' personal characteristics.

Bias Review Panels

All right, now that you have an idea of what test bias is, what should you do with that knowledge? First, for any really significant test (such as a state-mandated high-stakes test), you should find out whether the test's items have been evaluated by a *bias review panel*. Bias review panels are becoming quite commonplace these days for most high-stakes tests. Such panels, usually consisting of ten to twenty members, are composed of individuals (educators or laypersons) drawn from the various constituencies represented by the students who are being tested. For example, there might be African Americans, Native Americans, Asian Americans, and Hispanic Americans on the panel. Then, too, there should be both men and women because some test items contain a gender bias, and it typically takes both sexes to spot such items.

Fundamentally, what bias review panels do is consider each item carefully to see if it contains any content that might offend or unfairly penalize children because of their personal characteristics. If the panel identifies items that do display bias, then such items should be removed from the test.

In Your Child's Classroom

Clearly, classroom teachers aren't going to assemble bias review panels just for their own tests. Bias review panels are used only with significant district, state, or national tests. But classroom teachers *should* be attentive to the possibility of bias in their own tests. As a practical matter, I suspect that most busy classroom teachers just don't devote much time to bias-detection for their own tests. They really should.

So, if you have an opportunity to look over your own child's tests, you might want to carry out your own review of the test items on the basis of their freedom from content that might *offend* or *unfairly penalize* students because of a student's personal characteristics. In a sense, you can be a bias review panel of one.

Sometimes you won't have access to a teacher's classroom tests, of course, because the teacher will want to preserve "test security." If you *are* able to analyze a classroom teacher's test items, then you can look carefully to see if there are any items that might offend or unfairly penalize children because of their personal characteristics.

If you find items that seem to be biased, you might want to discuss that possibility privately with your child's teacher or, better yet, the school's principal. Perhaps your concerns are unwarranted, because what looks like test bias, when clarified, really isn't. In any such interchange with your child's teacher or principal, of course, it's desirable for you to display mountains of tact. You and your child's educators need to work *together* for your child's educational well-being. Confrontational clashes about test bias rarely serve that purpose.

What Do You Really Need to Know about This Chapter's Content?

All right, you've taken a quick trip through the heart of what makes educational testing work. You are now at least acquainted with a set of central concepts that will pop up frequently as you learn more about school tests and how those tests impact on your child. In the form of an ever-so-brief review, let me stake out the most important things you should recall from this chapter.

- Educational testing, also described as "assessment" or "measurement," revolves around the test-based interpretations that are made regarding students' status with respect to educators' curricular selections.

- *Curriculum* refers to the educational *ends* that educators hope students will achieve. *Instruction* represents the educational *means* employed to achieve curricular ends.

- Educators' curricular selections, usually described as objectives, goals, or content standards, can be cognitive, affective, or psychomotor. If the bulk of a teacher's tests are aimed at the lowest level of Bloom's Cognitive Taxonomy, that is, aimed at memorized knowledge, the teacher's curricular aspirations are probably too low.

- Validity refers to the accuracy of the score-based interpretations educators make about the cognitive, affective, or psychomotor status of children. In the classroom, *content validity*, that is, adequate representation of the teacher's significant curricular selections, is the most important kind of validity evidence.

- Reliability of educational tests describes the consistency with which a test measures whatever it's measuring. But there are several meaningfully different ways of thinking about a test's consistency of measurement. For an individual child, a test's standard error of measurement supplies a plus-or-minus error estimate about a given score's accuracy.

- An educational test is biased to the extent that it *offends* or *unfairly penalizes* any child because of the child's personal characteristics such as gender, religion, ethnicity, or geographic locale. All items on high-stakes educational tests should be carefully evaluated by a bias review panel. Parents should be attentive to the possibility that the classroom tests used with their children may contain biased items.

POSSIBLE PARENT ACTION–OPTIONS

If you intend to take any action based on the material covered in Chapter 2, here are a few options for you to consider.

1. You might find it illuminating to take a gander at an official curricular guide that's supposed to govern what your child learns. Ask an administrator in your child's school if you can borrow any official state or district curricular materials. You can inform the administrator that because you're trying to help your child at home, you need to have an idea of what should be emphasized in school. I'll be surprised if you don't find such curricular documents covering substantially more content than is likely to be taught in the instructional time available to teachers.

2. Attempt to collect several classroom tests used by teachers in your child's school, then review each item, one at a time. See if there are elements in an item that might offend or unfairly penalize a child because of the child's personal characteristics. If there are many such items, you might consider a conversation with the school's principal.

3. You might want to call one or more of the *Suggested Resources for Your Child's Teacher or Principal* to the attention of an educator who works with your child. Because the chapter you've just finished reading deals with the fundamentals of educational measurement, you'd probably want to exercise this third action–option only if an educator appears to be genuinely uninformed about educational assessment.

You can try to get a fix on an educator's knowledge regarding educational assessment simply by asking, ever so meekly, for explanations about concepts such as those you've just considered in this chapter. If the educator's response is way out of whack with what you've learned here, then it's likely that the educator in question has only a questionable knowledge about educational assessment.

SUGGESTED RESOURCES FOR YOUR CHILD'S TEACHER OR PRINCIPAL

Printed Materials

Bloom, B. S. et al. *Taxonomy of Educational Objectives: Handbook I: Cognitive Domain.* New York: David McKay, 1956. *This famous classification of educational objectives distinguishes among cognitive, affective, and psychomotor objectives, then subclassifies the cognitive domain into six levels of objectives.*

Keenan, Jo-Anne Wilson, and Anne Wheelock. "The Standards Movement in Education: Will Poor and Minority Students Benefit?" *Poverty & Race, 6,* no. 3 (May/June 1997): 1–3, 7. *This essay is a thought-provoking piece dealing with potentially adverse effects of the movement toward educational content standards.*

Marzano, Robert J., and John S. Kendall. *A Comprehensive Guide to Designing Standards-Based Districts, Schools, and Classrooms.* Aurora, CO: McREL (Mid-Continent Regional Educational Laboratory), 1996. *This carefully structured collection of practical guidelines will help those educators who are attempting to base their educational efforts on carefully delineated sets of content and performance standards.*

Popham, W. James. *Modern Educational Measurement: Practical Guidelines for Educational Leaders* (3rd ed.). Boston: Allyn and Bacon, 2000. *Chapters 3–6 provide educational leaders with a careful look at reliability, validity, absence-of-bias, and how a test can make an instructional contribution for teachers.*

Standards for Educational and Psychological Testing. Washington, DC: Author, 1985. *These widely used* Standards, *soon to be revised, provide educators with a series of guidelines regarding high-stakes testing. The* Standards, *because they are often used in court cases regarding testing, influence the nature of significant educational tests.*

Videotape Programs

Assessment Training Institute, Inc. *Creating Sound Classroom Assessments.* (50 SW Second Ave., Ste. 300, Portland, OR 97204). *This video clarifies what quality assessment means and how to achieve it. Rick Stiggins defines specific standards that can be used anywhere—from the classroom to the boardroom—to check the dependability of assessments and turn the assessment process into an effective teaching tool.*

Northwest Regional Educational Laboratory. *A Status Report on Classroom Assessment.* IOX Assessment Associates (5301 Beethoven St., Ste. 190, Los Angeles, CA 90066). *Specific strategies are given to teachers for improving the quality of classroom assessments. The realities of classroom life are contrasted with the assessment preparation provided in teacher education programs.*

3

THE MISUSE OF STANDARDIZED TEST SCORES AS INDICATORS OF EDUCATIONAL EFFECTIVENESS

*T*his chapter, and the one following it, both deal with standardized tests. The focus of each chapter, however, is decisively different. In this chapter, you'll learn why the use of students' standardized test scores to evaluate educational quality, although currently widespread, is absolutely wrong. In Chapter 4, you'll learn how to interpret the reports you receive when your own child takes a standardized test. Chapter 4, then, deals with the use of standardized tests with individual students, not as a reflection of educational quality.

Clearly, if your child is in a school setting where standardized tests are not used, or are not used yet because your child is still too young, then you might only want to skim-read Chapter 4 or, perhaps, skip it altogether. But the current chapter's focus on the misuse of standardized test scores will be relevant to the way you think about the quality of your local schools. Chapter 3 is a must-be-read chapter, then, for all parents with children in school.

What Is a Standardized Test?

Technically, a standardized test is any examination that's administered and scored in a predetermined, standard manner. There are two major kinds of standardized tests, *aptitude* tests and *achievement* tests.

Aptitude Tests

Testing Terms:
Standardized Test
Any examination administered and scored in a pre-specified, standard manner

Standardized *aptitude* tests predict how well students are likely to perform in some subsequent educational setting. In schools, the most common of these exams are the SAT (*Scholastic Assessment Test)* and the ACT *Assessment,* both of which attempt to forecast how well high school students will perform in college.

Standardized aptitude tests have a mission similar to those tests that, when I was first teaching, we used to call *intelligence* tests. From such tests we calculated what was called a student's *IQ,* that is, the student's intelligence quotient. Aptitude tests try to measure how "smart" a child is, at least how smart the child is with respect to the child's verbal and mathematical abilities. Because such abilities are believed to be pivotal in a student's subsequent academic success, academic aptitude tests deal almost exclusively with students' verbal and mathematical abilities.

Testing Terms:
Aptitude Tests
Examinations designed to predict how well a test-taker will perform in some subsequent situation, usually an academic setting

Achievement Tests

Standardized *achievement* tests, on the other hand, supposedly measure a student's knowledge and skills, usually in particular subject areas such as language arts, science, mathematics, and social studies.

Testing Terms:
Achievement Tests
Examinations designed to assess the knowledge and/or skills students possess in a particular subject field

Currently, there are five prominent standardized achievement tests distributed nationally: the *California Achievement Tests, Comprehensive Tests of Basic Skills, Iowa Tests of Basic Skills, Metropolitan Achievement Tests,* and *Stanford Achievement Tests.* Three test publishers sell and score these five tests: CTB/McGraw Hill, Riverside Publishing Company, and Harcourt Brace.

What most people rely on when they use test scores to judge schools is student performance on standardized *achievement* tests. Those tests are thought to assess the kinds of skills and knowledge that should be taught in schools. Although student performance on academic aptitude tests is occasionally used to evaluate schools, this is much less common. In this chapter, therefore, I'll focus on standardized achievement tests. It's really important for you to understand what these tests *can* do and what they *can't*.

Annual Ranking Rituals

Each year, depending on the time of the year that achievement tests are given in a particular locality (most such tests are administered in the spring), local newspapers typically use students' test scores to publish district-by-district and school-by-school rankings. Highly ranked schools, that is, schools whose students score well on standardized tests, are regarded as effective schools. Conversely, lowly ranked schools are thought to be ineffective.

Realtors often use these test-based rankings to convince prospective home-buyers that "if you buy a house in this school district, your kids will be going to top-ranked, effective schools." It's not surprising that because parents obviously worry about their children's well-being, the prospect of sending a child to a good school might turn out to be the final factor in clinching a house-purchase.

In California, for example, one company *(McCormack's Guide)* distributes each year a set of guidebooks featuring the "latest school scores" and urges people "before you move" to consider test-based school rankings. In each guidebook (published for the most heavily populated counties in California) there's a school-by-school breakdown of how each school's students have performed on standardized achievement tests for the past five years. Even though the *McCormack's Guides* are loaded with cautions about relying too heavily on a school's test scores, its authors nonetheless conclude that "it pays to move into a neighborhood with high-scoring schools."

And it's not just real estate salespeople who believe that schools with high standardized test scores are good schools. If you talk about effective schools to almost any person you run into, you'll find that such a belief is widespread. People think that schools in which students score high on standardized achievement tests are good schools.

Even more unfortunately, the belief that a school's standardized test results are an indication of the school's instructional effectiveness is a view that's shared by many educators as well. Teachers and administrators who operate a school with low test scores often believe that, unless their students' scores improve, there's something deficient about the quality of instruction they're providing to the school's pupils.

As I've already indicated, the belief that students' scores on standardized achievement tests accurately reflect a school's educational quality is mistaken. Let's see why.

Measuring Temperature with a Tablespoon

To get a meaningful idea about why it is that standardized achievement tests do not provide evidence of a school's instructional effectiveness, you need to know where these tests came from in the first place.

The *Army Alpha*'s Influence

During World War I, military officials in the United States were hard-pressed to identify suitable officer candidates. To fight a war of such unprecedented proportions, the U.S. Army needed many, many officers. And, shortly after the United States entered the war, it was apparent that the Army's current ways of picking out suitable officer candidates were not working.

Accordingly, U.S. military leaders contacted the American Psychological Association for assistance. A committee of that organization was assigned to the task and, after a week's work at the Vineland Training School in New Jersey, the committee developed the *Army Alpha*. The Alpha was a group-administrable *aptitude* test that presented Army recruits with verbal and mathematical problems so, based on recruits' scores, *the recruits could be ranked according to their relative intellectual abilities.*

Recruits who scored high on the *Alpha* were sent to officer training programs. Lower scorers were assigned to other military roles. As it turned out, the *Army Alpha* was a remarkably successful assessment instrument. It was administered to about 1,750,000 men during World War I. And it worked! At least it worked much better than anything the Army had previously used.

The fundamental function of the *Alpha* was to sort out recruits according to their relative abilities to deal with paper-and-pencil verbal and quantitative tasks. In essence, the mission of the Alpha was to "spread 'em out" so the most able could be identified. This is the way that any standardized *aptitude* test works.

However, because of the success of the *Alpha* assessment approach, subsequent efforts to create standardized *achievement* tests followed the test-development and test-refinement methods pioneered by creators of the *Alpha*. So, when early measurement experts constructed an achievement test to measure a student's knowledge and skills in, say, social studies, the test developers really tried to stick to the *Alpha* approach to assessment, but in a social studies context.

As long as the post-WWI standardized achievement tests allowed students to be sorted out according to their relative abilities (as was the case with the *Alpha*), then the creators of those tests were satisfied. But that mission for the tests, as you'll soon see, rendered those tests inappropriate for judging the quality of schooling.

The Importance of Score-Spread

If a standardized achievement test doesn't provide a reasonable spread of scores, then it can't do a good job in permitting relative comparisons among test-takers. Let me use the term *percentile*, one of the most readily understandable ways of describing a student's test score to explain this point. A percentile tells us how a student's test score stacks up against scores earned by students in some kind of comparison group.

Thus, when you hear from a teacher that, "your child scored at the 80th percentile on the nationally standardized test," you know that your child's score exceeded the scores of 80 percent of the students who were included in the national test's *norm group*.

A norm group for a national test is a large, representative group of students who, having already taken that test, provide a comparison basis for subsequent test-takers. So, when you learn that your child scored "at the 80th percentile," this means your child outperformed 80 percent of the children in the national test's norm group.

Because percentiles rely on an interpretation approach by which the meaning of a score is attained by "referencing" the child's score back to a norm group, standardized tests are sometimes referred to as "norm-referenced tests." In contrast, a test whose interpretation depends more on what students "can or can't do," rather than how they compare to other students, is called a "criterion-referenced test." Norm-referenced interpretations about students are *relative* interpretations. Criterion-referenced interpretations are *absolute* interpretations.

Testing Terms:

Percentile

The percent of students in a norm group outperformed by a child with a particular test score

Today's standardized achievement tests, consonant with their *Army Alpha* heritage, are constructed so that they produce a substantial spread of scores. Only if students' test scores are really spread out is it possible to make fine comparisons so that relative differences can be identified among students based on how their scores stack up against the scores of students in the norm group.

Take a look, please, at the two sets of test scores in Figure 3.1. Both graphic displays are intended to indicate the proportion of students who earned different test scores. The shaded areas represent the numbers of students who earned a particular score. The higher the columns, the more students there were who earned that score.

Notice that in the top set of test scores, there is a reasonable spread of scores over a range of twenty items correct. However, in the bottom set of test scores, all of the scores are bunched up over only a seven-point range of scores from a low of fourteen correct to a high of twenty correct. As a consequence, the set of scores at the bottom does not have sufficient score-spread to permit the kind of percentile-by-percentile contrasts among test-takers that was at the heart of World War I's *Army Alpha* and remains the overriding mission of today's standardized achievement tests. The top distribution in Figure 3.1 is much, much better for purposes of making student-by-student comparisons.

If standardized achievement tests do not produce a healthy score-spread, then relative comparisons among students' scores will not be possible. And if that happened, the companies that publish the tests would have more difficulty selling those tests because parents could not be informed that "Mary scored at the 49th percentile in mathematics," or "Billy scored at the 54th percentile in language arts." Consequently, sales of the

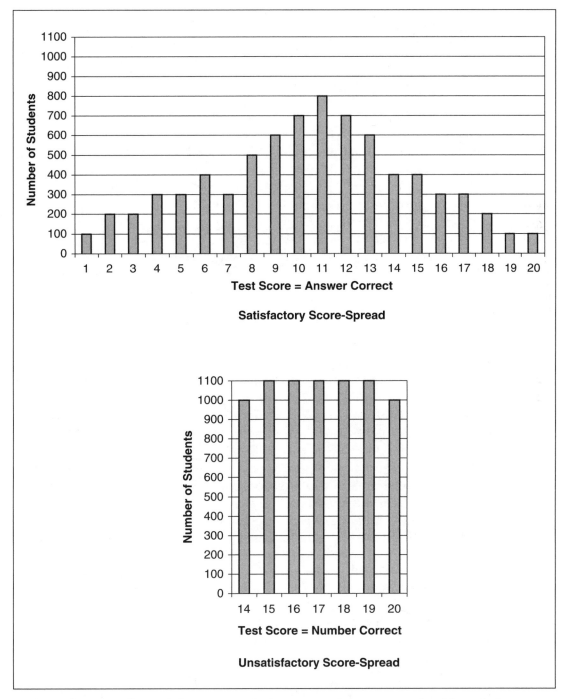

3.1 A satisfactory and unsatisfactory spread of test scores for purposes of making relative comparisons among test-takers

tests would decline. And such a result, from the perspective of the corporate officers who run test companies, would be less than wonderful.

The educational testing business, as you may already know, is very big business indeed. In 1997, for instance, the state of California began using a new standardized achievement test in all its public schools. The price tag for *one year's worth* of testing and scoring was about fifty million dollars. Yes, the companies that publish standardized achievement tests are definitely motivated by profits. And, to make profits, the standardized tests they publish must yield a reasonable amount of score-spread.

As you'll see shortly, when you look at the kinds of test items that are actually found in standardized achievement tests, the technical requirement to have these tests yield a substantial amount of score-spread leads the test's designers to include some genuinely troubling items—troubling, that is, with respect to using students' test performances as indicators of educational quality.

What Do the Items on Standardized Achievement Tests Measure?

If you had an opportunity to review, item-by-item, what's on one of the nationally standardized achievement tests, you'd be surprised by what you'd find. Typically, parents don't have a chance to study the items on standardized achievement tests. That's because the tests are usually re-used for a number of years, and test publishers quite naturally want to keep the tests "secure." Even teachers usually don't have access to the tests themselves between the times when the tests are supposed to be administered. (In all but a few settings, standardized achievement tests are administered by classroom teachers.)

Unless you are a student who's actually taking a standardized test, any item-by-item scrutiny of the items on standardized achievement tests is rare. But, because I've spent hours poring over the items in standardized achievement tests, I'm going to take you on a make-believe tour of these tests and tell you what you'd encounter if you and I could sit down for several hours and analyze the items we'd be apt to find in any of the nation's five major standardized achievement tests.

First off, if you gave any of the commercially published nationally standardized achievement tests a quick look-through, you'd find that the test usually has about four or five main sections. Typically, such tests contain separate sections dealing with reading, language arts (such as sentence formation, spelling, and punctuation), mathematics, science, and social studies. Each section contains about thirty-five to seventy items.

On first looking over the items, you'd probably conclude that the tests "look okay." After all, the science items seem scientific, the mathematics items are loaded with numbers, and the reading items require students to read. Everything appears to be what it should be.

And if I asked, "Would you like your child to be able to correctly answer the items on this test?" you'd probably respond, "You bet!" All parents would like their children to be able to answer the items on standardized achievement tests correctly. But because you might like your child to score 100 percent correct on a standardized achievement test's items does *not* mean that students' test scores should be used as a yardstick by which to measure instructional quality. As we continue our imaginary review of a typical standardized achievement test, let's see why.

The items on a standardized achievement test will reveal to you that those items are measuring one or more of the following three things:

- What's learned in school
- What's learned outside of school
- A child's inherited "school-smarts"

Let's look more closely at items measuring each of these three things. To help you see exactly what I'll be describing, I'm going to include examples of the kinds of items used in standardized achievement tests. All of the items I'll be using as illustrations represent slight variations of actual test items on standardized achievement tests. I've changed the items enough so that I don't violate test security, but the *essence* of the item is unaltered, that is, what it calls for the student to be able to do cognitively is exactly the same as it was in the original test item. (I'll indicate the correct answer with an asterisk. Actual items on standardized tests, of course, would be asterisk-free!)

What's Learned in School.   A good many items on standardized achievement tests measure precisely what most people think such items measure, namely, the knowledge and/or skills that teachers are trying to teach students. Consider, for example, the mathematics item in Figure 3.2. This item measures the sort of skill that teachers should be promoting for the students. The item assesses a student's ability to use multiplication and/or division to find out how long it will take for Tammy to finish a ten-mile bike race. It calls for use of the sort of real-world mathematics that people often must employ when they buy groceries, pay bills, or engage in other day-to-day activities. If they often take part in ten-mile bicycle races, of course, the item assesses a really relevant skill.

Parents might help their children to do homework that involves such mathematics problems, and parents may even help a child who's having trouble with this sort of problem. But few parents will set out to provide such math problems from scratch. No, this kind of item quite appropriately measures an important skill that teachers ought to be teaching children in school.

Look now at the sixth-grade geography item in Figure 3.3. It also deals with knowledge that should be taught in school. Although children

---

■ Tammy took part in a 10-mile bicycle race. She bicycled 4 miles in 36 minutes. Assuming she keeps racing at the same speed, how long will it take her to complete the entire race?

   A. 54 minutes

  *B. 90 minutes

   C. 72 minutes

   D. 87 minutes

   E. None of the above

3.2 The kind of mathematics item in a seventh-grade standardized achievement test that assesses *what's learned in school*

- Which of the following countries is located on the same continent as Brazil?

  A. Mexico

  B. Russia

  *C. Argentina

  D. Iran

3.3 The type of social studies item in a sixth-grade standardized achievement test that assesses *what's learned in school*

can certainly learn about geography outside of school, most children acquire their knowledge of geography in classrooms. If parents wrap their child's school-lunch sandwich in folded-up world maps instead of zipper-lock bags, then it's possible that the answer to the item in Figure 3.3 might be picked up during lunch, unless Argentina was covered with peanut butter. But, by and large, kids learn geography in school.

So, if we could return to our make-believe tour of a standardized achievement test, in reviewing all of a test's items, you'd find plenty of items similar to those in Figures 3.2 and 3.3. Such items assess the mainline cognitive objectives that teachers should be pursuing in school. But, and this is important, you'd also find plenty of items that don't!

What's Learned Outside of School.   As you carry on your review of the items on our fictional standardized tests, you'll find far too many items that assess things learned outside of school. To be more specific, these items measure skills or knowledge flowing from the kinds of experiences that are more common to children from higher levels of socioeconomic status (SES) than to children from lower SES levels. If a child is raised in an affluent family, the odds are that the child will be more likely to answer such test items correctly than if the child had been raised in a less affluent family.

And such items, I hope you'll agree, are not fair. Lower SES children don't get an equal chance to succeed on these kinds of SES-linked items. Beyond fairness, though, students' performances on such items should definitely not be used as an indicator of instructional quality. How can teachers be held responsible for the quality of the nonschool experiences that their students have? How can teachers be held responsible for the SES levels of their students?

- A plant's fruit always contains seeds. Choose the item below that is *not* a fruit.

  A. orange

  B. pumpkin

  C. apple

  *D. celery

3.4 The kind of science item in a sixth-grade standardized achievement test that assesses *what's learned outside of school*

Take a look at the sixth-grade science item in Figure 3.4 and you'll immediately see that students from a more affluent family get a real break on the item. What a child has to do is identify a plant without seeds. The first part of the item tells the child that a plant's fruits always contain seeds, so the child's challenge is to review the item's four options and pick the one that has no seeds.

Think about a child whose parents can routinely afford to purchase stalks of fresh celery or who always buy a fresh pumpkin to carve before Halloween. That child is likely to do better on this item than will a child whose parents must use food stamps. Advantaged kids will answer this item correctly more often than will kids from less advantaged settings. It is an SES-linked item.

Next, look at the fourth-grade social studies item in Figure 3.5. I have a number of concerns about this kind of item—an item-type often found on standardized achievement tests. For one thing, it is based on the kind of formal verbal analogy that people haven't really used all that much since the Middle Ages. When was the last time you personally used an analogy such as the one found in Figure 3.5? And, I assure you, I've never run into a teacher who actually teaches children how to deal with such formal analogies.

But the really serious defect in the item, as far as I'm concerned, is its link to the test-takers' SES. If a child comes from a well-to-do family that has been able to do some home remodeling, or even has been able to build a new home from scratch, you can bet that child will be well versed in a carpenter's use of a saw.

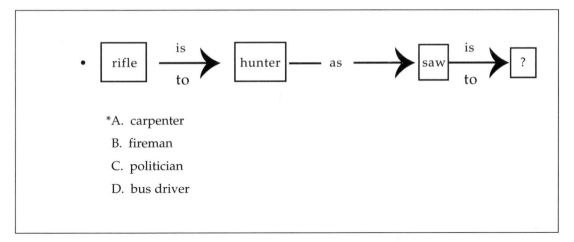

-

  rifle → (is / to) hunter — as → saw (is / to) ?

  *A. carpenter

  B. fireman

  C. politician

  D. bus driver

3.5 The kind of social studies item in a fourth-grade standardized achievement test that assesses *what's learned outside of school*

Moreover, the more magazines and television channels that are likely to be found in a middle or upper SES home also put the child from such circumstances in a far better position to answer this item than a child from disadvantaged circumstances. Articles about home-building are found in magazines and home-report TV shows abound on cable television. Children from low SES circumstances don't have those advantages.

The item in Figure 3.5 is too dependent on children's backgrounds. If a teacher's class consists chiefly of lower SES children, and if a standardized achievement test contains many SES-linked items such as the examples in Figures 3.4 and 3.5, can you see how unfair it would be to consider the teacher as instructionally weak on the basis of students' low performances on the standardized achievement test?

But, you might ask, "How many items of this sort are there on standardized achievement tests?" That's a reasonable question, and because I clearly anticipated you might be thinking of just such a question, only last month I spent a dozen hours going through every single item in a seventh-grade student test booklet for one of the five nationally standardized achievement tests.

I tried to be as fair as I could be, but I wanted to identify the items in which I thought the student's likelihood of answering the item correctly would be dominantly influenced by the student's SES. I'm not saying that everyone would agree with my item judgments, but here's what I came up with. The percent of items that I thought were too heavily linked to SES were:

Content Area	Percent of Items Influenced by Child's SES
• Reading	13%
• Language Arts	66%
• Mathematics	4%
• Science	47%
• Social Studies	45%

Even if my judgments were too stringent, and I really tried to be objective, suppose you cut in half my estimates about SES-linked items. Especially for science, social studies, and mathematics, that's still a fair proportion of a major standardized test in which the student's SES exercises a dominant role in determining the student's test score.

Remember, in higher-SES families, parents will usually have gone further in school than parents from lower-SES families. And children whose parents are better educated pick up a clear advantage over children whose parents are less well educated. As I reviewed the items in the language arts section of the test, I was surprised and dismayed to see how many were dependent on a student's ability to "hear" the way Standard American English ought to be spoken. Well, if a child's parents are well educated, there'll be more Standard American English spoken in the home. Kids from such homes have a leg up over kids from lower-SES families in which such language is less common. And how about children who grow up in families where English is not the first language?

When what's being measured is a student's socioeconomic status, not what the student has been taught in school, then it's clearly inappropriate to use the results of standardized achievement tests as indicators of educational quality. How can teachers or school administrators be held responsible for the composition of the students who attend their school?

A Child's Inherited "School Smarts."   When I was a high school teacher, over forty years ago, my fellow teachers and I all believed in what everyone referred to as "intelligence." And we surely believed that our students had different amounts of it. In those days, intelligence was thought to be something like an innate capacity for learning. Most of us regarded intelligence as a fixed amount of intellectual potential that each child was given at birth. In fact, educators would routinely calculate a child's intelligence quotient (IQ) by dividing the child's *actual age* (in years and months) into the child's *mental age* based on how well the child had scored on an intelligence test.

If a child who was actually ten years old scored as high as a typical twelve-year-old on the intelligence test, then we'd divide the ten into the twelve, and calculate that the child has an IQ of 120. An IQ higher than 100 was above average; an IQ lower than 100 was below average. But that entire view of intelligence as a person's inherited and immutable intellectual potential has gone the way of black-and-white TV sets. Its time has definitely passed.

More and more educators are now subscribing to the belief that there are *multiple* forms of intelligence. Based on the research of Professor Howard Gardner at Harvard, it is now widely thought that, instead of one big blob of intelligence, people possess various kinds of intelligence. I previously alluded to test items that measure a child's "school-smarts." Children who are school smart possess substantial amounts of *word-smarts* (verbal capabilities) and *number-smarts* (logical/mathematical capabilities).

In addition to school-smarts, there are other equally important forms of intelligence. For instance, Professor Gardner describes *inter*personal intelligence *(people-smarts)* as a form of intelligence that represents an individual's ability to discern subtle sentiments, views, and preferences of other people. Persons with strong people-smarts have finely tuned antennae that pick up other folks' personal inclinations.

Then there's *intra*personal intelligence *(self-smarts)*. This form of intelligence revolves around individuals' abilities to be in touch with their own motives, choices, and reasons for action. Persons who are self-smart understand what makes themselves tick, hence can act more wisely based on a heightened self-awareness.

Gardner's other forms of intelligence include musical intelligence *(music-smarts)*, bodily-kinesthetic intelligence *(body-smarts)*, and spatial intelligence *(picture-smarts)*. Clearly, today's conception of intelligence is a much richer view of the various capabilities a child possesses than my colleagues and I possessed more than four decades ago.

The reason I've spent several paragraphs describing today's view of multiple intelligences is that you must recognize within your own child there are those different kinds of capabilities. Few children are across-the-board superior on all seven forms of intelligence. And traditional "school-smarts" (word-smarts and number-smarts) by no means constitute the most important forms of intelligence. Some of today's most successful individuals may have been only so-so with respect to school-smarts, but have parlayed their people-smarts or self-smarts into highly successful careers.

Standardized achievement tests do *not* assess all of Gardner's seven varieties of intelligence. If standardized *achievement* tests were really going to do what their name implies, they wouldn't assess inherited capabilities at all. Instead, they'd measure the skill and knowledge *achievements* that a child makes in school.

So, do not be unduly disturbed if your child does not seem to display an abundance of word-smarts or number-smarts. Odds are that there are other forms of intelligence your child possesses, other forms of intelligence that can be just as important if not more important than school-smarts.

There's no such thing as a single, inborn commodity known as "intelligence." You dare not conclude that if your child doesn't have oodles of word-smarts or number-smarts, the child is not intelligent. Parents who convey such a perception to their children do those children a distinct disservice.

But what about the modifiability of any of the several varieties of intelligence? Take word-smarts, for example. If your child hasn't been very adept in using verbal concepts, even from an early age, does it mean that your child's deficiencies in word-smarts forever doom that child to mediocrity in the verbal realm? Absolutely not. If your child is well taught, there's the potential for real progress in the child's verbal knowledge and skills. But there may well be an upper limit to the child's verbal accomplishments. Or it may be that your child will take longer to achieve the levels of verbal achievement that, to other kids, might come more rapidly.

Let me be as honest as I can. For whatever genetic reasons, some children are born with different capabilities than others. I have four children. They differ meaningfully in which of the several kinds of intelligence they are strong in or weak in. Let me illustrate below using Child A and Child B. If I used *actual* names, sibling strife might still be induced. And they are grown-ups by now.

Child A	*Child B*
People-Smarts: Strong	People-Smarts: So-So
Number-Smarts: Weak	Number-Smarts: Strong
Word-Smarts: So-So	Word-Smarts: So-So

Note that Child A is weak in number-smarts. I really believe that there is an inherited limitation in Child A's ability to do mathematics. Does that indicate that teachers should have given up on Child A's math lessons? Of course not. In a sense, Child A inherited a range of potential quantitative accomplishments. I wanted to insure that Child A ended up at the absolute top of that range of potential quantitative achievement even though it might have taken Child A more time to learn the multiplication tables than it took for us to land a man on the moon.

Similarly, as a parent I wanted Child B to achieve at the upper limit of Child B's so-so people-smarts, strong number-smarts, and so-so word-smarts. That's what I hope all parents want for their children. Given whatever limits there are in a child's inherited potential to learn, we should be helping our children achieve to the very maximum of their potentials.

Returning to the kinds of items that you'd find as we continue our make-believe tour of a standardized achievement test, you'll run into a substantial number of items that, in the main, simply measure children's school-smarts, *not* what those children have been taught in school. Let me show you the kinds of items that you'd find in your review.

In Figure 3.6 you'll see a sixth-grade social studies item that seems to be dealing with the student's familiarity with the conservation of natural resources. Sounds pretty good, right? But if you look really closely at the item, you'll see that what sixth-graders really need to do, if they're going to answer this item correctly, is use their word-smarts. First, the child has to figure out that the phrase "to conserve resources" means to save them. Then, the word-smart child simply goes through the four response options, and concludes from a verbal analysis that in Choices A, B, and D, there's no savings that take place. Accordingly, the word-smart child will opt for Choice C even though there's never been any instruction in school regarding the conservation implications of writing on both sides of a piece of paper.

In other words, an item such as the sixth-grade social studies item seen in Figure 3.6 really assesses children's word-smarts, not any social

---

- If someone really wants to conserve resources, one good way to do so is to:

    A. leave lights on even if they are not needed.

    B. wash small loads instead of large loads in a clothes-washing machine.

    *C. write on both sides of a piece of paper.

    D. place used newspapers in the garbage.

3.6 The kind of social studies item in a sixth-grade standardized achievement test that assesses *a child's word-smarts*

studies learned at school. There are many such items in standardized achievement tests, items that present verbal problems for students to figure out. Students with sufficient word-smarts will typically be successful. Students with insufficient word-smarts typically won't.

There's another example in Figure 3.7. Here you'll see a seventh-grade mathematics item that assesses a child's ability to figure out how to create equal totals for two sets of number tiles. Look at the item for a moment, or even for a few moments, and you'll see that by switching the 4-tile and the 2-tile, each set of number tiles will sum to 16. So, Choice B is the correct answer.

Let's say a child who tackles that item does so on a "trial-and-error" basis by mentally exchanging the pairs of tiles represented in the four answer options. Number-smart kids can make those mental exchanges far

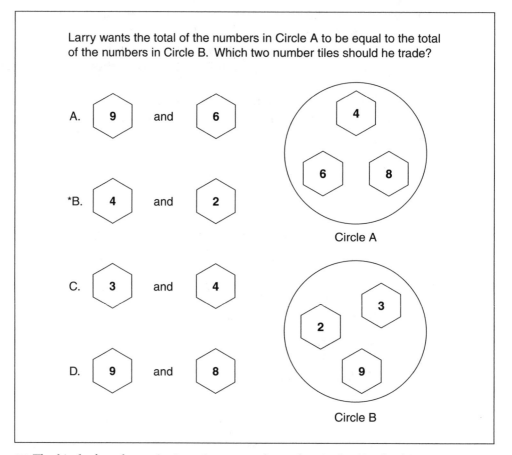

3.7 The kind of mathematics item in a seventh-grade standardized achievement test that assesses *a child's number-smarts*

better than kids who aren't as number-smart. I'm sure you can see that a number-smart child would not only be more likely to get the correct answer, but would be more likely to get that answer quickly, thus leaving more time to spend on subsequent items in the test. This item, even if the teacher did or didn't spend class time using number tiles, chiefly measures a child's number-smarts. The item in Figure 3.7 is a school-smarts item.

For a final item, please take a look at the two zoolike collections of animals in Figure 3.8. As you can see, in this fourth-grade science item children are asked to pick the animal that "moved the most" from Scene A to Scene B. (If you're in doubt about whether such items actually exist, I assure you that there *is* such an item in the science section of a currently published fourth-grade standardized achievement test.)

Now, unless you suffer from borderline blindness, you can see that only one of the four animals moved *at all* between the two scenes. Yes, it was good old Leo the Lion who hopped from the left of the tiger in Scene A to the right of the tiger in Scene B. Can you see that children who have spatial intelligence, that is, who are picture-smart, will be able to answer this item in a flash?

The item does *not* measure what children are taught to do in school. What sensible fourth-grade teacher would spend instructional time in

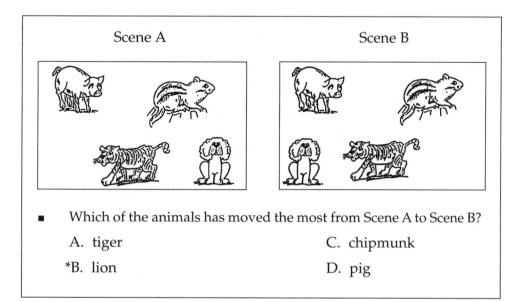

  ■   Which of the animals has moved the most from Scene A to Scene B?

    A. tiger   C. chipmunk

    *B. lion   D. pig

3.8 The kind of science item in a fourth-grade standardized achievement test that assesses *a child's picture-smarts*

science on such silliness? The item simply assesses children's picture-smarts, not what those children are taught in school.

A month ago, when I reviewed a current standardized achievement test, item-by-item, I identified the items that I believed were dominantly dependent on a child's school-smarts. I tried to be as fair to the test items as I could, but here are the percentages of such items I found in each of the five subject areas covered in the test:

Content Area	*Percent of Items Dominantly Assessing Children's School-Smarts*
• Reading	40%
• Language Arts	34%
• Mathematics	18%
• Science	52%
• Social Studies	53%

As you can see, the percentages of the items dominantly measuring children's school-smarts ranges from a low of 18 percent in mathematics to a high of 53 percent in social studies, followed closely by 52 percent in science. That's simply way too many items for which a student's correct answers are dominantly influenced by the student's inherited word-smarts or number-smarts. If you are only moderately "number-smart," you'll realize that 52 percent and 53 percent in a content area is *about half!*

You've now seen examples of the three kinds of items that you'll find in standardized achievement tests. There are items that do, indeed, measure what's learned in school. But there are also SES-linked items that measure what's learned outside of school. Finally, there are school-smarts items that measure the degree of a child's inherited verbal and quantitative abilities.

If a standardized achievement test contains many items significantly influenced by a child's SES level or school-smarts, the test is inappropriate to use in judging the quality of instruction. Items that are strongly tied to children's SES levels or to their school smarts *measure what children bring to school, not what they learn there.*

Why Do Standardized Achievement Tests Assess What They Do?

You might be wondering why it is that the folks who create standardized achievement tests include so many items that depend less on what's taught in school and more on what children bring to school. The answer is quite simple. Developers of standardized achievement tests rely so heavily on those two kinds of items because such items make the biggest contribution to the production of score-spread, the holy grail of standardized test publishers.

You see, if the creators of standardized tests actually loaded their tests with items covering content likely to be taught in school, too many students might perform well on the test. If the schools taught students the skills and/or knowledge measured by such a test, the vast majority of students would perform well on the test. As a result, there would be insufficient score-spread.

If you have the energy, take another look at Figure 3.1 on page 51. If too many students began to do too well on a standardized test's items, the resulting distribution of scores would look more like the scrunched-up set of scores at the bottom than the unscrunched set of scores at the top. Unscrunched scores provide sufficient score-spread needed for fine comparisons among students' relative performances. Scrunched-up scores don't.

Let me describe a related quandary faced by the creators of standardized achievement tests. The test items that do the best job in producing score-spread are the items answered correctly by about half the test-takers. Items that are answered correctly by too many students, for example, by 80 or 90 percent of the students, are typically not put on the test when it's first created, and are almost always removed from a test once it's revised.

But items on which most students perform well often deal with *the very content that teachers emphasize instructionally* because of that content's importance. The better the teacher teaches particular content, the better the students perform on that content. But the better students do on items measuring that content, the more likely it is that items covering such important and well-taught content will be discarded when the test is revised. There is, therefore, a systematic tendency to remove from standardized achievement tests those items covering the very most important content that teachers teach.

And this is done, of course, because of the standardized achievement test developer's constant quest for score-spread. I'm not suggesting that publishers of standardized achievement tests are unconcerned about the content preferences of subject matter specialists. Other things being equal, standardized achievement test publishers would just as soon have tests that measured most of the key content in each subject field tested. But other things are *not* equal, and soon the test-developer is faced with a choice between the measurement of key content and the creation of adequate score-spread. With few exceptions, you'll find the need for score-spread wins out.

Remember, standardized achievement tests are fairly short assessment instruments. Often, only forty or fifty items are used to assess students in a given subject field. So the test's designers have a truly difficult time in choosing items that effectively spread out students according to their relative performance levels. What ends up happening, as a consequence, is that many standardized achievement tests turn out to be almost impervious to detecting the effects of even first-rate teaching.

If many items on standardized achievement tests could be influenced substantially by teachers' instructional efforts, then score-spread would soon disappear. The "spread 'em out" mission of the *Army Alpha* and all subsequent standardized tests would fail. From a test publisher's perspective, the best items for standardized achievement tests are those that *can't* be influenced by even first-rate instruction.

When parents try to judge a school's educational quality by using standardized achievement tests, they really are trying to measure temperature with a tablespoon. It's the right job, but the wrong assessment tool.

What Standardized Achievement Tests *Can* Do

Standardized achievement tests should never be used to judge the instructional quality of a district, school, or teacher. Even so, those tests do have a potential contribution to make. Standardized achievement tests can help you, or your child's teacher, see how your child compares with a nationally representative sample of children with respect to what is measured by such tests. These kinds of comparisons can help, in a very rough way, to identify a child's relative strengths and weaknesses. For instance, you might find out that your child is strong in reading (a 90th percentile) but weak in mathematics (a 22nd percentile).

Those kinds of comparative judgments can be helpful to both parents and teachers. Yet, because of the small size of the content-sample in the test (with only forty to sixty items), parents should not race to the conclusion that a standardized-test score in a given subject area tells them what the child *really* knows about that subject. Remember, with all the items measuring students' SES level and school-smarts, there are very few items left to really give you an accurate fix on what your child knows in any subject.

Standardized achievement test scores give you a general, very sketchy idea about how your child stacks up against other children nationally with respect to the kinds of items included in the test. If you haven't reviewed the actual items on the standardized achievement test your child took—and you often will not have such an opportunity—*do not conclude* that your child's knowledge and/or skill in a particular subject area is well represented by the child's score on a standardized achievement test.

A Parent Puzzle

Here's another fictional interchange between a parent and an educator. Read the setting and the interchange, then decide what *you* would say next if you were the parent in the interchange. *After* you've decided how you might respond, you can see how I might have responded and why.

(Setting: Sunnyside Elementary School is located in a high-income suburb located just outside a major urban school district. Each year, in early summer, local newspapers rank each school in the state on the basis of student's scores on nationally standardized achievement tests administered at every other grade level. As usual, in this year's rankings, Sunnyside students score in the top 5 percent for the entire state.

The school's principal, Mrs. Billings, is appearing on a local radio's talk show to discuss this year's rankings. Most callers are parents of children in (1) the suburban district where Sunnyside is located or (2) the nearby urban school district. In response to a previous caller, Mrs. Billings has asserted that, "There's solid and continuing evidence that Sunnyside Elementary School's teachers are among the finest in the state." A new caller, a parent, is now on the line.)

Parent: "I'm pleased that you think the teachers at Sunnyside are so skillful, Mrs. Billings, because I have two children enrolled in the school. But I'm a little confused. What is the basis for your belief that your school's teachers are so good?"

Mrs. Billings: "As the school's principal, I have many opportunities to visit classrooms, and I'm constantly pleased by the first-rate instruction that I see going on there. But the chief reason for my belief appears in our local newspaper every July, as soon as students' scores on the state-selected standardized achievement test are published.

"The average scores of our third-graders and fifth-graders, the only two grades where tests are given in elementary school, are always at or near the top of the statewide test rankings. Yes, the most compelling evidence of our teachers' excellence comes from the excellence of our test results."

Parent: "But students' scores from nearby urban schools are always so much lower. Does that mean the teachers in those schools are not skillful?"

Mrs. Billings: "I wish I could give you another answer, but schools are created to help students learn, and if there's no learning that goes on, then I think those urban teachers are falling down. Don't you?"

*Parent: If **you** were the parent-caller, what would you say next?*

- -

My Response: If I were the caller, I might say something like this: "But Mrs. Billings, isn't it true standardized achievement tests contain many items that are more likely to be answered correctly simply because children come from advantaged families such as those served by Sunnyside? Perhaps there's fine teaching going on in the urban district, but students' scores on a standardized achievement test simply won't show it."

My Reason: It sounds, from what Mrs. Billings has said, that she doesn't understand about the inappropriateness of using standardized achievement test scores as a major indicator of instructional effectiveness. As a caller, I wouldn't have time "on air" to supply all of the points treated in this chapter. (That might require a lengthy infomercial!) But perhaps I can plant a seed of doubt in Mrs. Billings' mind. If she seems willing to listen—and to learn—then I might suggest that she consult one or more of the *Suggested Resources* you'll find cited at the close of the chapter.

Even with the limitations you've seen, however, standardized achievement tests can supply some useful insights to teachers and parents about particular children, not instructional quality. In the next chapter you'll learn how to make the most sense out of your child's score reports based on standardized achievement tests.

Are Educators Responsible for Student Growth?

I've been stressing that standardized achievement tests contain far too many items assessing what students bring to school, not what they're taught there. And, as a consequence, I've been arguing that standardized achievement test results should not be used to evaluate the quality of schooling. Does this argument lead to the conclusion that because students' standardized test scores are significantly influenced by factors outside the control of educators, those educators have no responsibility for increasing students' skills and knowledge? It does not.

Schools exist to help students learn. Teachers and school administrators must be held accountable for increased student learning, and they should produce credible evidence that students are, in fact, learning what they are supposed to learn. But credible evidence of educators' instructional quality will not come from students' scores on standardized achievement tests. Those tests are simply the wrong assessment tool for a terribly important job, namely, the assembly of solid evidence that children are being well taught. Later, in Chapter 13, I'll show you how teachers can collect credible evidence that students are acquiring increased knowledge, improved skills, or more appropriate affect.

Teachers should not be allowed to dodge their instructional responsibilities by saying "standardized achievement tests don't show our competence because they depend on the students we get." If standardized achievement tests are the wrong tool, then teachers had better use more appropriate tools to demonstrate, convincingly, that children are learning.

Your Responsibility

In view of what you now know about standardized achievement tests, do *you* have any responsibilities regarding the misuse of scores from these tests to indicate how well schools are performing? I think you do.

You'll learn in Chapter 11 that teachers, operating under enormous pressure to improve students' test scores on standardized achievement tests, sometimes succumb to such pressure. A limited number of teachers, victimized by the rules of an accountability game they can't win, engage in score-boosting activities that are not in the educational best interest of their students.

For example, some teachers spend far too much time in preparing their students for an upcoming high-stakes test. All that test-preparation time takes away classroom hours that ought to be spent on instruction. Even worse, some teachers end up teaching specifically toward the actual test items on standardized achievement tests. The result of such item-focused teaching is that students' scores on standardized achievement tests will be distorted by being artificially inflated. They'll no longer permit valid inferences about what students' real levels of achievement are.

There's more than a small chance these days that *your* child will be harmed by such an understandable, but inappropriate frenzy to boost scores on standardized achievement tests. You should do what you can to forestall such a situation.

First, you should let your child's teachers and principal know that you understand the inappropriateness of judging educators on the basis of standardized achievement test scores. You're apt to find that many educators have some kind of intuitive understanding that standardized achievement test scores aren't appropriate for determining educational quality,

but they're not sure why. If you need to, let them read this chapter or refer them to some of the *Suggested Resources* at the chapter's end. What you're really trying to do is "take the pressure off," that is, take the pressure off the educators who work with your child to boost scores on standardized achievement tests. The less pressure those educators perceive they're under to boost such scores, the more energy they'll be able to put into educating your child.

But one parent's voice is not as potent as many parents' voices. So, the second thing you should do is try to inform other parents about this issue, and encourage them to understand why it is that the present-day preoccupation with standardized achievement test scores can undermine the quality of the education their children receive. Show other parents the examples of items from standardized achievement tests you saw in this chapter. Explain why those items measure what students bring to school, not what they learn there.

Then those parents, now aware of the misuse of standardized achievement tests, can join you in decreasing the pressure on your school's educators to engage in score-boosting procedures that are educationally damaging to children. Anything you can do to correct this serious misuse of standardized achievement tests will, in the long run, have a positive influence on your child's education.

What Do You Really Need to Know about This Chapter's Content?

This is an important chapter for you and your child. If you really understand why it is that standardized achievement tests do not provide an accurate picture of instructional quality, you'll be able to relay that message to educators and other concerned parents. Presented below are the most significant features of the chapter.

- The most important lesson to be drawn from Chapter 3 is that standardized achievement tests should not be used to evaluate educational quality, that is, to determine the instructional effectiveness of a teacher, school, or district.
- Standardized *achievement* tests are supposed to assess the knowledge and skills children are taught in school; standardized *aptitude* tests are predictor tests designed to foretell how well students will perform in some subsequent educational setting.

- Today's standardized achievement tests are modeled after World War I's *Army Alpha*, a standardized *aptitude* test that was successful in identifying future officer candidates for the U.S. Army.
- To make the kinds of relative comparisons that are the chief function of standardized achievement tests, it is necessary for the tests to produce a substantial spread of students' scores.
- The items in standardized achievement tests measure (1) what's learned in school, (2) what's learned outside of school, and (3) a child's inherited school-smarts.
- Current thinking regarding children's inherited abilities suggests that there are multiple intelligences, not only the traditional academic capabilities based on children's verbal and quantitative abilities.
- Because of the substantial number of SES-linked items and items assessing children's school-smarts, the remaining items on standardized achievement tests offer parents only a very sketchy idea of their children's achievements in different subject areas.

POSSIBLE PARENT ACTION–OPTIONS

If you intend to take any action based on the material covered in Chapter 3, here are a few options for you to consider.

1. You can become sufficiently familiar with the contents of this chapter so that, at a future meeting of the teachers and parents in your child's school, you can get the following question on the meeting's agenda so it can be discussed: "Should our school's educational effectiveness be determined by students' scores on standardized achievement tests?" If the topic is considered, you can provide your own insights based on what you've read.

2. You can try to familiarize yourself with the actual items on standardized achievement tests by asking the principal in your child's school if you can review (at the school) a currently used standardized achievement test. Such tests are usually stored in the school under lock and key to preserve test security. Failing that, see if you can review a previously used form of a standardized achievement test. If you do gain access to a test for such a review, go through it item-by-item and try to answer the following questions for each item:

   - Is the knowledge or skill measured by this item truly *important* for children to learn?

- Will the probability of a student's answering this item correctly be *dominantly* influenced by the student's socioeconomic status?
- Will the probability of a student's answering this item correctly be *dominantly* influenced by the student's inherited school-smarts?

3. Let your child's teacher know that, because you have read about the misuse of standardized achievement tests as measures of instructional effectiveness, you are personally not going to be using such test-score results in arriving at your own estimates of educational quality. Encourage the teacher to supply other evidence of student growth. (See pages 263–281 in Chapter 13 for suggestions about how to gather such evidence.)

4. Set up a small parent study group to consider the contents of Chapter 3. By doing so, what you are hoping to accomplish is get more parents to understand the shortcomings of using students' standardized test scores as the chief indicator of educational quality. If possible, secure copies of current or earlier standardized achievement tests so your study group can review the actual items on these tests. Remember, it's the items that lead to students' test scores.

5. Encourage your child's principal to secure one or more of the *Suggested Resources* cited at the close of this chapter. Recommend that, if the principal considers it appropriate, the school's teachers might want to learn more about the inappropriateness of evaluating school quality using standardized achievement tests. Remember, many educators' professional reputations are wrongly damaged when people use standardized achievement test scores to determine educational quality.

SUGGESTED RESOURCES FOR YOUR CHILD'S TEACHER OR PRINCIPAL

Printed Materials

Cunningham, George K. *Assessment in the Classroom: Constructing and Interpreting Tests.* London: Falmer Press, 1998. *Chapter 8 of this introductory classroom assessment text provides a clear description of what standardized tests are and how they can be used by educators. Cunningham identifies some potential misuses of standardized test results.*

Popham, W. James. *Classroom Assessment: What Teachers Need to Know* (2nd ed.). Boston: Allyn and Bacon, 1999. *In an appendix provided at the end of this book, the appropriateness of standardized achievement tests as indicators of educational quality is analyzed on pages 315–321.*

Popham, W. James. *Modern Educational Measurement: Practical Guidelines for Educational Leaders* (3rd ed.). Boston: Allyn and Bacon, 2000. *The title of Chapter 15 in this measurement book written for educational leaders gives away its message: "Standardized Achievement Tests: Marvelous Measures—Often Misused."*

Weber, Ellen. *Student Assessment That Works: A Practical Approach.* Boston: Allyn and Bacon, 1999. *In Chapter 10, "Myths About Traditional Testing," Weber describes some of the difficulties associated with traditional testing. She identifies and repudiates ten popular myths about standardized tests.*

Videotape Programs

IOX Assessment Associates. *Criterion-Referenced Measurement: Today's Alternative to Traditional Testing.* (5301 Beethoven St., Ste. 190, Los Angeles, CA 90066). *This video describes the key elements a test must have in order for criterion-referenced interpretations to be made. Criterion-referenced interpretations are contrasted with norm-referenced interpretations.*

IOX Assessment Associates. *Norm-Referenced Tests: Uses and Misuses.* (5301 Beethoven St., Ste. 190, Los Angeles, CA 90066). *This video describes the nature of standardized, norm-referenced tests and isolates proper and improper use of such tests.*

4

MAKING SENSE OUT OF STANDARDIZED TEST SCORES

*Y*our child will be required to take standardized tests in school. There may be many. There may be few. But there *will* be standardized tests that your child will be obliged to complete.

What Tests to Expect

If you have a child in elementary school, the standardized tests your child will ordinarily be taking will be *achievement* tests such as the *Iowa Tests of Basic Skills,* the *Stanford Achievement Tests,* or the *Comprehensive Tests of Basic Skills.* Ordinarily, these tests are administered in the spring, but in a small number of localities, standardized achievement tests are given in the fall rather than the spring.

Sometimes, children in elementary school are also administered a standardized *aptitude* test. For instance, the *Cognitive Abilities Test* is a group-administered academic aptitude test employed to predict students' likelihood of future verbal and quantitative achievement in school. Group administered academic aptitude tests are being used less frequently by educators, so there's a strong likelihood that your child will never take such a test.

Individually administered aptitude tests are sometimes given by counselors or school psychologists, but only to students who are either gifted or, in contrast, appear to be intellectually handicapped. Very few teachers have been certified to administer individual aptitude tests. Students' scores on such tests are often used to develop an individual educational plan for special-education students who need individualized instructional attention.

Parents with children in middle schools (often called junior high schools) are apt to find that standardized achievement tests are still administered, but standardized aptitude tests are not seen all that often in grades six to eight.

When children reach high school, there may still be standardized achievement tests given, but usually at fewer grade levels than in elementary school. College-predictor aptitude tests such as the *Scholastic Assessment Test* (SAT), and the *ACT Assessment* are taken by many students in secondary schools, but usually at the student's choosing. A preliminary version of the SAT, the PSAT, is also available.

You might be interested to know that, in recent years, the term *aptitude* has definitely fallen out of favor with educators. That's because "aptitude" seems to imply a child's *fixed,* innate capacity to achieve. Fewer and fewer educators subscribe to the idea that a student has a fixed potential to learn. To illustrate, for years the formal name of the SAT was the *Scholastic Aptitude Test.* Then the publishers of that test scurried away from the "aptitude" label, renaming it the *Scholastic Assessment Test.* As you've now learned, the terms *test* and *assessment* mean essentially the same thing. Publishers of the SAT were so eager to escape the "aptitude," fixed-ability rap, that they accepted an obvious redundancy when retitling their test. They might just as well have called it the *"Scholastic Test Test,"* but that would have been a bit too obvious.

Well, when your child is in high school, if you plan for the child to attend college, you'll need to look into whether the SAT or ACT is most widely used where you live. The SAT is the more popular of the two aptitude tests for college-bound students, but there are some regions where most students sit for the ACT. Information regarding either exam should be available in the guidance/counseling office in your child's high school.

Reports, Reports

Whether your child takes a standardized achievement test or a standardized aptitude test, you should receive a report describing your child's performance. This chapter is intended to help you understand those reports better. Your child's teachers will also be getting reports about your child's test scores. I want you to know as much as they do about the way your child performed on those standardized tests.

Here's an advance tip on how this chapter is organized. First, you'll be introduced to the four most common ways that students' test scores are reported to parents. You'll be looking at *percentiles, grade-equivalent scores, scale scores,* and *stanines.* I want you to have an intuitive understanding about how these four ways of describing a student's performances work.

The reason you need to know how those scores function is that different score-reporting procedures are often used by different test publishers. And it's quite likely that your child will be taking several different standardized tests, distributed by different test publishers, while the child is in school.

Educators change standardized tests for a variety of reasons, such as trying to get tests that are most in line with a district's or a state's curriculum. Sometimes such test-shifts take place every few years. As a consequence, if you can master the fundamental meanings of the four major score-reporting mechanisms to be treated in this chapter, you should have little difficulty in interpreting what your child's scores mean, irrespective of which standardized achievement test or aptitude test is used.

After describing the four prominent score-reporting procedures, I'm then going to give you a brief guided tour through the most common kinds of parent score-reports used by test publishers. As you look at the typical sorts of parent-reports that you'll be receiving, you'll be able to employ what you've just learned about the four score-reporting methods. After you've seen some sample score-reports for individual students, you'll be readily able to make sense out of your own child's standardized test-score reports.

Two Straightforward, Easy-to-Learn Statistical Indicators

You'll often find that your child's scores on standardized achievement tests are reported in relation to a set of other students' scores (such as the scores in your child's class or school, or the scores of children who are in the standardized test's norm group). When your child's score is stacked up against the scores of other students, the other students' scores are typically described according to their *mean* performances and the *standard deviation* of their performances. The mean and the standard deviation are two statistical indicators often used by educators to describe students' test scores. You ought to know, at least in a general way, what educators are yammering about when they refer to the *mean* and *standard deviation* of a group of test scores. Accordingly, I'm going to give you a super-easy, nonthreatening mini-introduction to these two statistical indicators. Don't you dare be intimidated!

The *mean* is easy. It is simply the numerical average of a group of scores. Usually, the mean is calculated for a set of students' *raw scores*, that is, the numbers of test items that students answered correctly. If there were ninety third-graders in an elementary school, the mean performance for all the school's third-grade children would be calculated simply by adding together the ninety raw scores of the third-grade children, then dividing that

sum by ninety. The mean is the most commonly used way of describing how a group of scores, sometimes called a *distribution* of scores, is centered.

In addition to the mean of a distribution of scores, however, educators often wish to describe how "spread out" a distribution's scores are. The statistic most often used to describe a distribution's score-spread is the *standard deviation.* A standard deviation is something like the mean, at least in the sense that it is an *average.* The standard deviation actually represents an average of how far a distribution's raw scores are from the mean of that distribution. The more spread out a distribution's scores are, then the farther those scores will be from the distribution's mean. In that case, the standard deviation for the scores will be large. The less spread out a distribution's scores are, then the closer their scores will be to the distribution's mean. In that case, the standard deviation for the scores will be small.

Testing Terms:
Mean
The arithmetic average of a set of scores

I'd like you to be comfortable about where the standard deviation comes from, and how it's used. So, please look at Figure 4.1 if you will, and you'll see that a set of students' scores on a ten-item quiz are displayed graphically. Each student's score is represented by a shaded square. Notice that only one student answered all ten items correctly. (It was probably Sally Palmer, class smarty, who *always* gets the top score on tests.) There were five students who answered seven items correctly, and so on. Typically, someone "smooths" the top of the distribution so it looks more like

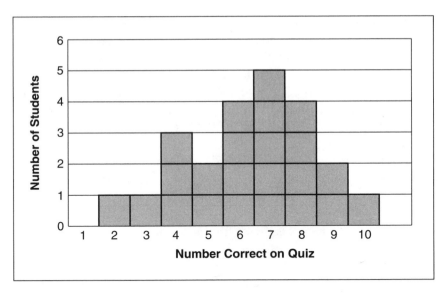

4.1 A distribution of 23 students' scores on a 10-item quiz

what you'll see in Figure 4.2, in which the tops of the several columns have been connected to make a single line or, as it's usually called, a "curve." Incidentally, the mean for the set of test scores portrayed in Figures 4.1 and 4.2 turns out to be 146 ÷ 23 = 6.3.

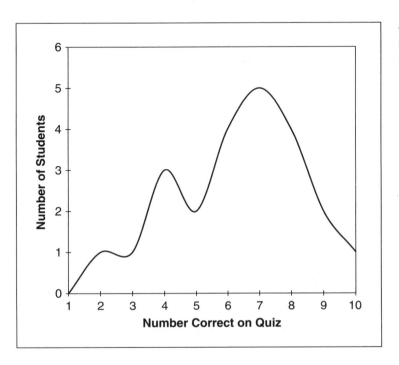

4.2 A smoothed curve representing 23 students' scores on a 10-item quiz

What you need to remember is that the *area* under the curved line represents the number of students who earned a particular score. So, notice in Figure 4.2 at the highest point in the curve, that is, where the area of the curve is greatest, on the baseline you'll see "7 correct." That's exactly what it was in Figure 4.1. So, if you see a set of scores represented graphically, and your child's score is included in that set of scores, then your child is represented somewhere by a small part of the area under the curved line.

Now, please look at Figure 4.3 in which you'll see two distributions of test scores presented, both of which have *identical* means. In the top distribution, you'll see the scores are more spread out. The standard deviation for those scores is shown graphically to the right of the distribution. In the bottom distribution, the less spread out one, the standard deviation is also shown graphically at the right. You'll see that it's smaller than the standard deviation for the top, more spread out distribution.

Earlier, I indicated that a standard deviation was sort of an average, much like the mean. Well, now you can see that the standard deviation

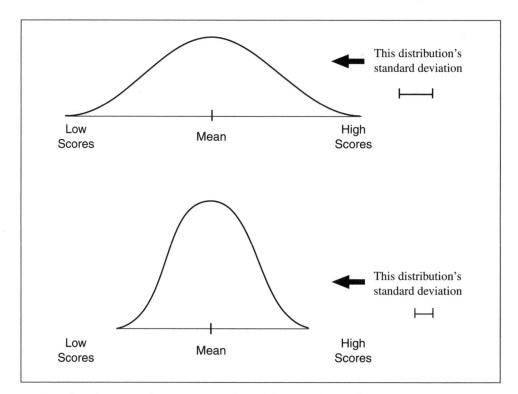

4.3 Two distributions of test scores with equal means but different standard deviations

represents something like an average of how far a distribution's raw scores are from its mean. The more distant (deviated) the scores are from the distribution's mean, the larger the average deviation of the scores. The less distant the distribution's scores are deviated from its mean, the smaller the average of the deviations. The standard deviation represents a kind of average spread of scores in a distribution.

One way that standard deviations are used to help interpret the meaning of your child's test performances is that a score distribution's standard deviation is used *something like a measuring stick* along the baseline of the distribution. If a standard deviation for a set of test scores were 3.6, for instance, then you'd have a measuring stick that was 3.6 in length. So, looking again at the top distribution in Figure 4.3, you'll see that if you were to use the standard deviation as a measuring stick, there would be room for about six standard deviations along the top distribution's baseline. Similarly, for the bottom distribution there would be room for about six of its standard deviations along its baseline.

Testing Terms:
Standard Deviation
A statistic reflecting the variability of a distribution of scores, the larger the standard deviation, the more distant are the distribution's scores from its mean

To repeat, larger standard deviations reflect score distributions that are more spread out (often referred to as distributions with more *variability*). Smaller standard deviations reflect sets of test scores with less variability, that is, less spread out. Thinking back to Chapter 3, in which you saw how important it was for the developers of standardized tests to spread students' scores out substantially, you'll realize that such test-developers try to create tests so students' performances will have large standard deviations. Score distributions with small standard deviations don't permit the fine comparisons that are at the heart of standardized testing.

All right, with the mean and standard deviation wrapped up, that is, now that you have a general idea about how those two statistical indicators work, let's look at the most common ways your child's standardized test performances will be described.

Four Score-Reporting Approaches

One of two interpretive frameworks is generally used to make sense out of students' test scores. Test scores are interpreted in *absolute* or *relative* terms. When you interpret a student's test score *absolutely*, you infer from the score what it is that the student can or cannot do. For example, based on a student's performance on test items dealing with mathematics computation skills, you can make an inference about the degree to which the student has mastered such computation skills. Teachers may even boil the interpretation down to an on–off classification, namely, whether the student should be classified as having *mastered* or *not mastered* the skill or knowledge being assessed. A mastery versus nonmastery interpretation represents an *absolute* interpretation of a student's test score. Classroom teachers often use absolute interpretive approaches when creating tests to assess a student's knowledge or skills based on a particular unit of study.

On the other hand, when you interpret a student's test score *relatively*, you infer from the score how the student stacks up against other students who are currently taking the test or have previously taken the test. For example, when a teacher says that Johnny's test score is "above average" or "below average" for his class, the teacher is making a relative test interpretation because the teacher uses the average performance of Johnny's classmates to make sense out of his test score.

As pointed out earlier, this chapter focuses on how parents can interpret scores on standardized tests. Because almost all standardized test scores require *relative* interpretations, the four interpretive schemes to be considered in the chapter are all relative score-interpretation schemes. Because the vast majority of standardized tests, whether achievement tests or aptitude tests, provide these sorts of interpretations, parents need to be especially knowledgeable about relative score-interpretation schemes.

Percentiles

The first interpretive scheme you'll consider, and by all odds the most commonly used one, is based on *percentiles* or, as they are sometimes called, *percentile ranks*. Percentiles are used most frequently in describing standardized test scores because percentiles are easily understandable to most people.

A percentile compares a student's score with those of other students in a *norm group*. A percentile indicates the percent of students in the norm group that the student outperformed. A percentile of 60, for example, means that the student performed better than 60 percent of the students in the test's norm group.

Let's make sure you understand what a norm group is. As indicated above, a percentile compares a student's score with scores earned by students in a norm group. This comparison with the norm group is based on the performances of a group of individuals who have already been administered a particular examination. For instance, before developers of a new standardized test publish their test, they will administer that test to a large number of students who then become the norm group for the test. Typically, different norm groups of students are assembled for all the grade levels for which percentile interpretations are made.

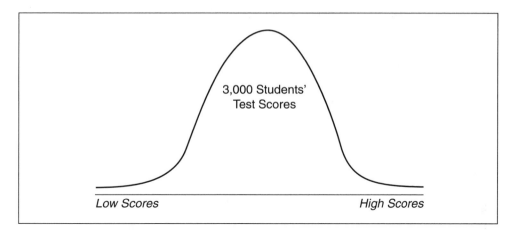

4.4 A typical norm group score distribution

Figure 4.4 shows a graphic depiction of a set of 3,000 students' scores such as might have been gathered during the norming of a nationally standardized achievement test. Remember, the students who participate in the initial norming of a standardized test are described as the test's norm group. The area under the curved line represents the number of students who earned scores at that point on the baseline. You'll notice that, and this is typical of a norm group's performance, most students score in the middle while only a few students earn very high or very low scores.

In fact, if the distribution of test scores in the norm group is *perfectly* normal, then, as you see in Figure 4.5, over two-thirds of the scores (represented by the area under the curved line) will be located relatively close to the center of the distribution—that is, plus and minus one standard deviation (SD) from the mean. (Here's one of the instances where a score distribution's standard deviation is used as a kind of measuring stick on the baseline of the distribution.)

Not all norm groups are *national* norm groups. Sometimes test publishers, at the request of local school officials, develop *local* norms. These local norms can be either state norms or school-district norms. Comparisons of students on the basis of local norms is sometimes seen as being more meaningful than comparisons of students based on national norms.

In many instances, local norms are quite different from national norms because the students in a particular locality are not representative of the nation's children as a whole. If there is a difference between local and national norms, then there will be a difference in a student's percentile ranks. A student's raw score—that is, the number of test items answered correctly—might be equal to the 50th percentile based on *national* norms

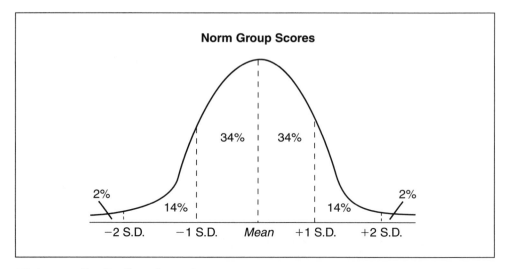

4.5 A normally distributed set of scores

but be equal to the 75th percentile based on *local* norms. That kind of situation would occur if the students in the local norm group hadn't performed as well as students in the national norm group. National and local norms often provide decisively different frameworks for interpreting standardized test results. When reviewing your child's test-score report, make sure you know whether your child's percentiles are based on national or local norms.

It's also true that some norm groups have been more carefully constituted than others. For example, certain national norm groups are more representative of the nation's population than are other national norm groups. There are often large differences in the representativeness of norm groups based on such factors as gender, ethnicity, geographic region, and socioeconomic status of the students in the groups. In addition, many standardized tests are renormed only every five to ten years. It is important to make sure that the normative information on which percentiles are based is both representative and reasonably current.

Grade-Equivalent Scores

Let's turn from percentiles to look at a *grade equivalent* or, as they're often called, *grade-equivalent scores*. Grade-equivalent scores constitute another effort to provide a relative interpretation of standardized test scores. A *grade equivalent* is an indicator of a student's test performance based on grade level and months of the school year. The purpose of grade equivalents is to transform scores on standardized tests into an index that reflects a student's grade-level progress in school. A grade-equivalent score is a developmental score in the sense that it represents a continuous range of grade levels and months of the school year.

Let's look at a grade-equivalent score of 4.5:

> A Grade-Equivalent Score:
> Grade Level → ④ . ⑤ ← Month of School Year

The score consists of the grade, then a decimal, and then a number representing months. The number to the left of the decimal point represents the grade level, in this example, the fourth grade. The number to the right of the decimal point represents the month of the school year, in this example, the fifth month of the school year.

Testing Terms:
Grade Equivalent
An indicator of a student's test performance expressed in terms of grade level and months of the school year

Many test publishers, using statistical schemes, convert raw scores on standardized achievement tests to grade-equivalent scores. These grade equivalents often appear on students' score-reports. Grade-equivalent scores are most appropriate for basic skill areas such as reading and mathematics where it can be assumed that the degree of instructional emphasis given to the subject is fairly constant from grade to grade. When standardized achievement tests are administered in the spring, most publishers indicate that the average score should be at the grade level plus eight months, for example, 5.8, 6.8, and so on.

The appeal of grade-equivalent scores is that they appear to be readily interpretable to both teachers and parents. However, many teachers and parents actually have an incorrect understanding of what grade-equivalent scores signify. To see why these scores are misunderstood, it's necessary to understand a bit about where they come from in the first place.

To determine the grade-equivalent scores that should be hooked up with a particular student's raw score, test developers typically administer the same test to students in several grade levels, then establish a trend line reflecting the raw score increases at each grade level. The test developers then *estimate* at other points along this trend line the grade equivalent for any raw score.

Let me illustrate this important point. In Figure 4.6, you will see the respective performance of students at three grade levels. The same eighty-item test has been given to students at all three grade levels: grades 4, 5, and 6. A trend line is then established from the three grades where the test was actually administered. The result of that estimation procedure is seen in Figure 4.7.

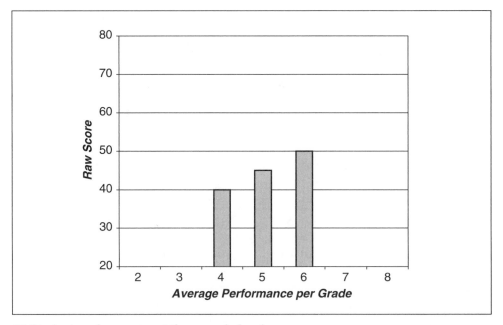

4.6 Student performances at three grade levels

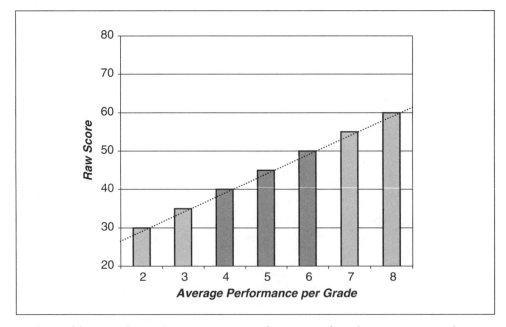

4.7 A trend line used to estimate average performance of students at nontested grades

In order for these estimated grade-equivalent scores to be accurate, several assumptions must be made. First, it must be assumed that the subject area tested is emphasized about equally at each grade level. It must also be assumed that student mastery of the tested content increases at a reasonably constant rate at each grade level over an extended period of time. And, as implied earlier, the assumption that the mastery of the test's content increases gradually over time is particularly difficult to support in subject areas other than reading and mathematics. (It's even a tough assumption to satisfy in those two subjects.)

The implied precision associated with a grade-equivalent score of 6.2, therefore, is difficult to defend. A 6.2 grade-equivalent score suggests a degree of accuracy that's simply not warranted. A parent–interpreter of a standardized achievement test's results may think that a 6.2 grade-equivalent score indicates the student's raw score represents a performance equal to that of a sixth-grade pupil in the second month of the sixth-grade year. Remember, most grade-equivalent scores are created on the basis of estimation, not real test-score data. Because substantial sampling and estimation errors are apt to be present, grade-equivalent scores should always be taken with several grains of salt.

Now that you understand grade-equivalent scores to be, at best, rough estimates, let's return to the potential misinterpretations that parents (and teachers, too) often make regarding grade-equivalent scores. Let's say a third-grade student makes a grade-equivalent score of 5.5 in reading. What does this grade-equivalent score mean? Here's a wrong answer: "The student can do fifth-grade work." Here's a *really* wrong answer: "The student should be promoted to the fifth grade." The right answer, of course, is that the third-grader understands reading skills that the test covers about as well as an average fifth-grader does at midyear. A grade-equivalent score should be viewed as the approximate place where a student is along a developmental continuum, not as the grade level in which the student should be placed.

If standardized achievement tests are used in your child's school district, and if those tests yield grade-equivalent scores, it is important for school officials to provide parents with an accurate description of what a grade-equivalent score means. Parents who have not been given an accurate definition of such scores frequently think that a high grade-equivalent score means their child is capable of doing work at the grade level specified. Some parents even use high grade-equivalent scores as a basis for arguing that their child should be promoted to a higher grade. Because many parents have a misconception of what a grade-equivalent score means, they may have an inflated estimate of their child's level of achievement.

The frequency of misinterpretations about grade equivalents is the reason that some districts have, as a matter of policy, eliminated grade-equivalent scores when reporting standardized test results.

Because grade-equivalent scores are supposed to refer to a child's developmental level of achievement, they are only used with standardized achievement tests, never standardized aptitude tests.

Scale Scores

Let's move, now, to the third of our four score-interpretation schemes: *scale scores.* A scale score constitutes yet another way to give relative meaning to a student's standardized test performances. Because the statistical advantages of scale scores are considerable, scale-score reporting systems have been used with increasing frequency in recent years. As a consequence, you need to become familiar with the main features of scale scores because such scores are very likely to be used when you receive reports of your child's performances on standardized tests.

A *scale* that is used for test scores typically refers to numbers assigned to students on the basis of their test performances. Higher numbers (higher scores) reflect increasing levels of achievement or ability. Thus, such a scale might be composed of a set of raw scores in which each additional test item correctly answered yields one more point on the raw-score scale. Raw scores, all by themselves, however, are very difficult to interpret. If your child's teacher told you that your child "had earned 34 points," you would have no idea what that meant. A student's score on a raw-score scale provides no idea of the student's *relative* performance. Therefore, measurement specialists have devised different sorts of scales for test-interpretation purposes.

Scale scores are *converted raw scores* that use a new, arbitrarily chosen scale to represent levels of achievement or ability. Shortly, you'll be given some examples to help you understand what is meant by converting scores from one scale to another. In essence, a scale-score system is created by devising a brand-new numerical scale that is often very unlike the original raw-score scale. Students' raw scores are then converted to this brand-new scale so that, when score interpretations are to be made, those interpretations rely on the converted scores based on the new scale. Such converted scores are called *scale scores.*

Testing Terms:

Scale Score

A representation of a student's raw score on a converted numerical scale, typically very unlike the original raw-score scale

For example, in Figure 4.8, you see a range of raw score points from 0 to 40 for a 40-item test. Below the raw-score scale, you see a new, converted scale ranging from 500 to 900. For a number of reasons, to be described shortly, it is sometimes preferable to use a scale-score reporting scheme rather than a raw-score reporting scheme. Thus, a student who achieved a raw score of 30 items correct might be assigned a scale score of 800, as shown in Figure 4.9.

One of the reasons that scale scores have become popular in recent years is the necessity to develop several equidifficult forms of the same test. For example, a basic skills test must sometimes be passed before high school diplomas are awarded to students. Typically,

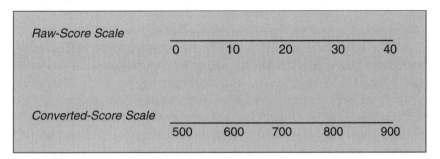

4.8 A raw-score scale and a converted-score scale

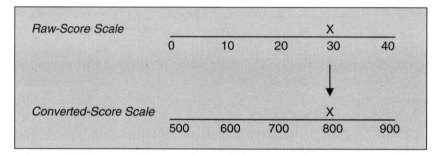

4.9 An illustration of a raw-score conversion to a scale score

those students who initially fail the test are given other opportunities to pass it. The different forms of the test that are used for such retake purposes should, for the sake of fairness, represent assessment challenges for students that are equivalent to those represented by the initial form of the test. However, because it is next to impossible to create test forms that are *absolutely* identical, scale scores can be used to help solve the problem. Scores on two test forms of differing difficulty levels can be statistically adjusted so that, when placed on a converted score scale, the new scale scores represent students' performances *as if* the two test forms had been perfectly equal in difficulty.

As indicated earlier, scale scores are difficult for parents to interpret intuitively, unless the scale scores are accompanied by percentiles or some other supporting information. Mistakes are also made in interpreting scale scores because parents assume that all scale scores are similar. For example, when the *Scholastic Assessment Test* was initially administered over forty years ago, the mean scale score on the verbal section of test was 500. (It was called the *Scholastic Aptitude Test* back then.) This does not signify that the mean score on the *Scholastic Assessment Test* today is 500 or that other tests using scale scores will always have mean scores of 500. Scale-score systems can be constructed so that the mean score is 50, 75, 600, 700, 1,000, or any number the scale constructor has in mind.

One kind of scale score that's being seen more frequently in the reports you might receive about your child is known as a *normal curve equivalent* (NCE). The testing company computes your child's percentile, then figures out what that percentile would be in a *normal* distribution of scores such as you saw in Figure 4.3. The child is then assigned a scale score that the child would have received if the distribution of test scores had been perfectly normal. NCE distributions usually have a mean of 50 and a standard deviation of about 20.

To illustrate, let's say your child's raw score on a standardized achievement test in math turned out to put the child at the 84th percentile. Now an 84th percentile, if the score distribution were normal, would put your child one standard-deviation-distance above the mean. (You can look back at Figure 4.3 if you think I'm pulling your leg.) So, if the NCE mean is 50 and the standard deviation 20, your child would be assigned an NCE of 70.

NCE distributions, as you see, are based on the assumption that students' mastery of the content (knowledge and skills) being assessed is distributed among children in a normal fashion. Rarely is that true. However, to the extent that such distributions approximate a normal shape, then NCEs can prove useful. Like all scale scores, however, NCEs are difficult for most people (parents and teachers alike) to interpret.

Stanines

The final kind of score-reporting approach you need to understand is an increasingly popular kind of scale score known as *stanine*. A stanine reporting system is formed by dividing a normal distribution along its baseline into nine equal parts. You can see how a stanine distribution is set up in Figure 4.10.

It will be apparent to you as you look at Figure 4.10 that children who score well on a standardized test (achievement or aptitude) are given higher stanines while those children who score less are given lower stanines. Some

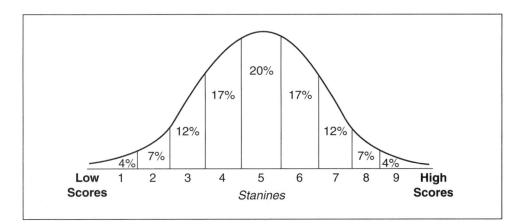

4.10 The approximate percent of scores in a normal distribution represented by stanines

test publishers describe the top three stanines (7, 8, and 9) as "above average," the middle three stanines (4, 5, and 6) as "average," and the bottom three stanines (1, 2, and 3) as "below average."

"Stanine" is a term formed by a combination of "standard" and "nine." (When first used, scale scores were referred to as "standard" scores. As with NCEs, stanines are scale scores that assume the existence of an essentially normal distribution of scores (in the general population) of whatever's being measured by a test.

The real virtue of stanines is that they are fairly *gross* reporting mechanisms. Rather than trying to give you a super-precise indication of how your child's performance compares with the performances of other children (such as is the case with percentiles), stanines provide you with only an approximation based on nine categories. It is the very grossness of stanines that has made a number of educators endorse this form of reporting.

Too many educators (and parents) mistakenly ascribe unwarranted precision to educational testing. Educational assessment is a far less precise

Testing Terms:

Stanine

A score-reporting procedure in which a student's raw score is converted to a nine-point scale score ranging from a low of one to a high of nine

game than most folks imagine. Stanines, because they make it clear that all children's test scores can be classified into one of nine fairly hefty chunks, make no pretense at precision. As a parent, you'll know that if your child gets a stanine of seven on a standardized test in reading, the child is doing better than average on the tests, but not decisively so. That's probably about the level of precision that you ought to be taking from your child's test-score reports.

One problem with stanines is that students who score very close to the demarcation lines in a stanine distribution will frequently be misclassified, that is, will be given a stanine that's one-too-high or one-too-low from what the student actually should get. For instance, take a look at Figure 4.10 again and you'll see that a student whose raw score was equal to a percentile of 60.5 would be assigned to the sixth stanine. But if the child had scored only one percentile lower, then a fifth stanine would have been assigned.

Some parents place far too much significance on the stanines their child receives on a standardized achievement test. Is a *borderline-high seventh* stanine really so much worse than a *borderline-low eighth* stanine? Probably not. So, if your child's standardized test results are reported as stanines, don't get too caught up in a competitive contest with other parents about whose child's stanines are spiffier. Stanines are rough indications of how children perform on standardized tests. They are not ammunition for a parental-pride showdown with other parents.

Contrasting the Four Interpretive Options

You've now considered four types of score interpretation schemes: percentiles, grade-equivalent scores, scale scores, and stanines. It's time to review and summarize what's really important about these four ways of making sense out of your child's test scores.

You first looked at percentiles. A *percentile* indicates a student's standing in relationship to that of a norm group. If a student's test score is equal to the 25th percentile, the student's performance exceeds the performances of 25 percent of the individuals in the norm group. One advantage of percentiles is that they're easy to interpret. And, for the most part, people's interpretations of percentiles are accurate. A disadvantage of percentiles is that the defensibility of the interpretation is totally dependent on the nature of the normative data on which the percentiles are based. Unrepresentative or out-of-date norm data yield potentially inaccurate percentile interpretations. As pointed out earlier, because percentile interpretations are so widely used, it's imperative for parents to be knowledgeable regarding such interpretations.

Percentiles

Advantage: readily interpretable

Disadvantage: dependent on quality of norm group

Next, you considered grade-equivalent scores. A *grade equivalent* indicates the nature of a student's test performance in terms of grade levels and months of the school year. Thus, a grade equivalent of 3.7 would indicate that the student's test score was estimated to be the same as the average of a third-grader during the seventh month of the school year. One advantage of grade-equivalent scores is that, because such scores are based on grade levels and months of the school year, they can be readily understood by parents. A significant disadvantage associated with grade-equivalent scores, however, is that they're frequently misinterpreted.

Grade Equivalents

Advantage: readily communicable

Disadvantage: often misinterpreted

Scale scores were then described. *Scale scores* are interpreted according to a converted numerical scale that allows test publishers to transform raw scores into more statistically useful scale-score units. A student who gets a raw score of 35 correct out of 50 items, for example, might end up with a converted scale score of 620.

Scale Scores

Advantage: useful in equalizing difficulties of different test forms

Disadvantage: not easily interpretable

Finally, stanines are yet another kind of scale score. They divide a normal distribution into nine equal parts along its baseline. High stanines (for example, 8 or 9) indicate that a student has scored well on a test; low stanines (for example, 1 or 2) indicate the opposite. The advantage of stanines is that their inherent grossness disinclines parents to ascribe too much precision to students' reported test results. Interpretive problems do arise, however, when a student scores close to the borderline separating one stanine from another.

Stanines

Advantage: approximate interpretations fostered
Disadvantage: potential misclassification of borderline scores

---

Now that you've seen the most common kinds of reporting schemes used for describing children's performances on standardized tests, it's time to look at some typical score reports for parents. Fortunately, because of the increasing importance placed on such test scores, as well as the growing demand from parents for more readily interpretable score-reports, most publishers of standardized tests are now making a concerted effort to explain their score reports in parent-palatable informational materials that accompany a child's test-score reports.

Many test publishers also supply sets of sample items to parents as well as detailed guidelines for interpreting the specific kind of score report being used in a district. (Typically, school-district officials have some choice regarding the particular kind of parent-report forms they wish the test publisher to use in their district.)

My advice to you, based on your familiarity with the four score-reporting schemes just described, is to read carefully any explanatory materials you receive along with your child's standardized test results. Most of these materials have already been revised and improved based on the reactions of parent groups to earlier versions of those materials.

A Parent Puzzle

Here's a fictional exchange between a parent and the parent's child. If this were your child, let's see how you'd deal with the situation.

(Setting: A fourth-grade child, Chandler, has just returned from school in the fall and is almost in tears. The child's teacher, Ms. Evans, has spent the last hour of the day telling students how they performed on the standardized achievement test that was administered during the previous April to all third-graders in the school.

Ms. Evans gave all children a slip of paper indicating their stanine scores in reading, language arts, mathematics, social studies, and science. Ms. Evans explained that the best stanine was a nine and the worst stanine was a one. Chandler's stanine scores for the five subject areas were less than wonderful. Those scores are, quite obviously, the reason that underlies the child's distress.)

Child: "I'm not very smart."

Parent: "Why do you say that, Chandler?"

Child: "We got our scores from the tests we took last year. I didn't do very well."

Parent: "What were your scores?"

Child: "I got my 'stanine' scores from Ms. Evans. She says that a nine is high and a one is low. I got a four in reading, a five in math, a four in language, a five in science, and a six in social studies."

Parent: "That sounds pretty good to me. Why are you so unhappy?"

Child: "All of my friends got higher scores. A bunch of them even got some nines. They're smart and I'm dumb. That's all there is to it."

Parent: If you were Chandler's parent, what would you say next?

My Response: If I were dealing with an upset child, I'd try to be honest but informative. I'd probably say something such as, "There are three things you have to realize, Chandler. One deals with the tests you took and one deals with what it means to be 'smart.' First, last spring you took what is called a standardized achievement test. These tests are not all that accurate, especially when they're administered to young children such as third-graders. And your stanine scores are all in the middle range. They definitely do not indicate that you're dumb.

   "The second thing is that there are all sorts of 'smarts.' Some children are smart in numbers or in reading, and some children are smart in sensing what makes other children act the way they do. Experts these days identify at least seven kinds of smarts. This test measured only a couple. You may be all right in those that were measured, but you may be wonderful at others.

continued

A Parent Puzzle *(continued)*

"Finally, what makes a child successful in school, Chandler, is *effort*. If you really try hard in all that you do in school, you'll be very successful. Don't worry about being smart or unsmart. What pays off in school is how hard you try. And however you do in school—*however*—I love you as high as the sky."

My Reason: I would want to get a child to recognize the limitations of standardized achievement tests, but also to realize that stanine scores of four, four, five, five, and six are perfectly normal, especially when a child is tested in the third grade.

Then I'd want Chandler to understand that there are different kinds of intelligence, not just traditional academic ones. I'd also want to stress the importance of effort. Finally, I'd make sure that Chandler knows there's unconditional love that will be forthcoming—irrespective of whether the child's stanines are closer to nine or to one.

Interpreting Your Child's Score Report

In the next few pages you'll find an example of a typical report that's given to parents about their child's performance on a standardized *achievement* test. Reports regarding students' standardized *aptitude* tests are similar, although such reports typically focus only on a student's *verbal* and *quantitative* aptitude.

On the left-hand page of two facing pages, you'll find a brief introduction to the type of score report that's presented on the right-hand facing page. I'll comment on several features of the score report, identified in that report by circled upper-case letters Ⓐ. When you've looked over the score report and the accompanying comments, simply do a page-turn and move on to the next score report.

Bar Graphs Featuring Percentiles

One of the more common ways of reporting students' performances on standardized achievement tests features the use of bar graphs such as you can see in Figure 4.11 at the right. The bars are sometimes vertical, as seen in the illustrative score report, or sometimes horizontal. Bar graphs are frequently combined with percentiles as seen in this example.

(A)   In all reports of a student's standardized achievement test results, there will be a section that includes identifying information regarding the child who took the test (for example, age and sex), the site where the test was given (district, school, and teacher), the date when the test was given, the form of the test administered, and so on.

(B)   Percentile ranks are typically arranged so that the bar graph can be interpreted according to them. Notice that as the percentiles get closer to the center, they are more compressed. In the center of the distribution, then, students can answer a few more items correctly and make a substantial improvement in their percentile rankings.

(C)   In this report you'll see both national percentiles and local percentiles (for the district only). Many district officials want to see how their students stack up nationally as well as locally. So, if this were the Parent Report for your child, you'd look at the two columns for Reading and conclude that your child outperformed 55 percent of students in the test's national norm group and outperformed 66 percent of the students in your local district. The numbers at the top of each bar signify the exact national and local percentile rank attained by each student.

   If you look at the differences between the national and local percentile ranks for all five subjects tested, you'll realize that, on average, the district's students don't do as well on this test as do students in the national norm sample. That's why the local percentile-rank bars are always higher than the national bars. Putting it another way, the local students don't represent as strong a comparison group as do the students in the national norm group.

(D)   Quite frequently, score reports will help parents recognize what constitutes an above-average, average, or below-average performance. Notice that these designations are based on the national norm group. Typically, an average performance is identified as a score somewhere between the 25th and 75th percentiles.

(E)   Without exception, test publishers provide explanations of what the chief features of their score reports mean. In some cases, the report attempts to personalize the report by stating that your child (sometimes the reports even give your child's name) "scored better in science than 44 percent of the national comparison group and better than 63 percent of the district comparison group."

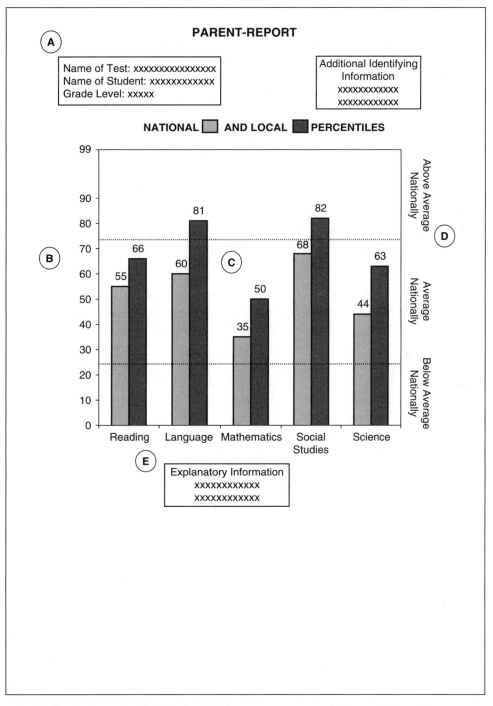

4.11 An illustrative standardized achievement test-report for parents based on national and local bar-graphed percentiles

Confidence Bands Focused on Skill Mastery

An increasingly popular way to inform parents about their children's standardized test results is to identify the specific performance level earned by a student on a skill, but to display that level in the middle of a *confidence band*. Such confidence bands are usually formed by use of the standard error of measurement associated with each subskill. You may recall from Chapter 2 that a standard error of measurement represents the reliability of an individual student's test performance. So, by forming a confidence band that extends one standard error of measurement above and below a student's actual performance, a more realistic range of achievement is presented that probably captures a student's true level of performance.

The illustrative score report presented in Figure 4.12 at the right describes how a child performed on a set of skills in reading and in language. The use of confidence bands emphasizes the less-than-unerring accuracy of this kind of educational measurement.

(A) The report at the right deals with a child's skills in two subjects, namely, reading and language. A full Home Report to parents would also include scores for any other subjects tested. Usually those subjects are mathematics, science, and social studies. Subskill reports typically are provided *in addition to* more general reports such as the bar-graphed percentiles seen previously in Figure 4.11.

Skills such as those identified in the sample report in Figure 4.11 could be broken down into even more discrete categories such as punctuation subskills dealing with commas, semicolons, and other forms of punctuation. As a parent, you need to make sure there are a reasonable number of items per skill or subskill so that the student's mastery of the skill or subskill is apt to have been assessed reliably.

(B) The numbers of items per skill are often provided in such reports. The smaller the number of items, the more shaky should be the inference about a student's mastery levels.

(C) The student's actual performance level is identified by the circle, but the circle is nestled in the midst of a confidence band that should guide parents to a more accurate, general estimate about a child's subskill performance. These bands sometimes overlap two of the designated mastery levels. Note that this fictitious child's Evaluative Comprehension skill in reading could reflect either "none" or "some" mastery.

(D) In many cases, beyond merely describing how parents should interpret a score report, an analysis of a student's strongest and weakest mastery levels is often provided by test publishers.

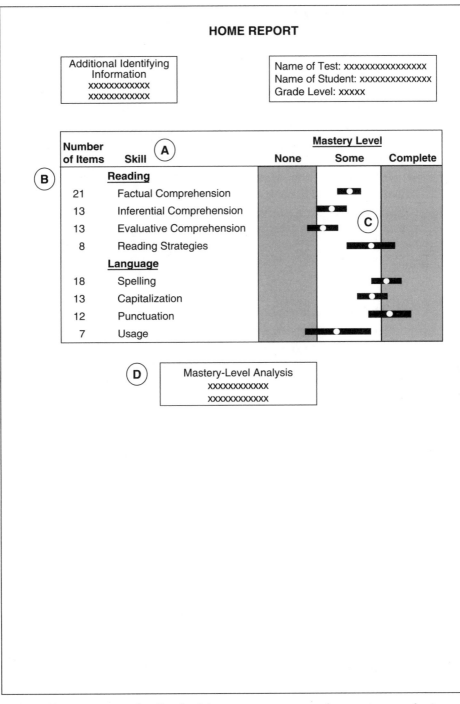

4.12 An illustrative standardized achievement test-report for parents employing confidence bands to portray a student's skill mastery

Numerical Reports Identifying Stanines, NCEs, and Grade Equivalents

Some reports regarding children's standardized test performances provide parents with a flock of numbers. Such number-laced reports can, at first glance, be fairly intimidating. (Even at second glance, they still can.) What you have to remember, however, is that you already understand the kinds of score-reporting mechanisms that are being used in such reports. In the illustrative parent-report for a fifth-grader presented in Figure 4.13 at the right, you'll see that, for a set of mathematics skills, parents are provided with their child's stanine, NCE, and grade equivalent. If you've forgotten how any of those work, read backwards in this chapter until you come to them. When appropriate, then read forward until you return to Figure 4.13.

(A)   This report provides the number of test items per skill and also the number of items that a student attempted to answer (No. Att.). You'll see that this fictitious student failed to answer three of the five items dealing with statistics/probability.

(B)   Stanines, as I hope you'll recall, are a special kind of scale score ranging from a low of one to a high of nine. This fictitious student seems to be pretty good in almost all of the mathematical skills measured.

(C)   These normal curve equivalents (NCEs) assume that students' scores on the mathematics items in this standardized achievement test will be distributed in an essentially normal fashion. You'll note (from the asterisked (*) footnote), that for this test the NCE mean is 50 and its standard deviation is 10. Thus, if your child received an NCE of 60, this would indicate that the child scored one standard-deviation's distance above the mean. Because both stanines and NCEs are based on assumptions of a distribution's normal shape, they are closely related.

(D)   Assuming that this test was administered to fifth-graders in the spring, we would expect that the "average" child (Is there such a thing?) would get a grade equivalent of 5.8. You'll see that this fictitious child gets much higher grade equivalent scores for most skills except Numerical Relations. And, as indicated earlier, there was Statistics/Probability for which three of the five items weren't even attempted.

(E)   Parent-reports often contain personalized comments about a child's strong and weak performances. In this fictitious instance, there might have been a comment such as, "In three of the skills (computation, algebra, and problem-solving), this child's performance was barely lower than the next higher stanine. Accordingly, the total array of stanines may underestimate the excellence of the child's performance in mathematics."

REPORT FOR PARENTS

Test Name: xxxxxxxxxxxxxx
Subject Area: xxxxxxxxxxxxx
Student: xxxxxxxxxxxxxxxx
Grade Level: xxxxx

Additional
Identifying Information
xxxxxxxxxxxxx
xxxxxxxxxxxxx

| | (A) | | (B) | (C) | (D) |
Mathematical Skills	No. Items	No. Att.	Stanine	NCE*	Grade Equiv.
• Numerical Relations	6	6	5	51	5.8
• Estimation	5	5	7	61	8.4
• Computation	8	8	7	62	8.6
• Measurement	6	5	6	57	7.3
• Geometry	7	7	9	70	9.2
• Statistics/Probability	5	2	4	35	4.4
• Algebra	6	5	7	62	8.6
• Problem Solving	7	6	8	67	9.1

* NCE Mean = 50, Standard Deviation = 10

(E)

Strengths and Weaknesses
xxxxxxxxxxxxxxxxxxxxxx
xxxxxxxxxxxxxxxxxx

4.13 An illustrative standardized achievement test-report for parents identifying a fifth-grade student's stanines, NCEs, and grade equivalents

Different Strokes

Most test publishers make available to local educators an enormous menu of different sorts of score reports for teachers as well as parents. The teachers, of course, must receive information about all of their students. For parents, the focus is only on one child's test performance.

But, given the variety of score-reporting systems that are available, it would be impossible to supply you with all possible score reports about your child that might be sent to you. What I hope this chapter has done is clear away some of the mystery associated with standardized test-score reports.

The descriptive information accompanying students' standardized test reports is becoming more and more readily interpretable. If you recall what's in this chapter, and if you read carefully any explanations accompanying your child's score report, I'm confident you'll be able to make sense out of it. If you can't, then it's time to ask your child's teacher or principal just what the report's various parts really mean.

What Do You Really Need to Know about This Chapter's Content?

I readily confess that this chapter was fairly tough reading. There were oodles of numbers and, for many readers, more than a few new ideas. But the chapter's purpose was to familiarize you in a general way with the kinds of concepts and display techniques that are likely to be used when you try to interpret a score report about your child's standardized test scores. Here, then, is what you really need to recall about the chapter.

- The most common way to describe a distribution of test scores is by calculating its *mean,* that is, its numerical average, and its *standard deviation,* that is, a kind of average about how far a distribution's raw scores are from its mean. The standard deviation is also used in several score-interpretation schemes as a sort of measuring stick along the baseline of a distribution of scores.
- Four frequently used score-reporting schemes for parents are percentiles, grade-equivalent scores, scale scores, and stanines. Brief descriptions of all four, along with the chief advantage and disadvantage of each, were provided on pages 93–95.
- The actual score reports you receive for your child will almost always contain explanatory information regarding the interpretation of the

one or more reports you'll be sent. Typically, those explanations should suffice. If not, do not be reluctant to ask your child's teacher or school administrator to clarify anything about which you have doubts. If you're willing to spend a bit of time studying your child's score report, it should make sense to you. If it doesn't, it's the report's problem, not yours.

POSSIBLE PARENT ACTION–OPTIONS

In a sense there are two kinds of action–options you can take when dealing with your child's score reports. First, you can try to understand the report more completely if you have any doubts about how it is to be interpreted. Second, once you're clear about what the report means, you could set up a conference with your child's teacher to see if there are things you could do as a parent based on your child's test performance to help out at home.

1. As indicated earlier, you might seek clarification if there are doubts you have about the meaning of any aspect of a score report. Your child's teacher is a natural source of such clarification, but not all teachers are truly at ease when explaining how to interpret test-score reports. If your child's teacher seems uncomfortable or unsure, check with the principal to see if a school administrator or, perhaps, another teacher might help.

2. A conference with your child's teacher *may* turn out to be useful, but you need to be cautious about trying to derive very targeted test-based information about your child, information that you can act on at home. As you saw in the previous chapter, and as you'll understand better when you read about teachers' score-boosting activities in Chapter 11, standardized achievement tests simply do not provide either teachers or parents with the kind of information that translates into on-target instruction, in school or at home.

   The best you can usually do is identify your child's relative strengths or weaknesses—certainly in subject areas such as math or science. And, if there are enough items measuring particular skills within subject areas, such as inferential reading or literal reading, then relative comparisons of a student's strong and weak skills may be helpful.

   But do not think that, after discovering your child is weak in one or more standardized achievement test areas, you will easily be able to "fix" such shortcomings. As you'll see in Chapter 11, standardized achievement tests do not yield the kind of information needed so that parents can set up very helpful skill-focused instructional activities.

3. If your child's teacher or principal seems to display something less than a satisfactory understanding of standardized achievement tests and how to interpret them, you could refer them to one or more of the items in the *Suggested Resources* cited next.

SUGGESTED RESOURCES FOR YOUR CHILD'S TEACHER OR PRINCIPAL

Printed Materials

Cunningham, George K. *Assessment in the Classroom: Constructing and Interpreting Tests.* London: Falmer Press, 1998. *In Chapter 4, Cunningham provides educators with a tidy summary of what's needed to interpret test results.*

Gronlund, Norman E. *Assessment of Student Achievement.* Boston: Allyn and Bacon, 1998. *Chapter 10 contains a lucid explanation of the common kinds of score-reporting methods used with standardized achievement tests.*

Hopkins, Kenneth D. *Educational and Psychological Measurement and Evaluation* (8th ed.). Boston: Allyn and Bacon, 1998. *Chapter 14, "Standardized Achievement Tests," provides an in-depth look at how educators can judge the quality of standardized achievement tests. Descriptions are provided of how to interpret students' performances on such tests.*

McMillan, James H. *Classroom Assessment: Principles and Practice for Effective Instruction.* Boston: Allyn and Bacon, 1997. *In Chapter 13, McMillan describes how to administer and then interpret standardized tests. Brief consideration is given to statistical measures of central tendency and variability, as well as to measures of relationship. The typical score-reporting procedures for standardized tests are also considered.*

Videotape Programs

IOX Assessment Associates. *Making Sense out of Standardized Test Scores.* (5301 Beethoven St., Ste. 190, Los Angeles, CA 90066). *This videotape describes the role of percentiles, grade equivalents, and scale scores when interpreting students' standardized test scores. Strengths and weaknesses of each are identified.*

Northwest Regional Educational Laboratory. *Understanding Standardized Tests.* IOX Assessment Associates (5301 Beethoven St., Los Angeles, CA 90066). *From this video, educators learn how standardized achievement tests are designed and how the norming process provides a comparative basis for score interpretations.*

5

Common Classroom Tests: When Students Choose Their Answers

*T*his is the first of four chapters intended to familiarize you with the kinds of classroom tests your child is likely to be taking in school. I want you to become at least moderately knowledgeable about these sorts of classroom assessment instruments. More specifically, first I want you to know what the strengths and weaknesses of each type of test are. Second, I want you to learn at least a bit about the most common mistakes that are made when teachers construct the items to use in those tests.

A Test-Reviewer to Be Reckoned With

The reason that I'm asking you to become more familiar with various sorts of classroom tests is that you'll find the tests your child receives are an efficient and accurate reflection of what goes on *instructionally* in the classroom. The single most accurate indicator of what is transpiring instructionally in your child's classroom is often the tests that your child is required to take. The more you learn about those tests, the more you'll know what's occurring in the classroom.

Assessing the Tests

You have every right to review the tests your child takes. But, of course, you'll probably have to wait until *after* the tests have been completed. Most teachers are, quite properly, reluctant to have parents preview tests prior to a test's administration.

Sometimes you'll find that teachers send their students' completed tests home so that the results can be reviewed by parents. More often than not, however, you'll need to ask if you want to review the kinds of tests being used with your child.

In many instances, if you ask your child's teacher for an opportunity to review your child's tests, you may have to do so at school rather than at home. Most teachers, quite properly, don't want their tests circulating in the community. But if you know what to look for (and you will after reading this book), an hour or so of test review will give you all sorts of insights about what the teacher is *testing* and, as a consequence, you'll have a good idea about what the teacher is *teaching*.

There's apt to be an immediate dividend of your asking to look over your child's tests "so you can get a better idea of how you can help at home." If teachers know that parents will be reviewing their classroom tests, you can expect an immediate improvement in the quality of the tests being used with your child. Teachers are like everyone else. If they know their efforts are to be reviewed, they'll often put more energy into whatever's being scrutinized, in this instance, the teacher's classroom tests.

But you won't be a "know-nothing" parent who's looking at the teacher's tests. On the contrary, after finishing this book, you'll be reasonably well versed about what kinds of test items should be used and, if those items are used, how they should be constructed. In short, you'll be a test-reviewer to be reckoned with. And such test-reviewers usually stimulate stronger classroom testing.

Talking with Teachers about Their Tests

Suppose an acquaintance of yours, after running into you at a local grocery store, pulls you aside for a brief conversation. The conversation actually turns out to be a scolding. Your acquaintance starts to scold you about how you are raising your child. How do you think you'd respond?

Obviously, not many parents would be delighted, or even civil, if blasted about the caliber of their child-raising. Few people really enjoy being harshly criticized about an area of their responsibility. Educators are no different.

If you've looked over some of your child's tests and you believe those tests are less than wonderful, you need to bring that to the teacher's attention or to the principal's attention, but not in a confrontational manner. What you want to see happen is an improvement in the tests that your child is taking. You should not set out to embarrass or discount your child's teacher. That kind of an approach is apt to make the teacher or principal defensive. A discounting approach will rarely modify the test practices about which you're concerned.

So, I'd definitely start off a conversation with a teacher somewhere along these lines:

> "I really appreciate your taking the time to see me. I'd like to talk with you about my child's classroom tests. What I'm interested in is the nature of the tests themselves. I'm certainly no expert in educational testing, and you probably know much more about educational testing than I do. But I've just finished a book for parents about educational testing. And, after looking over my child's classroom tests, I ran into a few things that I hope we can discuss. I really don't mean to be forward, but I'm sure we both want what's best for the children. Now, let me raise several concerns that I wanted to bring to your attention. . . ."

What you are trying to do throughout the conversation with the teacher is get the teacher's classroom tests improved. You won't accomplish that mission if you threaten the teacher. Most fundamentally, you are trying to get the teacher to improve that teacher's classroom tests as a direct consequence of the teacher's knowing that you and, perhaps, other parents are looking at the classroom tests. (You can let another parent borrow this book. Actually, the publisher would probably prefer that you encourage other parents to *buy* their own copies.)

External scrutiny of one's efforts almost always leads to higher quality efforts. Teachers are no different. If you and other parents are reviewing the teacher's classroom tests, these tests will improve.

Frankly, if you believe the principal in your child's school is capable, it might be preferable to bring any concerns about the quality of your child's tests to the principal. If principals are skilled, when they hear of potential deficiencies in teachers' efforts, they'll intervene without identifying that it was a parent—more specifically, you—who brought the problem to their attention. The principal can, as part of the principal's required supervisory responsibilities, deal with such test-related issues in a routine manner. If you have doubts about a principal's capabilities, however, you may need to speak directly with your child's teacher.

In any event, whether you choose to speak to your child's teacher or your child's principal, you really ought to *prepare* for such an intervention. Get out a sheet of paper and identify the main points you want to make. Be sure to identify the *constructive* suggestions you intend to make. You might even write yourself a note or two such as "Confrontations lose" or "Adversarialism rarely wins." But, above all, plan how you're going to behave during any test-focused conversation with educators.

And there's one more thing to remember. After you've finished this book, there's a good chance you'll know more about educational testing than the educator to whom you're speaking. If you sense that you possess a stronger understanding of educational assessment than the teacher or principal to whom you're talking, be careful. It will be tempting to "lord it over" such an educator. But tread softly. You're trying to improve your child's education, not win some trivial interpersonal contest.

An Important Assessment Distinction: Student-Selection versus Student-Construction

Testing Terms:

Selected-Response Items

Test items calling for students to choose an answer from two or more options

Testing Terms:

Constructed-Response Items

Test items calling for students to create answers to test items or to generate responses to assessment tasks

In all educational testing, there's a significant option available to the person who is creating the test. Items can be used in which students *choose* their answers from two or more options presented to them. The most common examples of such items are True–False items or multiple-choice items. This chapter will describe three types of items that involve students' choosing their answers. Most assessment specialists usually refer to such items as *selected-response* test items.

A second category of test item calls for students to *create* their own responses to some sort of task. Essay tests and short-answer items, for instance, call for students to construct their own answers rather than choose among already provided options. Assessment specialists typically describe such items as *constructed-response* test items.

Pros and Cons

Cognitive Challenge.   There are truly important differences between these two categories of item-types. For openers, there is a fundamental intellectual difference involved when a child is asked to *create* an original answer (as is required in constructed-response tests) versus when a child is asked to *choose* from two or more already presented options (as is required in selected-response tests). Clearly, the generation of a brand new response by a child is tougher than merely spotting the correct answer from a set of options that are already sitting there.

So constructed-response items, in general, present more cognitively challenging tasks for students than would be represented by selected-response tests. However, that's not always so. Suppose, for example, a teacher directed students to memorize a short poem, then asked them to write it from memory on a test. That would be a constructed-response test item, but it would only be classified at the "memory only" knowledge level of Bloom's Cognitive Taxonomy.

Similarly, although many selected-response items demand little more than rote memory from students, it's also possible to create clever selected-response test items that are very challenging indeed. Selected-response items can definitely be built to measure higher cognitive levels in the Bloom Taxonomy.

So, although it is generally true that constructed-response items represent a more cognitively challenging chore for students than selected-response items, you really must look at the particular items themselves to be certain.

Ease of Scoring.   There's a second important difference between selected-response and constructed-response items, and that's the energy it takes teachers to score students' tests. Imagine for a moment that you are a teacher and you're correcting your twenty-nine fifth-graders' midterm exams in social studies. If the midterm exam were a forty-item True–False test, you'd probably be able to score all twenty-nine papers in about ten minutes. If the midterm exam were an essay test, you'd be obliged to spend several hours in scoring the tests. And those hours would be hours you couldn't spend in planning your instructional activities.

It's a practical issue, of course, but the necessity to spend considerable time on the scoring of students' responses disinclines many teachers to rely on constructed-response tests. Most teachers would like to preserve at least partial sanity, and the need to score too many constructed-response tests has driven more than one harassed teacher onto the couch of a psychotherapist.

Selected-response tests, in general, also require less time for students to complete. Less test-taking time, of course, leaves more time for students to be taught. It's always possible, of course, for a teacher to go overboard on the length of even selected-response tests.

What many teachers do is employ selected-response tests whenever there's a knowledge objective being assessed, because a substantial amount of knowledge can be efficiently assessed *and scored* using selected-response tests. For example, teachers can quickly measure a child's retention of historical information with an easily scored True–False test. Teachers can then tap higher levels of student cognitive skills by using constructed-response items. It's a reasonable sort of mix-and-match assessment plan.

As a parent, if you review your child's tests and find that a teacher uses *only* selected-response items or, in contrast, uses *only* constructed-response items, that should alert you to the need to chat about the relative virtues of both categories of items with your child's teacher or principal.

Several "Teacher Shouldn'ts"

Before dealing with three specific types of selected-response items, you should be aware of several item-writing guidelines that apply to *either* selected-response or constructed-response items. Here, briefly, are four things teachers shouldn't do when they create classroom assessments.

- Unclear Directions: *Teachers shouldn't provide unclear directions for their tests. Any directions that are not crystal clear to students are poor directions. Because teachers know very well what they want students to do on a test, they sometimes fail to make it clear to students how a test-taker is supposed to respond.*

- Unintended Clues: *Teachers shouldn't incorporate elements in their test items that unintentionally give away the correct answer. Remember, the teacher should be trying to arrive at a valid interpretation about students, and if there's something in an item that gives away a proper response, even if the test-taker couldn't have arrived at that response without the unintended clue, then the teacher won't know whether the child's correct answer stems from the child's achievement or the give-away clue.*

    For instance, in True–False items it is usually the case that if the test item includes an always *or a* never, *the item will be False. There are so few absolutes that are true. An alert student will spot a* never, *and opt for a False answer in a heartbeat.*

- Complex Sentences: *Teachers shouldn't create classroom tests containing complicated sentences. Classroom tests do not provide teachers with a platform to strut their sentence-structure suave. Simple sentences are needed, because students may be confused by complex sentences loaded with piles of clauses, phrases, and a major collection of commas. To make valid interpretations of students' responses, a teacher's classroom tests should never contain complicated sentences.*

- Difficult Vocabulary: *Teachers shouldn't load their classroom tests with vocabulary terms the children are not apt to know. If it's a vocabulary quiz, of course, the teacher might want to find out if students know the meaning of* superfluous. *But if* superfluous *isn't the focus of the test, then it's not the kind of word that should be found in a classroom test. Teachers can't make valid interpretations about children's capabilities if the children don't know what some of the test's key words mean.*

If you do have an opportunity to review the classroom tests your child takes, be on the lookout for these four "teacher shouldn'ts," namely, unclear directions, unintended clues, complex sentences, and difficult vocabulary. It's understandable if these test-construction flaws are found occasionally. Even experienced teachers should be allowed a few test-building goofs. But if your child's tests are really peppered with such problems, then this suggests the need for a conversation with your child's teacher or principal.

Let's turn, now, to the first type of selected-response item that teachers often employ in their classroom tests.

Two-Choice Items

Testing Terms:

Two-Choice Item

A selected-response item in which the student must choose between two options (Synonym: *Binary-choice item*)

One of the most common kinds of items used in classroom tests is a *two-choice* item such as a True–False item. The student gets an item, for instance, a statement that may or may not be true, then the student must indicate whether the item's statement is true or false. Testing specialists sometimes refer to two-choice items as *binary-choice* items because *binary* is simply a more high-class way of saying *two.*

One suspects that teachers have been using two-choice items ever since teaching began. In Figure 5.1 you'll see a few True–False items that might have appeared in ancient times.

Although True–False items are the most commonly encountered form of the two-choice item, students can also be obliged to choose between Right–Wrong, Correct–Incorrect, or Yes–No. The

---

True or False?   1. The sabertooth tiger that ravaged our village today had no incisor plaque or other serious forms of dental deterioration.

True or False?   2. According to Socrates, *Plato* was a Greek serving dish used for special meals.

True or False?   3. Helen of Troy spent most of her leisure time riding large wooden horses.

5.1 Illustrative, but fictitious, "ancient" True–False test items

important thing about a two-choice test item is that the child gets only two discrete choices; there are no in-betweens.

Strengths and Weaknesses

Positives.   The most significant strength of a two-choice item is that its brevity permits teachers to cover a substantial amount of content without taking up much testing time. For example, a student might be able to complete a forty-item True–False test in less time than it would take for the student to write one fairly hefty response to an item in an essay test.

Two-choice test items are especially useful when classroom tests are intended to find out the amount of knowledge that students have acquired, such as a set of important scientific facts a teacher has been trying to promote. A set of True–False items can efficiently tell teachers what students know, and what they don't.

Another excellent application of two-choice items arises whenever what the teacher has been teaching revolves around a two-category classification scheme such as might be found when students are being taught the difference between *fact* and *opinion* in a reading class or between *organic* and *inorganic* compounds in a science class. Two-choice items simply provide students with an example of one of the two categories, then let students choose which of the two categories is being exemplified.

For example, a Fact–Opinion item might present a statement such as "The book about school testing, written for parents by W. James Popham, is the finest book available on this topic." (Fact or Opinion?) If I were in control of the answer key for this test, I'd indicate that the correct answer is emphatically a Fact. Who said authors need to be nonpartisan?

Negatives.   The greatest "deficit" of two-choice items is *not* that it's too easy for students to guess the correct answer. Many people think that, because there are only two options from which students are to choose, students can come up with a correct answer 50 percent of the time simply by means of a mental coin flip. But while that may be true for *one* True–False item, it is definitely not true when there are twenty or even ten such items involved. The odds of a student's guessing correctly all items in a ten-item two-choice test is less than 1 in 1,000. No, the "ease-of-guessing" criticism is a bad rap that's laid on two-choice items.

The most serious weakness of two-choice items is that they are most typically focused on rote memory, that is, items measuring cognitive behavior at the lowest level of Bloom's Taxonomy. If your child's teacher is predominantly testing students with two-choice items, you should be somewhat concerned. It is *possible* to make two-choice items assess higher

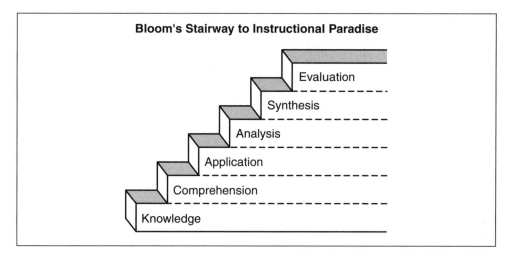

5.2 The six levels of Bloom's Cognitive Taxonomy

levels of students' cognitive achievements. But, as a practical matter, it's rarely done. Teachers who rarely stray from two-choice items are teachers who rarely push students higher on Bloom's Taxonomy, represented in Figure 5.2.

A less serious weakness of certain kinds of two-choice items, especially True–False items, is that there are many things in life that aren't decisively true or definitively false. Yet, True–False items don't offer children the option of asserting that something is "almost true" or "fairly false." The necessity for items that evoke one response or its opposite can sometimes distort reality for students.

Item-Writing Errors

As you saw, earlier in the chapter, there are several *general* "teacher shouldn'ts" that apply to all test items, whether those items are of the selected-response or the constructed-response variety. There are also item-writing errors that teachers sometimes commit when they are creating two-choice test items. Briefly, here they are.

- Negatives: *Two-choice items should rarely use negative statements and never use double negatives. Negative sentences can too easily confuse students, even knowledgeable students so that, in the case of True–False tests, it's not clear whether a True or a False is most appropriate.*
- Double-Concept Jeopardy: *Two-choice items should never include two concepts in a single statement. The problem with two or more concepts in a single two-choice item is that one concept can be true, while the other concept can be*

false. Even knowledgeable students are apt to be confused. Unknowledgeable students will almost certainly be confused, and thus might answer correctly!

- Unequal Category Representation: *Because there are two categories being used as the basis for the items (for example, True or False), each of the two categories should be represented by approximately equal numbers of items.*

  I remember once, when I was a high school teacher, creating a True–False test that had only false items. Shrewd students figured out what silliness I was up to, and had no trouble racing through the test. Less shrewd students, beginning to feel wary about the absence of "True" responses, ended up by tossing in a few true responses before they finished. It was a really dumb assessment idea. My assessment skills, at the time, were way less than wonderful.

- Dissimilar Item Length: *If, in a set of two-choice items, all items representing one category are lengthy, while all items representing the other category are short, many students will figure out what's going on, and therefore be able to answer the items correctly even if they know very little about the content measured in the test. So, let's say you're looking over your child's classroom exams and you find a two-choice test in which the statements in the items are meaningfully different in length. The false items all consist of short statements while the statements in the true items, because they contain so many qualifiers, are all long. For such a two-choice test, the likelihood of drawing a valid inference about students' status is significantly reduced.*

If you find that your child is taking a ton of two-choice test items, you should look over the items carefully. The *first* thing you should do is see if the items are only measuring a student's memorized knowledge. If that's all the teacher's tests are assessing, then it's likely students are primarily being taught to memorize factual information.

Second, you should see if many of the two-choice items contain the kinds of item-writing errors cited here. If there are such errors, then it may be time to have a brief, constructive conversation with your child's teacher or principal.

Common-Stimulus Two-Choice Items

A useful variation of the traditional two-choice item presents the student with a set of stimulus material, followed by several two-choice items based on that material. In Figure 5.3 an example of these kinds of items, known as *common-stimulus two-choice items,* is presented for a "descriptive statistics" item in a seventh-grade mathematics class.

As you can see, all of the four True–False items are based on the set of ten quiz scores that the test-taker has not previously seen. The presence of

Suppose that you are a member of a seventh-grade self-study group that is trying to learn about mathematics by a "cooperative model" in which each student's individual grade is based, at least in part, by the whole group's average performance. Last week your self-study group took a ten-item quiz. Here are the scores your group's students earned on the quiz:

5, 6, 7, 7, 7, 7, 8, 8, 8, 8, 9, 10

Now, using these twelve quiz-scores, decide whether each of the following statements is true or false.

1. The median for your group's quiz scores is 7.5. (True)

2. The mode for the set of quiz scores is 8.0. (False)

3. The range of your group's quiz scores is 5.0. (True)

4. The median for the set of quiz scores is different than the mean. (False)

5.3 An illustration of common-stimulus two-choice items for a seventh-grade mathematics class

previously unencountered stimulus material makes it clear that this set of two-choice items is assessing more than memorized information.

Teachers should use common-stimulus two-choice items that require students to deal with brand new stimulus material (such as the set of twelve quiz scores in Figure 5.3), then draw on that material as they answer a set of two-choice items.

In general, common-stimulus two-choice items possess the same strengths and weaknesses, and suffer from the same potential item-writing flaws, as the more typical one-at-a-time two-choice items. However, because common-stimulus two-choice items almost always oblige children to *apply* new information, they tend to foster less memorization-focused teaching.

Multiple-Choice Items

Perhaps the most popular selected-response item for educational tests is the *multiple-choice item.* Such an item usually presents the student with *a question* or *an incomplete statement,* along with three, four, or five answer choices. The student's job is to choose an answer from the options presented.

Multiple-choice items have been used for decades. (The *Army Alpha*, for example, employed such items.) Multiple-choice items are the most prevalent kind of item you'll find in standardized tests, either standardized achievement tests or standardized aptitude tests. In my experience, multiple-choice test items are also an especially common kind of item found in many teachers' classroom tests.

Testing Terms:

Multiple-Choice Item

A selected-response item in which the student must choose among three or more answer—options

Many teachers have seen such items so often as they grew up that they seem to believe a really "respectable" classroom test ought to have at least a dollop of multiple-choice items. So, if you're going to be reviewing your child's classroom tests, don't be surprised if you run into a number of multiple-choice items such as the ones you'll find in Figure 5.4. As you can see, the top item is a direct-question item, while the bottom item uses an incomplete statement format.

The first part of a multiple-choice item, that is, the material preceding the answer choices, is referred to as the item's *stem*. The potential answers are referred to as *options, alternatives,* or *choices.* Wrong options are usually described as *distractors.*

Direct-Question Form (best-answer version)

Which of the following modes of composition would be most effective in explaining to someone how a bill becomes a law in this nation?

  A. Narrative

  *B. Expository

  C. Persuasive

  D. Descriptive

Incomplete-Statement Form (correct-answer version)

Mickey Mouse's nephews are named

  A. Huey, Dewey, and Louie.

  B. Mutt and Jeff.

  C. Larry, Moe, and Curly.

  *D. Morty and Ferdy.

5.4 Illustrative multiple-choice items

Sometimes a multiple-choice item will ask students to select the *correct answer* from the alternatives. Sometimes a multiple-choice item will ask students to select the *best answer* from the available options.

As far as the number of answer options to be presented to the students, you'll usually find that four or five are used, although with younger children such as those in grade three or lower, a multiple-choice item may include only three options.

Now that you know something about the inner workings of multiple-choice items, let's look at their virtues and vices.

Strengths and Weaknesses

Positives. As with other types of selected-response items, multiple-choice items can be easily scored. Increasingly, schools are installing electronic scoring-machines so that teachers can command computers to scan and score students' answers to multiple-choice tests. However, even if teachers are scoring students' tests " by hand," the scoring of multiple-choice tests is really quite rapid.

A distinctive advantage of multiple-choice items (especially an advantage over two-choice items) is that the alternatives can be constructed so the options differ in their *relative* correctness. So, when teachers construct items in which students must choose the best answer from several competing options, the student is often obliged to make subtle (hence, challenging) discriminations among several answer–choices.

Multiple-choice items can be constructed so that they really only require students to show what they have memorized. However, multiple-choice items can be created so that they oblige students to engage in genuinely higher levels of thinking. The highest level of Bloom's Cognitive Taxonomy is "evaluation," and a well-written multiple choice item can require students to evaluate which of several "correct" answers is really "most correct."

Negatives. The greatest weakness of this form of selected-response item stems from the fact that the student is only obliged to *recognize* a correct answer, *not generate* it. Surely, in the interest of economy, teachers will often decide to use a multiple-choice item rather than asking the student to create a response from scratch. But the ability of a student to choose a correct answer from *already-presented* options is *not* the same as the ability of a student to generate an original response.

For instance, consider a reading test in which students are being assessed to see if they can read a passage and determine its main idea. Because I used to direct a test development company that created state-level tests, I have personally created hundreds of such "main-idea" items. Because the tests were to be administered to all students in a state, we were required (because of financial limitations) to use only multiple-choice tests. I wrote a great many main-idea items for those tests. They worked pretty well. (I am most likely biased in the appraisal of my own test items.)

The skill being measured was an important skill, namely, the skill of a child to read something, then comprehend what its main idea was. But, *in real life*, nobody reads something and is then given four choices, one of which happens to be a correct statement of the main idea. *In real life*, people must read a passage and then, without an accompanying set of answer–options, figure out the main idea of what they've read.

And that gets us back to the validity of score-based interpretations again. Can a teacher who relies exclusively on multiple-choice tests arrive at a valid interpretation about a student's ability to generate, without answer–option crutches, an accurate statement of the main idea of what the student has read? I personally doubt it.

So, despite the substantial efficiency that multiple-choice items (or, indeed, any kind of selected-response item) offer to educators, if a judgment is being made about your child's possession of an important skill, then the classroom assessment (that's being used to help the teacher make this judgment) should coincide as closely as possible with the nature of the skill as it must be used *in real life*.

Item-Writing Errors

Here are some of the more common mistakes that teachers make when they whip out multiple-choice items.

- **Unstuffed Items:** *A good multiple-choice item will have most of the content in its stem, thus permitting students to more efficiently review briefly stated answer–choices and select a winner. If a multiple-choice item uses only a single-sentence stem, and four answer–options—all of which are lengthy, multisentence paragraphs—then the student will be obliged to do too much reading (because of the lengthy answer–options). Lengthy stems and brief alternatives are winners. Brief stems and lengthy alternatives are losers.*
- **Answer-Length Clues:** *Sometimes teachers will give away the correct answer to a multiple-choice item by making the correct alternative much longer than the distractors. Students tend to choose the lengthier alternative simply because it stands out so distinctively. Besides, they get so many more words for their choice!*

But there can be give-away clues in the other direction as well. Sometimes the correct answer is super-short and all of the alternatives go on forever. What teachers should do, of course, is make all alternatives about the same length. However, it's okay if in a four-option multiple-choice item there are two short options and two long options. That arrangement doesn't supply an unintended clue to students.

■ Unspread Answer–Options: *There's a strong tendency for teachers to overuse certain alternatives as the correct answers in a multiple-choice test. In a four-option item, teachers tend to overbook on Choice C as the correct answer. That's because teachers are reluctant to use Choice A all that often because it seems to the teacher that the student won't need to review the other options. Even Choice B gets neglected a bit for the same reason. And Choice D is sometimes avoided because it's the "last choice" and teachers don't want students to choose it for that reason alone. As a consequence, Choice C gets overused as the correct answer–option.*

All teachers have to do to correct this error is make sure that the correct answers are divided in approximately equal proportions among all of the answer–choices.

■ Negatives as a Confusion Source: *It has been alleged, particularly by overly cautious individuals, that "one robin does not spring make." Without debating the causal relationship between seasonal shifts and feathered flyers, in multiple-choice item-writing we could say with confidence that "one negative in an item stem does not confusion unmake." Negatives are strange commodities. A single* not, *tossed casually into a test item, can drive students crazy. Besides, because* not *is such a tiny word, and might be overlooked by students, there's a chance that a number of students (who didn't see the* not) *will be trying to ferret out the best alternative for a positively stated stem. It's okay if you find that your child's teacher occasionally uses negatively stated stems in multiple-choice items. But if that's done, then the negatives should be clearly identified with italics, underscoring, or boldface type.*

■ The All-of-the-Above Error: *Multiple-choice test items should never include an "all-of-the-above" option as the students' final choice. There are a pair of important reasons for not using this common option.*

First, assume that "all-of-the-above" is the last and the correct answer in a four-option multiple-choice item; this means that the first three alternatives must all be correct. So, when many students see that Choice A is correct, they will simply mark it as correct and move on to the next item without ever seeing that Choices B and C are also correct, thereby making Choice D the winning option.

Second, even if a student doesn't know that all of the item's options are correct, the student can get by with partial information. Suppose, for example, that there was a five-option multiple-choice item and that, because the first four options are all correct, the fifth "all-of-the-above" option was really the correct answer. Let's say that a student doesn't know anything at all about Choices A and B, but does recognize that both Choices C and D are correct. Thus, even though the student only knows what's involved in about half of the options, the student is able to choose Choice E, "the all-of-the-above" option. Because Choices C and D are correct, Choice E must be the winning answer.

However, although the "all-of-the-above" option is a clear loser, there are many times when a "none-of-the-above" alternative works quite well in multiple-choice items. For instance, in mathematics computation problems, if there were only four alternatives, one of those choices would have to be the correct answer, so students might be able to guess their way to a correct choice even with computational errors.

But with a "none-of-the-above" option, if the student's initial computation doesn't work out so it coincides with one of the item's options, then it may well be that the correct answer really is "none-of-the-above." The net effect of the addition of the "none-of-the-above" option to multiple-choice items is that it makes the items much more difficult for students. They are not able to pick the best answer from a set of answer–choices. Rather, they must be certain they're correct.

In recent years there has been a fair amount of "multiple-choice test-bashing" by critics who believe those items would be better described as "multiple-guess" items. Nevertheless, if skillfully employed by your child's teacher in classroom tests, these items can efficiently and effectively measure important skills and knowledge.

Matching Items

Testing Terms:

Matching Item

A selected-response item in which the student must match entries on one list with appropriate entries on a second list

A *matching item* consists of two parallel lists of words or phrases that require the student to match entries on one list with appropriate entries on the second list. Entries in the list for which a match is sought are referred to as *premises*. Entries in the list from which selections are made are referred to as *responses*. Usually, students are directed to match entries from the two lists according to a specific kind of association that is described in the test directions. Presented in Figure 5.5 is an example of a matching item.

Notice in the illustrative matching item that both lists are *homogeneous;* that is, all of the entries in the column at the left (the

---

Directions: On the line to the left of each military conflict listed in column A, write the letter of the U.S. president in Column B who was in office when that military conflict was *concluded.* Each name in Column B may be used no more than once.

Column A

(H) 1. World War I
(G) 2. World War II
(C) 3. Korea
(E) 4. Vietnam
(A) 5. Persian Gulf

Column B

A. Bush
B. Clinton
C. Eisenhower
D. Johnson
E. Nixon
F. Roosevelt
G. Truman
H. Wilson

5.5 An illustrative matching item

premises) are U.S. military conflicts and all of the entries in the column at the right (the responses) are names of U.S. presidents. Homogeneity of list entries is an important attribute of properly constructed matching items.

Although matching items are sometimes found in teachers' classroom tests, they are found with far less frequency than two-choice or multiple-choice items.

Strengths and Weaknesses

Positives.   An advantage of a matching item is that its compact form makes it possible to cover a substantial amount of content without taking up too much space. Another advantage of matching items (along with all selected-response items) is that the scoring of students' answers is relatively easy. All a teacher needs to do is hold a list of the correct responses alongside the students' responses and spot any errors.

Negatives.   A disadvantage of matching items is that, as with the two-choice items, they tend to encourage students' memorization of low-level factual information that is often of debatable value. The sample matching item in Figure 5.5 illustrates that point. Although the format of a matching item nicely represents the student's task of linking up U.S. presidents with

A Parent Puzzle

(Setting: A parent has been looking over a series of completed classroom tests that the parent's fourth-grade child, Ashley, has taken. Ashley has been scoring well on the tests, always earning grades of A or B. But the parent is concerned that there are only two kinds of items that ever appear on the tests, namely, True–False items (usually about 20) and multiple-choice items (usually about 15). The parent, being concerned about the exclusive use of selected-response items, stops by Ashley's classroom one afternoon after calling Ashley's teacher to see if a brief meeting is possible. Here's what went on at the session.)

Teacher: "I'm so pleased you could stop by this afternoon. Ashley's been doing very well in class. You should be proud. But I'm sure you are. Now, what would you like to talk about?"

Parent: "I am pleased with Ashley's progress, and I'm certain you're doing a good job in teaching her. Thanks for all your hard work. But I did want to raise a concern with you about the tests that Ashley has been bringing home.

"I've seen that all the items are always of two types—True–False items or multiple-choice items. I've been wondering whether the use of only those two item-types is really letting you find out what Ashley knows— *and doesn't know.*"

Teacher: "I'm delighted that you've taken the time to look over Ashley's tests. You're right. All of my tests employ only multiple-choice or True–False items. But if you look closely at the items, especially the multiple-choice items, you'll see that the items are measuring far more than Ashley's ability to memorize factual information. Was that your concern?"

Parent: "Yes, I'm concerned that if only these two types of items are used, items that I believe educators refer to as selected-response items, Ashley won't be sufficiently challenged."

Teacher: "That's a legitimate concern. Too many times we see teachers using only selected-response tests because they are exclusively concerned with measuring what students have memorized. And I'm sure that many of my True–False items are of that sort. But that's why I use the multiple-choice items as well. In the last test that Ashley took, for example, 10 of the 15 multiple-choice items measured intellectual skills that were well beyond most memory. Doesn't that deal with your concern?"

Parent: If you were the parent, how would you respond?

My Response: First off, I'd note that the teacher does not seem to be defensive. That's a clear plus. Some teachers, if a parent raises *any* questions about the teacher's tests, the teacher's instruction, or even the teacher's choice of wardrobe, will become mildly to tyrannically defensive. The teacher in this fictional interchange does not appear to be defensive.

Accordingly, I would feel free to say something such as, "I really appreciate the fact that your test's multiple-choice items are measuring more than memorized

continued

A Parent Puzzle *(continued)*

information; that's quite appropriate. But so we both find out if Ashley can *generate* original responses instead of only *recognizing* the correct answers in the multiple-choice items, couldn't you devote at least a portion of some of your tests to constructed-response items?"

My Reason: Because this teacher seems willing to listen, and is clearly concerned about an overemphasis on items that measure mere memorization, I think the teacher might entertain a constructive suggestion that, at least occasionally, some constructed-response items could be included in Ashley's classroom tests.

Remember, constructed-response tests take far more time to score, so you'd be asking the teacher to put in some extra effort. But if you only ask for the occasional addition of constructed-response items, this represents a more reasonable request. If you remain pleasant, not critical, and make it clear you want what's best for Ashley and the rest of the students, you might just see some constructed-response items creeping into Ashley's future tests.

U.S. military conflicts, who really cares? In other words, is the cognitive task represented by the illustrative item really one that you'd want your child to be able to perform?

The illustrative item assesses a student's knowledge; but is that knowledge truly significant? I'd say it isn't. What you ought to be asking yourself if you find yourself reviewing the classroom tests taken by your child is this: "Does this item assess a skill or body of knowledge that my child really needs to learn?" Sometimes, unfortunately, teachers become so attached to a particular kind of item format that they'll use that format even though what's being tested isn't all that worthwhile.

Item-Writing Errors

Here are a few of the item-writing errors that you are apt to find if your child's teacher uses matching items, but doesn't do a great job in the building of such items.

- Lengthy Lists: *The lists of premises (on the left) and responses (on the right) ought to be relatively brief. That's because students should not be spending an eternity checking out a long list of responses to see which one best fits a premise. A list of ten or so responses is about the upper limit. If there were twenty responses, that would be way too many. Incidentally, if one of the lists contains short words or phrases and the other list contains long ones, shorter words or phrases should be in the list at the right (the response list). That's because the student will be reading a premise, then scanning the response list for a suitable match. The list to be scanned should, of course, be more scannable.*

■ **Heterogeneous Lists:** *As indicated earlier, each list in a matching item, that is, the premise list and the response list, should consist of homogeneous entries. Not just any old list of assorted entries should be used in a matching item. That's because if there are three or four different kinds of subsets within a response list, for instance, three U.S. presidents, three British prime ministers, and three Russian presidents, the student's task is much too easy. The student will often only need to choose from a subset of the response list, not from the entire list.*

Thus, if either the premises or the responses in a matching item are heterogeneous, *that is, consist of different sorts of entries, this constitutes an item-writing error for matching items.*

■ **Equal Length Lists:** *Equality is such a good thing that most of us applaud equality whenever it rears its lovely head. But, in the case of matching items, equality of length in the premise and response list constitutes an item-writing error. You see, if there are exactly the same number of responses for a premise list, then when the student is nearly finished with the matching of premises, there'll only be a few responses left. And it will be too easy to guess which of the remaining few responses is correct.*

Suppose for example, that there were seven premises and seven responses. If your child knows the match for five of the seven premises, then there are only two responses remaining. A mental coin flip will help the child come up with two correct answers about half the time.

So, there should always be at least two or three more responses than premises in a matching item. If you find matching items in which there are lists of equal length, you've found a matching item that's flawed.

It's really difficult to imagine a teacher's classroom test consisting only of matching items. After all, there are many sorts of cognitive skills, or many types of knowledge, that simply won't fit into this kind of item format. More often than not, therefore, you're likely to find that matching items might constitute a part, but not all, of a classroom test. That's probably an appropriate role for this type of selected-response item.

Even though selected-response items have been criticized in recent years for their failure to assess students' cognitive capabilities as those cognitive capabilities must be used in real life, selected-response test items will surely be used in educational tests. As a parent, therefore, you need to be familiar with the major strengths, weaknesses, and typical defects of the most common types of these items.

What Do You Really Need to Know about This Chapter's Content?

You've now considered the three most frequent kinds of selected-response items used in teachers' classroom tests. I suggest that the following points are the ones you really need to take away from this chapter.

- A parent who knows about educational tests what you'll know when you finish this book can, by reviewing a child's classroom tests, play a meaningful role in improving those tests (if improvement is needed). This improvement function will usually require a conversation with your child's teacher or principal about the tests. This conversation will typically require advance planning on your part.

- A significant distinction in educational testing is the difference between selected-response items and constructed-response items. Selected-response items call for students to identify correct answers from already presented alternatives. Constructed-response items oblige students to generate their answers. Selected-response items can be easily scored, but do not oblige students to create their responses. The most popular kinds of selected-response items are two-choice items, multiple-choice items, and (to a lesser extent) matching items.

- A two-choice item, such as the True–False item, has the advantage of covering much content efficiently. Its chief disadvantage is that it encourages only memorization of factual information.

- A multiple-choice item can assess the student's memorized knowledge of content as well as genuinely high-level cognitive skills. Its alternatives can represent relative degrees of correctness, thereby presenting a challenging intellectual task to students. A major weakness of this type of item is that it still only requires students to recognize an already present correct response, not generate one.

- A matching item's strength is that it can efficiently cover a good deal of content, although it often encourages rote memorization of information by students.

POSSIBLE PARENT ACTION–OPTIONS

The most likely options for you to consider stemming from this chapter's content all revolve around the classroom tests that your child takes.

1. At the least intrusive level, you could simply look over any tests that your child is allowed to bring home. If you find that the tests are exclusively selected-response in nature, or that there are many item-writing errors in those items, you might wish to send a brief note to your child's teacher or the school principal. In that note, you could *tactfully* register your concerns and ask if it would be possible to make some changes in future tests.

2. Another course of action would be for you to contact your child's teacher by telephone or note to see if the teacher will allow you to come to the school to look over the past tests your child has taken. One of the reasons for doing so is to understand better just what kinds of skills and knowledge are being promoted so that you can provide more focused help at home.

   Assuming the teacher agrees to your proposed test-review session, you might determine that the tests too heavily rely on selected-response items or that the test's selected-response items display a number of item-writing flaws. If so, then some subsequent comments to the teacher or the principal, perhaps framed in the form of questions, might stimulate the teacher to think twice about the use of certain kinds of assessment items.

3. Suggest to your child's principal or teacher that one (or more) of the *Suggested Resources* could help teachers improve the quality of their classroom tests.

SUGGESTED RESOURCES FOR YOUR CHILD'S TEACHER OR PRINCIPAL

Printed Materials

Gronlund, Norman E. *Assessment of Student Achievement*. Boston: Allyn and Bacon, 1998. *In Chapters 4 and 5, Gronlund describes how teachers can create multiple-choice items, True–False items, matching items, and a type of selected-response item he refers to as an interpretive exercise.*

Haladyna, Thomas M. *Developing and Validating Multiple-Choice Test Items*. Mahwah, NJ: Lawrence Erlbaum Associates, 1994. *From this introductory book, educators can learn about key principles to follow in developing and appraising multiple-choice items.*

Hopkins, Kenneth D. *Educational and Psychological Measurement and Evaluation* (8th ed.). Boston: Allyn and Bacon, 1998. *In the ninth chapter of this book, "Constructing Objective Tests," Hopkins describes how teachers should build the most common kinds of selected-response items. He also considers short-answer items to be "objective," so describes item-construction approaches for these items as well.*

Stiggins, Richard J. *Student-Centered Classroom Assessment* (2nd ed.). Upper Saddle River, NJ: Prentice-Hall, 1997. *In his Chapter 6, Stiggins provides a clear set of suggestions about how teachers can generate selected-response items. He regards selected-response assessment as both flexible and efficient.*

Videotape Programs

Assessment Training Institute, Inc. *Common Sense Paper and Pencil Assessments.* (50 SW Second Ave., Ste. 300, Portland, OR 97204). *This video shows how traditional paper and pencil tests can build student achievement. It demonstrates effective strategies, suggests steps for involving students, and shows how tests can be used in a successful assessment plan.*

IOX Assessment Associates. *Creating Challenging Classroom Tests: When Students Select Their Responses.* (5301 Beethoven St., Ste. 190, Los Angeles, CA 90066). *Three easy-to-follow rules are presented to help teachers create selected-response classroom tests that call for higher-level thinking.*

Northwest Regional Educational Laboratory. *Paper and Pencil Test Development.* IOX Assessment Associates (5301 Beethoven St., Ste. 190, Los Angeles, CA 90066). *This videotape shows teachers how to plan tests, select the content to be tested, and write high-quality test items.*

6

COMMON CLASSROOM TESTS: WHEN STUDENTS CONSTRUCT THEIR ANSWERS

*I*n this chapter you'll be learning about two kinds of constructed-response classroom tests, namely, those containing *short-answer items* and those containing *essay items*. I would be astonished if, over the years, your child didn't do battle with many such items in teacher-made classroom tests. Short-answer items and essay items are a mainstay of many classroom assessments.

The Realism of Constructed-Response Items

If you recall the discussion of selected-response items versus constructed-response items in the previous chapter, you'll remember that although selected-response items are far easier to score, they fail to require students to employ their skills and knowledge in the same way that the real, post-school world does.

When children finally leave school, they will need to read a newspaper article and understand what it means without the aid of four multiple-choice options, one of which happens to capture the article's main idea.

When children finally leave school and, as they apply for a job, are asked to write a brief description of their interests and educational background, those descriptions must be written from scratch. There isn't any set of True–False items that can be answered as a substitute.

So, almost without exception, if teachers assess students' knowledge and skills with constructed-response items, the measurement method will more closely parallel what those students will be required to do later in life. So, if that's true, you might be wondering, why don't teachers create *all* of their tests so that students are required to construct their responses?

There are two answers to that question, both of which have merit. Answer number one is the *objectivity of scoring;* answer number two is the *time requirements of scoring.*

Objectivity of Scoring

The longer that students' constructed-response answers to test questions are, the greater the risk that teachers will score those answers inaccurately. Imagine, for a moment, that Mr. Melton, a sixth-grade teacher, was scoring his students' two-page responses to an essay question asking why the Allies were victorious in World War II. Clearly, Mr. Melton's students could head in numerous directions during their two-page diatribes about the causes of Allied victory. How confident would Mr. Melton be when scoring those responses that he could arrive at accurate distinctions in the quality of the essays? How confident would Mr. Melton be that if he had to *re-score* all of those essays—with his initial scores hidden—he would come up with the same scores?

Many teachers have genuine doubts about their ability to score students' constructed responses objectively. They fear that, when judging students' responses, they'll recognize a "bright" student's handwriting and unconsciously give that student an unwarranted high grade. Or, conversely, a teacher might spot a "slow" student's scrawling script and, without recognizing it, give that slower student a lower score than deserved.

Clearly, when teachers contrast the scoring-objectivity associated with a multiple-choice test versus an essay test, there's certain to be less objectivity in scoring students' essays. And it is this fear of nonobjectivity that disinclines some teachers to employ constructed-response tests. They want to be fair with their students, and they believe selected-response tests are far more fair.

It is true, as you'll see in the next chapter, that through the use of carefully developed scoring guides, teachers can score student's constructed responses more accurately. But such accuracy-inducing scoring guides are not only difficult to create, they take substantial time to use. And that brings us to the second reason teachers often opt for selected-response items in their classroom tests.

Time Requirements of Scoring

It would be delightful if teachers had small classes and ample preparation time so that they could provide the most effective instruction of which they were capable. But that's not today's reality. Most teachers are working at the very edge of their energy limits. No matter at what grade level, you'll rarely find teachers who have enough time to do what needs to be done with their students.

It takes time to plan an effective instructional sequence. It takes time to assemble the information and the materials that students need. It takes time to work with students individually or in small groups so that student's individual potentials can be realized. It takes time for teachers to determine whether a given instructional activity was effective so that, when next the activity is used, they know whether it should be deleted, reused, or revised. *And it takes time to score students' constructed responses.*

The time that it takes a teacher to score students' essay tests constitutes time that must be taken away from the teacher's planning efforts. And if instruction isn't well planned, then it's apt to be ineffective. So, because teachers don't want to offer students instruction that's less effective than it should be, many teachers opt to employ the time-saving alternative of using selected-response tests—tests that can be scored in a fraction of the time it takes to score students' constructed responses.

If you find your child's teacher is using classroom tests that appear to focus too heavily on selected-response tests, remember that there are legitimate reasons why the teacher may be doing so. The legitimacy of those reasons, however, need not prevent you from encouraging the teacher to devote at least a portion of the teacher's classroom tests to the use of items that elicit responses closer to the responses required in the real world.

Short-Answer Items

One kind of constructed-response item that you're likely to see in your child's classroom tests is a *short-answer item.* Short-answer items call for students to supply a word, phrase, or sentence in response to a direct question or an incomplete statement. If the student's response to an item is to be a paragraph or longer, such items are usually regarded as essay items.

Testing Terms:

Short-Answer Item

A constructed-response item calling for students to supply a word, phrase, or sentence in response to a direct question or incomplete statement

In order to help deal with the two chief reasons that some teachers avoid constructed-response items, that is, concerns about objectivity of scoring and the time requirements of scoring, many teachers who use short-answer items prefer to use items that call for *really* short responses from students such as a single word or a very short phrase.

In Figure 6.1, you'll see several examples of short-answer items for an elementary-school U.S. geography test. Notice that, in the first two items, the student is to supply answers in the spaces at the end of the item. In the final two items, students are to fill in the blanks in incomplete statements. All four of the items ask students to supply only names of specified states.

In Figure 6.2, there's another pair of short-answer items that, unfortunately, indicate how trifling the content of such items can be. Short-answer items *can* require students to think. But short-answer items can also deal with truly trivial content. The items in Figure 6.2 prove it.

Strengths and Weaknesses

Positives. Short-answer items represent an efficient way to assess relatively simple kinds of learning such as the student's ability to produce the

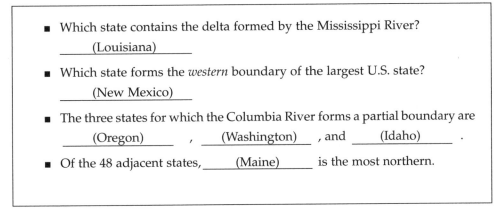

- Which state contains the delta formed by the Mississippi River?
  _____(Louisiana)_____

- Which state forms the *western* boundary of the largest U.S. state?
  _____(New Mexico)_____

- The three states for which the Columbia River forms a partial boundary are
  _____(Oregon)_____ , _____(Washington)_____ , and _____(Idaho)_____ .

- Of the 48 adjacent states, _____(Maine)_____ is the most northern.

6.1 Illustrative short-answer items in geography

names of states in the geography items seen in Figure 6.1. But carefully crafted, short-answer items can also be used to measure higher level cognitive skills than mere memory.

The really big advantage of a short-answer item is that it requires a student to *produce* a response, not merely recognize an appropriate response from a set of already present alternatives. To produce a correct response typically requires a student to possess more completely the knowledge or skill being assessed. Sometimes, partial knowledge or partial possession of a skill will allow your child to recognize the correct answer from the alternatives presented in a selected-response item. That's not possible with a short-answer item.

A special virtue of short-answer items, especially those that ask for responses of only words or phrases, is that the brevity of the student's response makes for more speedy scoring and more objective scoring. In fact, short-answer items in classroom tests can be remarkably close to selected-response items when it comes to efficiency and objectivity of scoring.

- In which of the six states that were the answers to the items in Figure 6.1 is Popham Beach found? _____(Maine)_____

- Who would care? _____(Any Self-Respecting Popham)_____

6.2 Illustrative short-answer items dealing with less-than-significant content

For larger-scale tests, such as high-stakes statewide or nationally standardized achievement tests, because short-answer items still require human scorers, they add considerably to the costs of scoring. However, recent advances in computer-based scanning of student's responses to short-answer items suggests that soon it will be possible to electronically score not only students' selected responses, but also their constructed responses to short-answer items.

Negatives. The chief disadvantage with short-answer items is that they do take more time to score than their selected-response counterparts. And there is also the potential for more subjectivity-induced scoring errors by teachers. Actually, these problems can typically be avoided if the teacher constructs items so that the response sought is only one or two words in length, and there is really only a single correct answer that must be supplied by the student.

But those very items where there's only *one* correct answer often elicit memorized factual information. And that is the danger of seeking students' super-short answers. The teacher will often be tempted to measure low-level, memory-only knowledge.

So, if you find that your child is being asked to respond to at least some short-answer items, you should be pleased. But before you get too smug, look at the items to see what's really being assessed. Is the item measuring high-level or low-level cognition? Short-answer items, as you see, have the potential to tap higher-order thinking on the part of your child. In many classroom tests, however, that potential is not realized.

Item-Writing Errors

Here are a few of the errors you may see in any short-answer items found in your child's tests.

- Testing for Trivia: *If teachers are going to go to the trouble of scoring students' constructed responses, they should certainly expend that energy in measuring more than students' memorized information. If you are reviewing a test containing short-answer items, see if the items are measuring anything other than knowledge, the lowest level of Bloom's Taxonomy.*
- Swiss-Cheese Items: *For incomplete-statement types of short-answer items, there should rarely be more than one or two blanks. The presence of more than two blanks in an incomplete statement makes it difficult, if not impossible, for the student to know what the teacher is getting at. Take a look at the following item to see how a profusion of blanks can render a short-answer item*

almost indecipherable: "After a series of major disasters, in the year
_____ *, the explorers* _____ *and* _____ *, accompa-*
nied by their _____ *, discovered* _____ *." Can you see why*
such item-writing travesties are referred to as "Swiss-cheese items?"

■ Linear Inequity: *When teachers use a short-answer item, they should be try-*
ing to get the student to display knowledge or skill the student possesses. To
the extent that there are any unintended clues in the item itself, the teacher's
test-based interpretation about the student will be less accurate. For short-
answer items, one form of unintended clue is unequal lines provided for stu-
dents to respond.

If teachers are looking for a brief response, they sometimes toss in a
super-short line. If they're expecting a longer response, they provide a length-
ier line. Thus, line-length becomes an unintended clue to the answers sought.
This is an easy defect to eliminate. All blank spaces for students' answers
should be equal in length.

Incidentally, in incomplete statements, it is better to place the item's
blanks toward the end of the statement rather than at the statement's begin-
ning. Statements that begin with a blank can frequently confuse students.

So, if you never see short-answer items used in your child's classroom
tests, you might want to ask the teacher or principal, "Why?" However, if
you do find that your child has been receiving short-answer items, then be
attentive to the item-writing errors just described.

Essay Items

Testing Terms:

An Essay Item

A constructed-response item calling for a paragraph or longer response to a question or directive

Essay items have been used to test students since the Middle
Ages. Today, in many nations, the most common type of educational test item still used is the essay item. An essay item is a
constructed-response test item that calls for students to write a
response of a paragraph or more to a question or directive intended to measure students' skills and/or knowledge.

In Figure 6.3 you'll find several examples of the kinds of
essay items your child might have to deal with in classroom
tests dealing with social studies. Notice that the first and third
examples of test items in Figure 6.3 are *directives* rather than
questions. A directive simply assigns a task for the student to
complete. The middle item in Figure 6.3 is framed in the form of a question. Usually, with a bit of rewording, an essay item written as a question
can be reformulated as a directive, or vice-versa.

- In your own words, prepare an essay of about 400 words indicating why President Harry Truman replaced General Douglas MacArthur at the height of the Korean conflict.

- Why is there usually a much lower turnout of voters for U.S. elections during the years when no president is to be elected? (Answer in the space provided.)

- In less than 50 words, give a strong argument for the "division of powers" among the executive, judicial, and legislative branches of our governmental system.

6.3 Illustrative essay items

Notice also in Figure 6.3 that all three items give students an idea about how extensive their responses are supposed to be. In the first and third item, the desired number of words is identified. In the second item, the student is told to answer "in the space provided." As you'll see, when essay items fail to provide students with an idea about how extensive their response should be, this constitutes an item-writing error.

Writing Samples: A Special Case

There's a special kind of essay item that I want you to set aside for a moment. The kind of essay item I'm referring to calls for an essay to be written in order for teachers to judge the quality of the student's ability to compose an essay. We'll look more extensively at this kind of item in Chapter 8.

Such essay items are generally referred to as *writing samples*. Writing samples are intended to reflect how well students can write, either in general or in specific kinds of writing such as the student's ability to write a narrative essay or a persuasive essay.

When students are asked to compose an essay in order to display how well they can write, this task is regarded as a type of *performance test*. We'll devote all of Chapter 8 to performance tests—one of the most widely used performance tests being those calling for students to produce writing samples to measure a student's compositional skills.

The kinds of essay items you should be thinking about as you read this chapter are the essay items you might find your child's teacher using in order to measure what your child has learned about science, social studies, language arts, and even mathematics. For example, your child could be asked on a mathematics exam to, "Write a brief essay describing the

connections among the four computational operations of addition, sub-traction, multiplication, and division."

Strengths and Weaknesses

Positives.   Essay items can be used to assess students' ability to engage in higher-level cognitive thought, for example, to analyze and to synthesize. Suppose an English teacher gives students a poorly written poem, then asks the students to write brief essays analyzing the poem's weaknesses and offering suggestions about how to improve the poem. That's the kind of intellectual undertaking that you simply can't pull off with selected-response items.

The use of essay items to measure students' higher-level thinking skills coincides more directly with the kinds of intellectual operations they'll be called on to use throughout their lives. For instance, suppose an elementary school teacher were showing students how to use a five-step *systematic* decision-making process that could be employed whenever they faced important decisions in their lives. The five steps might be: (1) identify and clarify the decision to be made, (2) generate possible decision options, (3) analyze or collect evidence regarding the appropriateness of the decision options, (4) choose and implement a decision, and (5) evaluate the appropriateness of the decision according to its consequences.

Well, if the teacher really wants to see whether students thoroughly understand this five-step process, all the teacher needs to do is describe a new kind of decision to be made (one that hasn't been discussed in class), then ask students to write an essay describing, step-by-step, how they would *systematically* go about making a decision.

That kind of step-by-step application of the decision-making process is precisely what the teacher hopes students will do when school's over. In other words, the essay item's question or directive can be responded to using exactly the same intellectual operations that are called for in real life. And that, of course, is what allows educators to make *valid* interpretations about the real-world skills that students possess.

Negatives.   As with most things in life, an essay item's greatest strengths are its greatest weaknesses. That's because in order to elicit student responses allowing educators to assess students' higher-level cognitive skills, somebody has to score those essay responses. As with all constructed-response items, such scoring takes time and runs the risk of insufficient scorer objectivity. Because essay responses are the most lengthy of the constructed-response answers that students must supply, this means the scoring of students' responses takes much longer and the likelihood of arriving at inaccurate scores surely soars. (Try to say, "Sorry scores surely soar," three times aloud in *rapid* succession. If you can, you get A+ in pronunciation.)

Because the scoring of students' essay responses takes so much time, teachers really need to be selective in their use of essay items, restricting such items to the measurement of really significant skills (for instance, the student's ability to compose an explanatory essay).

As far as scoring students' essays with accuracy, we'll deal with the use of scoring guides in the next chapter. You will see that it is possible to devise a defensible method of scoring students' essay responses, but that the creation of first-rate scoring procedures is, in itself, quite a time-consuming task.

What I hope you'll realize as you complete this chapter is that constructed-response items can play a powerful role in helping your child's teacher *and you* in determining your child's current knowledge and skills.

Essay items are especially useful in measuring a child's higher-order cognitive skills. But essay items take time to construct (more time than is usually thought) and they lead to student responses that take scads of time to score accurately.

Because teachers simply don't have unlimited time at their disposal, they rarely have the option of relying exclusively on constructed-response items. You wouldn't want your child's teacher to devote so much time to testing that there was insufficient time to plan and deliver high-quality teaching, would you?

And that, of course, creates the need for *balance* in the kinds of test items a teacher ought to use for classroom tests. Dramatic overbooking on either selected-response or constructed-response items is probably not in your child's best interest. If you find, on reviewing your child's tests, that the teacher has gone overboard in either direction, then it's time to tactfully raise a concern or two with the principal or the teacher.

It's not that your child's teacher needs to have different kinds of test items just for variety's sake. Different is not necessarily dandy. But you've now seen that the greatest payoff of constructed-response tests, namely, the requirement for students to generate responses, also requires teachers to spend a considerable amount of time in scoring students' responses. Selected-response tests can be used much more efficiently. With a blend of the two types of tests, teachers can engage in simultaneous cake-having and cake-eating. Your child will be getting an appropriate mix of item types in classroom tests.

Item-Writing Errors

Let's look at a few of the more serious item-writing errors associated with essay items.

- Assessing Knowledge: *A student's memorized knowledge can be efficiently measured via any of the selected-response items you considered in Chapter 5. It is simply an unwise use of essay items to assess a student's knowledge. For example, suppose your child's teacher used a social studies essay item that asked students to, "Write an essay identifying the original 13 states in this nation, then indicate whether each of these states sided with the North or the South in the Civil War." Surely your child could write an essay for that directive. (It would take a goodly chunk of time, of course, for students to do so.) Surely the teacher could score all the students' responses. (It would take a goodly chunk of time, of course, for the teacher to do so.) But surely the same low-level knowledge (that's all it really is) could be assessed far more efficiently with a series of selected-response items or short-answer items. Using an essay item for assessing such knowledge is like trying to eliminate a housefly with a hand grenade.*

- Failure to Communicate Desired Extensiveness of Response: *A second serious item-writing error for essay items is a teacher's failure to let the student know just how extensive the student's response ought to be. It's simply not fair to deny the student this important information.*

    Responses to essay items can be really lengthy or quite terse. A properly written essay item will, in one way or another, give students an estimate of the extensiveness of the response that the teacher is seeking. Sometimes this is done by putting essay items in test booklets so that a given area for the student's response is clearly staked out. Sometimes the item itself will specify an upper-word limit or an approximate length desired. All three of these approaches were used in Figure 6.3's illustrative items.

    Without clarified expectations regarding the approximate length of an essay item's response, the student is really at sea. Some students will overestimate what the teacher wants, take too much time answering early items, and run out of time for later items. Other students will underestimate the desired extensiveness of the items and respond too briefly, that is, end up with "blah-blah," when the teacher was expecting, "blah-blah-blah-blah!"

In this same vein, it is especially helpful if teachers can suggest about how much time students should devote to each item on an essay-item test. And if the teacher plans to weight students' responses to certain items more heavily than responses to other items, then the teacher should definitely let students know in advance *about this important intention.*

■ Inadequately Described Tasks: *Perhaps the most prevalent item-writing error for essay items involves a lack of clarity on the part of the teacher regarding precisely what it is that students are to do in their essay responses. Teachers who write essay items, of course, know precisely what they are looking for in the way of students' responses. That considerable advance understanding, however, sometimes limits the teacher's ability to, figuratively, sit at the student's desk and determine how the student will interpret an essay item's question or directive.*

If you and your child are looking over a completed essay item, and your child says, "I wasn't sure what I was supposed to do on this one." Chances are that the item's task wasn't sufficiently well described. The student's essay task must be unambiguously *described. If it isn't, that's a solid demerit for the essay item.*

A Parent Puzzle

(Setting: Mrs. Smith has been looking over Lee's classroom tests. Lee is in the sixth grade and does reasonably well in school. Even so, though, Lee constantly complains about the lengthy essay exams that are given weekly in class. Whether it's social studies, science, or language arts, Ms. Cole, Lee's teacher, seems to rely almost exclusively on essay tests. When Mrs. Smith looked seriously at Lee's completed tests, she decided a visit with the school principal was in order. Here's what happened during their late-afternoon meeting.)

Principal: "Thanks for calling to arrange this meeting, Mrs. Smith. We always appreciate it when parents take time to spend time with us about their kids. What was it you wanted to talk about today?"

Parent: "Actually, I was delighted that you could arrange time in your schedule to see me. I'm sure you have lots of problems you have to deal with. I'll not take long with mine."

Principal: "You have a problem, Mrs. Smith? Is it about Lee's progress? Ms. Cole mentioned to me only last week that Lee was doing quite well in class."

continued

A Parent Puzzle *(continued)*

Parent: "What I want to talk about with you concerns Ms. Cole. I hope you'll be able to treat my remarks as confidential."

Principal: "I'll certainly try to. Please go on."

Parent: "Well, it's Mrs. Cole's tests. As you may know, she tests Lee and the rest of the students quite frequently. And she always uses essay tests. Those tests are the cause for my concern."

Principal: "I'm surprised to hear you say that, Mrs. Smith. Most of our other teachers have nothing but admiration for Ms. Cole's exclusive commitment to essay tests. They know how much time it takes to score those tests. And I've heard Ms. Cole say, on more than one occasion, how exhausted she sometimes gets just scoring her students' essay exams. I'd think you'd be pleased that Lee is being tested with exams that stretch his mind."

*Parent: If **you** were the parent, how would you respond?*

My Response: I'd be a bit cautious in this situation, because the principal apparently thinks that all essay exams are "mind-stretching." That would be my clue the principal isn't all that familiar with the virtues and vices of essay exams.

I'd probably say something such as, "Early in the school year, Lee's father and I were really pleased that Lee was going to be tested with frequent essay exams. In the fifth grade, Lee rarely got a chance to try a hand at coming up with essay responses. But in recent weeks we've been carefully analyzing Ms. Cole's essay items. And we've seen that almost all of those items are only measuring Lee's memorized knowledge. That's the kind of outcome that could be measured most efficiently with selected-response items.

"It's no wonder that Ms. Cole becomes exhausted from scoring her students' tests. If she's only assessing knowledge, perhaps multiple-choice or short-answer items would do the job, and save her time.

"I hope Ms. Cole continues to use essay tests, but I'd like you to consider working with her so that those tests really measure the kinds of high-level cognitive skills that such tests are ideally suited for. I suspect that when you have an opportunity to look over some of the items in Ms. Cole's essay tests, you'll agree with our concerns."

My Reason: What I'm trying to get the principal to do is look at the teacher's test items, but after having been sensitized to the problem that a powerful constructed-response sort of test item is being used to measure memorized information. It's the wrong tool for this task. If Ms. Cole is testing her students exclusively with memory-only kinds of items, it's very likely that her instructional program is focused too heavily on students' memorization of information. Lee and the other students in Ms. Cole's class aren't being appropriately challenged. There's lots more to school than mere memorization.

If you don't find that your child's classroom tests contain, at least occasionally, some constructed-response items, you ought to be somewhat concerned. Remember, the purpose of educational testing is to allow teachers *and parents* to arrive at valid interpretations about children's level of knowledge and skills. The closer that such knowledge and skill parallels what children have to use in later life, the better.

But, because selected-response choices are rarely presented to people in the real world, constructed-response test items elicit the kinds of evidence about students that will help you make more valid inferences about whether your child can carry out the kinds of skill-based and knowledge-based activities required by the postschool world. A total absence of constructed-response items, therefore, robs you of the opportunity to get an accurate fix on whether your child possesses the skills and/or knowledge that the child truly needs.

Assessing Young Children

Constructed-response assessment is also particularly appropriate for very young children in kindergarten through grade three. But the "constructions" teachers of young children need to look at are generally not a child's response to an essay or short-answer item.

Instead, teachers of young children should characteristically rely on *embedded* assessments, that is, assessments that are incorporated into the instructional process. For very young children, it would be ideal if children never knew they were being assessed.

The timing for assessing young children is also critical. Assessment of such youngsters should be *developmentally appropriate*, that is, suitably meshed not only with the typical developmental level of children at a specific age, but also aligned with the developmental status of a *particular* child. What this means, of course, is that the assessment of young children should be individually tailored.

Teachers will need to use assessment methods that rely heavily on systematic observations of children in ongoing instructional activities. Assessments should be undertaken at times when, in the teacher's judgment, the child is developmentally ready to be assessed.

This focus on developmentally appropriate assessment means, without dispute, that the use of standardized achievement tests with children, at least until the end of the third grade, is a definite no-no. The validity of score-based inferences that such testing will yield is likely to be inadequate.

Until children reach grade four, the use of traditional paper-and-pencil tests should be sharply limited.

What Do You Really Need to Know about This Chapter's Content?

Now that you've considered the two most common kinds of constructed-response items, it's time to review the chief elements in this chapter. I think the four points below are the ones you really need to have in mind when you think about classroom tests that call for students' constructed responses.

- The major dividend of constructed-response items is that they require children to display cognitive capabilities more consonant with the requirements of real life.
- The two chief drawbacks of constructed-response items are: (1) the reduced objectivity of scoring, and (2) increased time requirements for scoring students' responses.
- A short-answer item's advantage is that it requires students to produce rather than recognize correct answers. Such items do take somewhat more time to score, however, and there is increased subjectivity of scoring over that found with selected-response items.
- An essay item's major advantage is that it can be used to measure genuinely high-level cognitive outcomes. Its chief disadvantages are, as with most constructed-response items, it takes substantial time to score students' responses and there is a considerable loss in objectivity of scoring.

POSSIBLE PARENT ACTION–OPTIONS

If you intend to take any action based on the material covered in Chapter 6, here are a few options for you to consider.

1. If you find that your child's teacher rarely, or never, uses essay items or short-answer items in classroom tests, then a conversation with the principal would seem warranted. Or, if such tests are used, but include many of the item-writing errors identified in this chapter, a conversation with the principal is still appropriate.
2. If essay tests are used in your child's classroom, you might try to find out how well your child understood what the items called for. If there's insufficient clarity regarding what's sought in the items, a brief talk with your child's teacher might be suitable.
3. If you think that your child's teacher could use a bit of professional development in the "care and feeding of constructed-response test items," you might suggest one or more of the *Suggested Resources* cited below.

SUGGESTED RESOURCES FOR YOUR CHILD'S TEACHER OR PRINCIPAL

Printed Materials

Hopkins, Kenneth D. *Educational and Psychological Measurement and Evaluation* (8th ed.). Boston: Allyn and Bacon, 1998. *In Chapter 8, Hopkins provides a detailed picture of how teachers should construct and use essay items.*

Linn, Robert L., and Gronlund, Norman E. *Measurement and Assessment in Teaching* (7th ed.). Upper Saddle River, NJ: Prentice-Hall, 1995. *"Measuring Complex Achievement: Essay Questions" is the title of Chapter 9 in this widely used measurement text. Linn and Gronlund do a solid job in describing how to build and score essay items.*

Stiggins, Richard J. *Student-Centered Classroom Assessment* (2nd ed.). Upper Saddle River, NJ: Prentice-Hall, 1997. *In Chapter 7, this book provides an incisive treatment of essay examinations and how to get the most educational benefit from them.*

Videotape Programs

Assessment Training Institute, Inc. *Assessing Reasoning in the Classroom.* (50 SW Second Ave., Ste. 300, Portland, OR 97204). *This video provides a clear illustration of what it means to be a proficient reasoner and problem solver. It also suggests practical ways to transform this vision of achievement into quality classroom assessments that help teachers teach reasoning and help students succeed as problem solvers.*

IOX Assessment Associates. *Assessing Young Children: A Guide for Educators and Parents.* (5301 Beethoven St., Ste. 190, Los Angeles, CA 90066). *Because the assessment of children in grades K–3 invariably calls for the use of constructed-response assessments and observations, this video describes why standardized testing of such young children will lead to invalid inferences. The role of developmentally appropriate practice as it influences assessment is also considered.*

Northwest Regional Educational Laboratory. *Measuring Thinking in the Classroom.* IOX Assessment Associates (5301 Beethoven St., Ste. 190, Los Angeles, CA 90066). *Clear and careful delineation of the cognitive skills to be assessed is the first step in creating classroom assessments that tap students' higher-order thinking. This video describes several strategies for integrating assessments of children's thinking into the instructional process.*

IOX Assessment Associates. *Creating Challenging Classroom Tests: When Students* Construct *Their Responses.* (5301 Beethoven St., Ste. 190, Los Angeles, CA 90066). *In this video, the focus is on the generation of constructed-response test items that elicit students' higher-level cognitive efforts. The use of rubrics for scoring students' responses is also treated.*

7

Rubrics: Potentially Useful Scoring Tools

*M*any years ago, when I was a high school teacher, I used essay tests, at least some of the time. Most of my fellow teachers also, on occasion, employed essay items in their tests. Essay items, at that time, were commonly found in classroom tests. They still are.

But, as I think back to the essay tests I routinely dispensed to my high school students, I have a confession to make. (Having been raised as a Catholic, I fully understand the dividends of confession.) What I want to confess is that when I tossed an essay item into a test, I rarely had more than a murky idea of how I expected my students to respond to it. And I'm pretty sure that most of the other teachers in my school were equally unclear about how they would be judging their students' answers to essay items.

Sure, if I asked students to write a brief essay in my American Government class describing "how a bill becomes a law in the U.S. Congress," I had a general idea that students should describe the bill-to-law legislative sequence fairly accurately. But that was as far as my thinking ever went *until* I started correcting my students' tests. Then, usually triggered by some sort of unanticipated answer (students' answers to essay items are almost as unpredictable as a lottery), I'd find I had to think carefully about what sort of responses should be graded an A, what sort should be graded a B, and so on.

As I say, most of my fellow teachers were, truthfully, equally unclear—*in advance*—about how they were going to evaluate students' responses to essay items. If you think back to the essay tests that you took in school, I'd be willing to bet that your teachers had only a general idea—in advance—of how they'd grade your responses.

Enter Rubrics

But loose, even casual evaluation of students' essay responses is becoming less and less common in our schools these days. That's because more teachers are beginning to use *rubrics* to score students' essays. It's very likely that your child's responses to essay items will, in the near future, be scored by teachers using a rubric. That's why you need to learn what a rubric is. Even more importantly, you need to learn what a *good* rubric is.

A *rubric* is simply a *scoring guide* to be used in judging the quality of students' constructed responses. Such scoring guides help teachers distinguish among students' responses by setting forth the important things that should be included in the student's response, and then indicating how to judge the relative quality of those things. A well-written rubric is almost as easy to use as a good cookbook. For example, if there is a maximum of five points that could be earned by a student's essay response, a well-written rubric will clearly set out what a student's response needs to contain in order to earn five points, to earn four points, to earn three points, and so on.

When and Why—Rubrics?   Rubrics first started to be used in the United States during the 1970s. Originally, rubrics were the scoring guides that were employed when educators tried to judge the quality of students' composition skills. In other words, rubrics were really born in an effort to more systematically score students' writing samples.

I've always wondered why the original developers of such scoring guides simply didn't refer to a scoring guide as a "scoring guide." I suppose that "scoring guide" would have been too easy for people to understand, so a more opaque label was chosen. Some specialists enjoy enshrouding their work in mystery. At any rate, rubrics slowly became more popular among educators until, after a time, educators began to encourage the use of rubrics for scoring any kind of extended student response, not only writing samples.

And, because educators became entranced by rubrics, so too did test publishers and textbook publishers. In the 1990s, more and more standardized achievement tests and the tests that are distributed along with textbooks began to be accompanied by rubrics. Rubrics, it is apparent, are eminently fashionable at this time.

Whence the Name?   As I indicated, odds are that you'll be running into one or more of your child's teachers who use rubrics. So that you become more able to deal with those teachers when rubrics are discussed, I want you to learn what a rubric is and how to tell a super rubric from a shoddy one. That's because, as you will see, a well-formed rubric can be a powerful asset to your child's *instructional* success. A poorly constructed rubric won't be any help at all.

But, before getting into the nuts and bolts of rubrics, I thought you might like to know something that your child's teacher is *not* apt to know, namely, where the name *rubric* came from in the first place. Then, if you really get stuck in a rubric-related conversation with a teacher, you can casually toss in a line or two about the origins of the term. A typical teacher ought to snap to attention after your mini-tour of rubric etymology.

Actually, before the scorers of writing samples latched onto the term *rubric* with such gusto in the seventies, a rubric had historically meant a *category* or a *description of a certain class of commodities,* such as when a scientist might classify things under the three *rubrics* of animal, vegetable, or mineral.

That meaning of rubric, a meaning that existed for centuries, came to us from the Middle Ages. During medieval times, before the invention of the printing press, all Christian missals and other books were hand-copied by monks who dedicated their lives to that activity. (Book-copying, incidentally, is a psychomotor skill.) If you've ever seen pictures of the written-in-Latin books produced by these medieval copyists, you may recall that the copyists almost always started off a chapter or a section of a book with a huge *red* letter.

The Latin word for "red" is *ruber.* And it was because those monks always commenced a new section of their Latin missals with a *ruber* letter that *rubric* became a word to signify sections or categories.

Why it was that the scorers of students' writing samples decided to steal a perfectly good term and use it instead of the more readily understood phrase, "scoring guide," I simply don't know. Is it possible their first scoring guides were initiated with a large red letter?

Let's take a look, now, at the important elements of a rubric. Although there are minor variations in the rubrics used by different teachers, if you understand the rubric components about to be described in this chapter, you'll have little difficulty in dealing with different varieties of rubrics.

Components of a Rubric

Evaluative Criteria.   The most important part of a rubric consists of the *evaluative criteria* by which the quality of a student's response is to be judged. For example, the earliest rubrics that were employed to score students' writing samples included evaluative criteria such as *content* (the information included in a student's composition), *organization* (the manner in which the content was structured in the composition) and *mechanics* (the composition's spelling, punctuation, and sentence structure).

So, for example, if a teacher were judging your child's ability to write a brief essay in a science class describing how to conduct a scientific experiment, the teacher's rubric might include evaluative criteria focusing on the quality of (1) statement of the problem, (2) the hypothesis to be tested, (3) data to be collected regarding the hypothesis, (4) data analysis, and (5) conclusion. For each of these evaluative criteria, the rubric might indicate whether a certain number of points (for example, 0, 1, 2, 3, or 4 points) could be earned *per criterion*.

Incidentally, although you should not make a big deal out of it if your child (or your child's teacher) misuses the word *criteria*, I'd like you to know that the Latin word *criterion* is singular and refers to *one* evaluative factor such as the "organization of an essay." The Latin word *criteria* is plural and refers to two or more evaluative factors, such as an essay's "content" and its "mechanics."

Now if your child's teachers ever *misuse* the singular (*criterion*) or plural (*criteria*) form of that term, that is no time for you to chide those teachers by splashing the Latin singular/plural distinction on them. In the long haul, that's not going to do your child any good. I would suggest, however, that on hearing a teacher say "the criteria is . . ." or "the criterion are . . . ," you display a subtle, yet ever-so-condescending smirk.

Testing Terms:
Evaluative Criteria
The key factors in a rubric that are used to judge the quality of a student's response

All right, singulars and plurals aside, the heart of a rubric is its set of evaluative criteria. In plain language, a rubric's evaluative criteria are simply "the key things a teacher looks at to tell how well the student has done."

You'll find that different labels are sometimes given to evaluate criteria. They might be called *dimensions, traits, factors,* or some other synonymous descriptor. What you need to keep in mind is that these are the major things used to judge your child's performance.

Analytic versus Holistic Use of a Rubric

When teachers use a rubric's evaluative criteria, they can use them *analytically* or *holistically*. When a rubric is used *analytically*, points are awarded to the student's response on the basis of *each* evaluative criterion. For instance, suppose there are four evaluative criteria in a rubric, and that there are zero, one, two, or three points that can be awarded for each criterion. Super responses earn three points per criterion, while sluggo responses get zero points. The teacher may or may not total up those points for the entire response. In this illustration, a total score could range from a low of zero (four evaluative criteria times zero) to a high of twelve (four evaluative criteria times three).

The payoff in using a rubric analytically is that there is considerable attention given to the rubric's individual evaluative criteria, and a series of criterion-by-criterion judgments about points-per-criterion must be made. Analytic rubrics usually take a great deal of time to use. It's tough to make criterion-by-criterion point allocations in the twinkling of an eye.

Testing Terms:

Analytic Scoring

When the evaluative criteria in a rubric are used to obtain a set of criterion-by-criterion scores

In contrast, although a *holistic* use of a rubric will find a teacher being attentive to the rubric's evaluative criteria, that attention will be much more general. The teacher considers the rubric's evaluative criteria when making an overall judgment, but makes one overall judgment about the quality of a student's response, not a series of criterion-by-criterion judgments.

So, for example, if your child's teacher were using a rubric to judge a persuasive essay the child wrote, the teacher might be keeping in mind the rubric's several evaluative criteria, but would assign a single, overall evaluative judgment to the essay, possibly using a zero to five score-point scale.

Testing Terms:

Holistic Scoring

When the evaluative criteria in a rubric are used more generally to obtain a single, overall score

The advantage of a holistic rubric is that it takes far less time to score student's responses. An analytic rubric, however, typically provides more diagnostic information for teachers, students, and parents because there's a criterion-by-criterion breakdown on the student's performance.

Should you, as a parent, always be pushing for the analytic use of rubrics in your child's classes? Not if you're wise. You see, if the analytic use of rubrics proves to be so time-consuming that the teacher rarely uses rubrics at all, then that result would be instructionally unfortunate for your child. As you'll soon see, a *well-formed* rubric can really help your child learn. Thus, you'd like to see the frequent use of rubrics to assess the quality of your child's constructed responses.

So, it's really better if teachers use more rubrics, even if those rubrics are employed holistically, rather than only an occasional analytic rubric. What some teachers have done to deal with this serious time-consumption problem is to score *all* students' responses holistically, then re-score analytically only the weakest responses because those students surely need the most focused help.

Quality Descriptions

In order for a rubric to be really useful in evaluating students' constructed responses, it is necessary for each evaluative criterion to be accompanied

The Daily News

EDUCATIONAL ASSESSOR BURNED AT STAKE!

While sizzling, evaluated quality of flames using a 5-point holistic rubric

Yesterday, educational assessors were generally considered to be members of the education profession. Granted, educational assessors deal with a very specialized aspect of the educational enterprise, namely, measuring students' cognitive, affective, or psychomotor status. Nevertheless, educational assessors don't measure the tensile strength of steel cables or the distance between Earth and Jupiter. Almost without exception, educational assessors measure students. And, if the adjective *educational* signifies anything, the

assessing done by educational assessors ought to have a direct bearing on education. Yet, I believe that large scale assessors are deliberately distancing themselves from the central mission that guides the profession to which they belong. The central mission of education is the education of children. To the extent that the large-scale-assessment community remains seemingly oblivious of education's central mission, then I think that large scale assessment is headed in a dysfunctional direction.

The fundamental function of almost all educational assessment is to measure students so that we can make assessment-based inferences about their status with respect to educationally relevant cognitive, affective, or psychomotor domains. There are varied uses to which these assessment-based inferences can be put, but I believe the two most important uses of large-scale assessment-based inferences are the following: *Educational Accountability*, that is, the accumulation of evidence to help determine if educational expenditures are achieving the intend

by a description of what, according to that criterion, constitutes a strong student response. Sometimes, especially for rubrics that are to be used analytically, there will be a description for each quality level available. For instance, if there are four different levels of quality for each evaluative criterion, then there will be a different description of what the student's response should look like (with respect to that criterion) in order to earn each of the four point allocations.

In other instances, especially for holistic rubrics, a general description will be given for each evaluative criterion according to what constitutes a strong versus a weak response, for example, the evaluative criterion of "mechanics" that is often used to judge students' compositions. A general quality description for that criterion might read something like this: "Strong compositions will contain few, if any, errors in spelling, punctuation, or capitalization. Weak compositions will contain frequent errors in spelling, punctuation, and/or capitalization."

The combination of the evaluative criteria and the quality descriptions associated with each criterion provides the scoring *clarity* that is the real contribution of a rubric. That clarity can be enormously helpful to teachers in planning their instruction. *That clarity can be enormously helpful to students and to their parents.*

Putting it simply, if teachers are clear-headed about where they are going instructionally, they're more apt to get there. Well-formed rubrics help teachers clarify the nature of the responses they hope to elicit from students. The clarity that well-formed rubrics provide for teachers will help those teachers put together more effective, on-target instructional activities for their students.

Similarly, the more clear-headed that *students* are about what's expected of them, the more likely it is that they'll achieve what is intended. But that means, of course, students must have in-advance access to the rubrics that will be used to judge the quality of their performances. The rubrics might be rephrased in more student-understandable language, because some rubrics are fairly technical in nature. But it would be instructionally absurd for teachers to go to the trouble of using well-formed rubrics, yet not let students in on the secret of how those students are going to be judged.

Similarly, if you are going to try to support a teacher's efforts at home, then *you* should definitely have access to the rubrics that will be used to evaluate your child's performances. If you don't know the basis of the evaluation system being used to appraise your child's work, how can you really be expected to help?

Testing Terms:

Quality Description

A rubric's criterion-by-criterion description of what constitutes a weak and strong response according to that evaluative criterion

A Rubric is Not a Rubric is Not a Rubric

The earliest rubrics that the nation's teachers encountered were, almost without exception, rubrics designed to score children's writing samples. And those rubrics were well-formed, in the sense that the rubrics contained evaluative criteria that could be addressed instructionally by teachers.

For instance, take the evaluative criterion, "organization," which was typically found in the early rubrics that were used to score students' writing-samples. Not only is the evaluative criterion of "organization" something teachers can use to judge student's compositions, it is also something that can be *taught*. Teachers can teach their students that well-organized compositions usually have an introduction, a body, and a conclusion. Teachers can teach their students that the body of a composition can be organized in logical, chronological, order-of-importance, or other ways. In short, teachers can teach their students how to write compositions that, when evaluated with a rubric containing an evaluative criterion of "organization," will be evaluated positively.

A Constructed-Response Item as a Skill-Representer

To understand why it is so important that rubrics contain evaluative criteria that can be tackled instructionally, you need to recall why it is that we give children educational tests in the first place. (If you need a brief refresher about the validity of test-based interpretations, feel free to dip into Chapter 2 again, pages 19–43.) Educators use tests in order to arrive at accurate inferences about the knowledge or skills children possess. In the case of constructed-response tests (such as essay exams), the teacher is almost always measuring *skills*. That's because, frankly, students' knowledge (memorized information according to Bloom) is more efficiently measured by selected-response tests.

So, in Figure 7.1 you'll see the relationship between a cognitive skill that a teacher is trying to get students to acquire and a constructed-response test that's intended to measure the student's skill-mastery. Notice that the constructed-response test consists of a student's *generated* response to a task (such as "Write a persuasive essay in favor of, or opposed to, a county sales tax.").

As you look at Figure 7.1, it is important for you to recognize that the skill (the circle at the left) is applicable to many, many tasks in addition to the *one task* contained in the constructed-response test (the circle at the right). The purpose of the test is to *represent* the skill so that, based on how well students do on the test, it is possible to make a valid interpretation about students' levels of mastery for the skill that the test represents.

For example, if the skill involved is a student's ability to write a narrative essay, there are literally hundreds of narrative essay writing tasks that the teacher could assign. Only one task typically comprises the test. Based on the child's response to that one task, the teacher makes an interpretation about the child's ability to write *any* narrative essay.

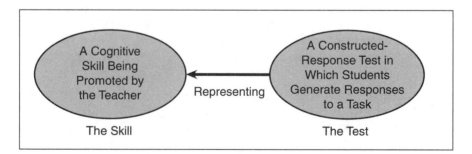

7.1 The relationship between a cognitive skill and a constructed-response test intended to assess students' mastery of the skill

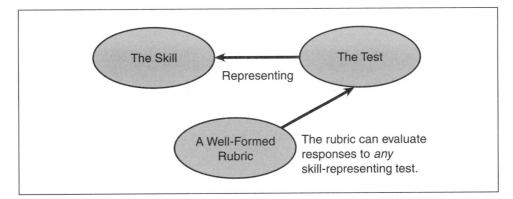

7.2 How a well-formed rubric can be used to evaluate students' responses to *any* skill-representing test

In Figure 7.2 therefore, you'll see that a well-formed rubric will apply to the skill itself, not the particular task that happens to have been used in the test. A good rubric, at least a rubric that can make an *instructional* contribution, will contain evaluative criteria that apply to the appraisal of students' responses to *any* task representing the skill being promoted by the teacher.

Task-Specific Rubrics

Unfortunately, if you review the rubrics that are being used to judge your child's efforts, it's possible that you'll find those rubrics are *task-specific*. A task-specific rubric is one whose evaluative criteria focus only on the specific task embodied in the constructed-response test item. Such evaluative criteria supply no instructional guidance to teachers, students, or parents.

An instructionally useful rubric contains evaluative criteria that give students a framework against which they can judge the quality of all future responses requiring the use of the skill being measured. But a task-specific evaluative framework will only help students judge the quality of their responses to a single test item, not the skill itself. How can students make use of an evaluative framework that only applies to a single test item? Obviously, task-specific rubrics are of little instructional value.

Suppose, for example, that a constructed-response essay item in a history class asked students to analyze the reasons underlying America's lack of preparedness for the Japanese

Testing Terms:

Task-Specific Rubric

A scoring guide whose evaluative criteria are aimed exclusively toward judging students' responses to a particular task

Empire's attack at Pearl Harbor on December 7, 1941. The skill involved is the ability to analyze underlying causes of historical events. The essay item's requirement that students write an historical analysis dealing with the Pearl Harbor attack is only one instance in which that historical analysis skill could be demonstrated.

Now, presented below are two illustrative evaluative criteria that might be incorporated in a rubric as one of several factors by which to judge a student's essay response to the item about the Pearl Harbor attack. Look both evaluative criteria over, then decide which one would have the greatest *instructional* payoff.

- *Evaluative Criterion A:* The student's essay should indicate that U.S. officials misjudged Japan's willingness to take military action in 1941 prior to a formal declaration of war.
- *Evaluative Criterion B:* The student's essay should recognize that one nation's special economic or political needs can sometimes incline it to take actions that are unforeseeable by other nations.

I think that if you'll study the two illustrative evaluative criteria for a moment, you'll see that Evaluative Criterion A is applicable only to the specific 1941 Pearl Harbor incident. The evaluative criterion does not apply to the other kinds of historical analyses that students might be called on to make in school or in life. Evaluative Criterion A, therefore, is *task-specific* and, as such, provides little instructional guidance for teachers, students, or parents.

Evaluative Criterion B, on the other hand, would apply to a variety of historical analyses involving two or more other nations. In essence, this criterion suggests that when dealing with other nations, it is necessary to recognize relevant economic and political factors that could motivate those nations to act. Failure to do so represents an error. A student's response to such historical analyses should attend to this concern. If students understand Evaluative Criterion B, they can apply that criterion in a variety of settings.

Skill-Focused Rubrics

A rubric whose evaluative criteria are applicable across different kinds of skill-determining tasks can be described as a *skill-focused* rubric. Such rubrics are aimed at the skill, not at judging a student's response to a particular task. The early rubrics that were used to judge students' writing-samples were all skill-focused. Many of the rubrics I've seen in the past few years, however, and I'm referring both to those developed by classroom

Testing Terms:

Skill-Focused Rubric

A scoring guide containing a manageable set of instructionally addressable evaluative criteria that can be used to judge students' responses to all skill-determining tasks

teachers as well as those developed by textbooks and test publishers, are absolutely task-specific. Such rubrics will help teachers score students' responses because a task-specific rubric spells out what's being looked for in a particular response to a particular test item. From an instructional perspective, however, task-specific rubrics are a total washout. And the *instructional* yield of a well-formed rubric is really its greatest contribution.

Instructional Addressability.   A skill-focused rubric, as noted above, contains evaluative criteria applicable to all students' responses that are intended to show whether the student has mastered the skill. In addition, however, all of a skill-focused rubric's evaluative criteria must be *instructionally addressable*, that is, must be capable of being taught to students by the teacher. If, for example, one of the evaluative criteria in a skill-focused rubric for judging students' compositions is *proper punctuation*, then a teacher can directly instruct students about instances when commas should be used and when periods are required. If a skill-focused rubric is going to make a positive impact on what students learn, then every evaluative criterion in that rubric must be capable of being *taught*.

A Manageable Set of Evaluative Criteria.   If a skill-focused rubric is likely to help children learn better, then it ought to contain a small set of evaluative criteria, not a lengthy list of such criteria. If a rubric contains eight or nine evaluative criteria, you can be pretty sure that there'll be too many evaluative criteria for the student to pay attention to, and too many evaluative criteria for *you* to pay attention to if you're helping your child at home.

A good skill-focused rubric will rarely have more than four or five evaluative criteria. And each evaluative criterion will be *concisely labeled* so that teachers, students, and parents can readily readily refer to an evaluative criterion as the student is in the process of mastering a skill.

A well-formed rubric, that is, a skill-focused rubric, can be enormously helpful to (1) *children* as they learn to master skill, (2) *teachers* as they plan and deliver instruction promoting the skill, and (3) *parents* as they help their children move toward skill-mastery. If your child and your child's classmates aren't having their constructed responses judged by skill-focused rubrics, that situation should be altered.

Hyper-General Rubrics

In addition to skill-focused rubrics (great!) and task-specific rubrics (ghastly!), there is one remaining variety of rubric you're apt to find teach-

ers using when they score your child's constructed responses. I refer to that sort of rubric as a *hyper-general rubric* because it's way too imprecise to do anyone any real good.

A hyper-general rubric does little more than indicate that a really excellent response by a student is, well, "really excellent." A student's average response might be described as "reasonably acceptable, but neither good enough to be excellent nor bad enough to be weak." A really weak response is, as you've probably guessed, "really weak."

Hyper-general rubrics typically employ different words than the fun-poking phrases I used in the previous paragraph, but not all that different. Hyper-general rubrics do little more than restate what each of us already knows when we think about the differences among the traditional grades teachers give when they assign an A, B, C, D, or F.

But why do teachers, textbook publishers, and testing companies ever use such excessively general, almost meaningless rubrics? The answer is easy. It's because rubrics are increasingly popular these days, so some test publisher or textbook publisher feels compelled to produce rubrics, even hyper-general rubrics. These publishers are saying to themselves, in a sense, "if educators want rubrics, then rubrics they will have."

Testing Terms:
Hyper-General Rubric
A scoring guide whose evaluative criteria are excessively vague

A Parent Puzzle

(Setting: Your tenth-grade child, Shelby, is enrolled in an English class in which the teacher, Mr. Ballard, routinely evaluates students' written work with rubrics. According to Shelby, Mr. Ballard told his students that this is the first year he's used rubrics, but he now is a firm believer in their value.

Mr. Ballard sends all of his rubrics home with his students, so "parents can get a feel for what I expect of my students." Accordingly, you have had an opportunity to look over those rubrics. To your dismay, you discover that all of the rubrics are hyper-general. They offer you and Shelby little more than a collection of platitudes about "strong student responses being strong" and "weak student responses being weak."

You decide to speak to Miss Prichard, the principal at your child's high school. Because you work during school hours, you've made an appointment to talk with Miss Prichard by telephone during your lunch hour. Here's how the conversation got underway.)

Parent: "Thanks for taking some time away from your schedule, Miss Prichard. I know how busy you are. And I do wish I could come in to meet with you in person, but my work schedule really interferes."

Miss Prichard: "I understand all too well. A good many of our parents have to deal with us by telephone. It's no problem. Now, how can I help? I assume you're calling about Shelby."

Parent: "That's right. To be more specific, I'm calling about Shelby's English class, the one taught by Mr. Ballard. As you may know, Mr. Ballard relies very heavily on the use of rubrics to judge his students' work. He seems very pleased with rubrics. I understand from Shelby that this is the first year Mr. Ballard has used rubrics."

Miss Prichard: "Yes, he's described his use of rubrics to our high school's other teachers at a faculty meeting. He really is enthusiastic about rubrics."

Parent: "And that's my concern, Miss Prichard. I've had several opportunities to look over the rubrics that Mr. Ballard uses in class. Without exception, they are remarkably general. Other than offering a series of vague statements about 'good being good' and 'bad being bad,' the rubrics really don't isolate how Shelby's work will be evaluated. Isn't that what rubrics are supposed to do?"

Miss Prichard: "Actually, and I'm not sure that this is common knowledge, Mr. Ballard uses rubrics that are supplied by the publisher of the textbook that he's using in Shelby's class. And that publisher is one of America's leading textbook publishers, so I'm confident that the rubrics for the book were developed by top-flight professionals."

Parent: If you were Shelby's parent, how would you respond to Miss Prichard?

My Response: "Miss Prichard's reaction would trouble me. She's evidently assuming that simply because some publisher, even a "leading" publisher, distributes a rubric, the published rubric is automatically a good one. Miss Prichard doesn't appear to know that rubrics can vary meaningfully in their quality. I'd probably proceed fairly

continued

A Parent Puzzle *(continued)*

gingerly, therefore, because I'd be bringing new information to a school administrator, and many school administrators are reluctant to accept any "professional" suggestions from "nonprofessionals."

I might say something like, "I've been doing some serious reading about rubrics, Miss Prichard, because they seem to be popping up in a number of Shelby's classes. One of the educators who writes about the role of rubrics in the classroom seems to be saying rubrics that are as vague and general as the ones Mr. Ballard uses are of almost no value from an *instructional* perspective. Would you have any interest in looking at what I've been reading?"

My Reason: What I'm trying to do with my response is raise some warning flags for Miss Prichard. Based on my estimate that she's not all that conversant with rubrics, I'm suggesting that there are "authorities" who would find Mr. Ballard's rubrics reprehensible.

If I can entice Miss Prichard to read one of the items in this chapter's *Suggested Resources*, perhaps that will incline her to help Mr. Ballard sharpen his hyper-general rubrics. Given her current knowledge, Miss Prichard is not apt to intervene with Mr. Ballard. I'm hoping to get her to learn more about instructionally relevant rubrics, then use that knowledge with Mr. Ballard. This is a situation where a soft sell is required.

However, because there are so many different kinds of intellectual skills to be promoted by teachers, and there would often be significant differences among the rubrics associated with each skill, creators of hyper-general rubrics believe they have created a useful "one-size-fits-all" rubric, that is, a scoring guide that will be useful for judging students' responses to tasks designed to assess students' mastery of many different skills. Unfortunately, "one-size-fits-all" rubrics don't work instructionally.

The most serious drawback of hyper-general rubrics is that they convey no clear idea to the teacher, student, or parent about how to judge the caliber of a child's work. Remember, there are few more powerful instructional approaches than simply letting students know what is being sought of them. A hyper-general rubric conveys no genuine clarity of expectation to anyone other than "Good is good, while bad is the absence of good." Hyper-general rubrics embody *pretend precision*. They are too general to help anyone, but they masquerade as genuine clarifiers.

So, if you find your child's constructed responses are being evaluated with a hyper-general rubric, then you know that a great opportunity has been missed. Well-formed rubrics can help children learn. Hyper-general rubrics are scoring guides without substance.

Well, this just about wraps up your visit to the rubric factory. What I want you to realize is that not only are rubrics being used with more frequency these days by educators, but rubrics *should* be used with more frequency. Your child's responses to essay items, for example, should be appraised by a teacher who uses a rubric. And that's because the increasing widespread support of rubrics has made teachers more attentive to the factors they use to judge the quality of their students' work.

Rubrics, for the education profession, are relatively new things. At a casual glance, parents might regard rubrics as little more than glitzy scoring guides. But, as you've now seen, a skill-focused rubric can provide teachers, students, and parents with the kind of clarified expectations that can really yield big *instructional* dividends.

You've also seen that not all rubrics are good ones—at least they are not likely to help your child master worthwhile skills. If teachers, desperate to get aboard the rubric bandwagon, are employing skill-specific or hyper-general rubrics, such rubrics are unlikely to help students. Moreover, such unsound rubrics will tarnish the reputation that rubrics, at least well-formed ones, should have. Your child will learn better if skill-focused rubrics are employed as part of the child's education. Try to see that such rubrics are used.

What Do You Really Need to Know about This Chapter's Content?

For most parents, *rubrics* represent an unfamiliar concept. But, as indicated above, rampant rubricity is rolling forward in the field of education. If you carry the following key points with you when leaving this chapter, you'll know more than enough to deal with rubrics when your child runs up against them.

- *Rubrics* are scoring guides that are ever more widely being used by educators to score students' responses to constructed-response types of test items, particularly items that call for students to produce an extended response (such as an essay).
- The chief components of a rubric are (1) its *evaluative criteria,* that is, the key factors to be used in judging the quality of a student's response, and (2) each evaluative criterion's *quality descriptions,* that is, the delineation for each evaluative criterion about what constitutes a strong or weak response from students.
- Rubrics can be employed either *holistically* or *analytically.* Analytic scoring requires a separate score for each evaluative criterion. Holistic

scoring is a global attempt to incorporate all evaluative criteria, but in a more general, overall fashion.

- A *skill-focused rubric* employs a relatively small number of concisely labeled evaluative criteria, all of which are *instructionally addressable* and all of which apply to the evaluation of any kind of skill-determining response by students.

- A *task-specific rubric* makes little contribution to instruction because its evaluative criteria apply only to the particular task (or test item) to which the student responds.

- A *hyper-general rubric* is of little instructional utility because, in attempting to function as a one-size-fits-all scoring guide, its depictions of what constitutes good and bad student responses are too vague and inexact.

POSSIBLE PARENT ACTION–OPTIONS

If you intend to take any action based on the material covered in Chapter 7, here are a few options for you to consider.

1. The most fundamental option available to you regarding rubrics is to get copies of the rubrics being used with your child. If there are rubrics being used with your child's classroom tests, then most teachers would view with favor a parent's request for rubrics so you can help your child master what the teacher is attempting to promote.

2. Once you obtain copies of any rubrics being used with your child, then you can review them to see whether your child's responses are being scored by skill-focused, task-specific, or hyper-general rubrics. If anything other than skill-focused rubrics are being used, then a few questions to your child's teacher or principal might encourage a bit of rethinking about the nature of the rubrics being used.

3. Although rubrics are becoming more and more popular among educators, some teachers and school administrators are still fairly unfamiliar with them. Moreover, some educators are touting the virtues of instructionally shoddy rubrics such as task-specific or hyper-general rubrics. For any of those educators, you might encourage the use of one or more of the items in the *Suggested Resources* section.

SUGGESTED RESOURCES FOR YOUR CHILD'S TEACHER OR PRINCIPAL

Printed Materials

Busick, Kathy, and Rick Stiggins. *Making Connections: Case Studies for Student-Centered Classroom Assessment.* Assessment Training Institute, Inc. (50 SW Second Ave., Ste. 300, Portland, OR 97204). *This case study workbook by Kathy Busick and Rick Stiggins provides challenging real-world assessment issues for professional development training. The cases present provocative assessment concerns, such as evaluating grading practices and developing effective scoring criteria.*

Falk, Beverly, and Susanna Ort. "Sitting Down to Score: Teacher Learning Through Assessment." *Phi Delta Kappan, 80,* no. 1 (September 1998): 59–64. *Through the use of well-designed rubrics, teachers who take part in sessions to score students' responses can gain powerful instructional insights. This article describes how.*

McMillan, James H. *Classroom Assessment: Principles and Practice for Effective Instruction.* Boston: Allyn and Bacon, 1997. *As part of Chapter 7, McMillan describes how to develop rating scales and scoring criteria for the appraisal of students' constructed responses.*

Popham, W. James. "What's Wrong—and What's Right—with Rubrics." *Educational Leadership,* 55, no. 2 (October 1997): 72–75. *This is an essay I wrote for teachers and administrators. It addresses most of the points made in the chapter, but relies on examples designed for educators. When it was first published in 1997, it attracted a fair amount of attention from educators.*

Weber, Ellen. *Student Assessment That Works: A Practical Approach.* Boston: Allyn and Bacon, 1999. *In Chapter 12, Weber devotes brief attention to rubrics. Specifically, she describes how to construct a rubric for appraising a research paper.*

Videotape Programs

IOX Assessment Associates. *The Role of Rubrics in Classroom Assessment.* (5301 Beethoven St., Ste. 190, Los Angeles, CA 90066). *Educators learn in this video what a rubric is and how to distinguish good rubrics from bad ones. Sample rubrics are included for discussion purposes.*

Northwest Regional Educational Laboratory. *Writing Assessment: Issues and Answers.* IOX Assessment Associates (5301 Beethoven St., Ste. 190, Los Angeles, CA 90066). *This video describes how holistic, analytic, and primary trait scoring approaches can be employed to judge the caliber of students' writing samples.*

Northwest Regional Educational Laboratory. *Writing Assessment: Training in Analytical Scoring.* IOX Assessment Associates (5301 Beethoven St., Ste. 190, Los Angeles, CA 90066). *The Northwest Regional Educational Laboratory has been at the forefront in promoting the use of a rubric to score students' writing based on a six-criterion model. This video describes how the six-criterion model should be used.*

8

PERFORMANCE TESTS

*I*n this chapter you'll be learning about *performance tests*. Although performance tests could be used to measure students' knowledge, such tests are almost always employed to assess students' *skills*. A performance test consists of a *task* that's presented so students can make a *response* to the task. The student's performance, as displayed in the response, is then used to arrive at an interpretation about the student's level of mastery regarding the skill being assessed by the performance test.

What Is a Performance Test?

In schools, the most commonly used educational performance tests are those employed to assess a student's composition skills. Educators have used such performance tests for well over twenty years, and it is increasingly rare to find children's composition skills measured by anything other than a performance test calling for students to compose an original writing sample.

To illustrate the chief features of such a performance test, let's suppose the skill being measured is a student's ability to write narratively, that is, to create an original composition that tells a story. The chief features of this performance test would be the following:

Skill: **Narrative Writing**

Task: Student must write an original, 500-word essay telling about "What happened on one of my most favorite days."

Scoring: Students' essays are evaluated on the basis of a rubric. The rubric could focus only on (1) how to judge narrative essays or (2) how to judge any kind of essay.

Interpretation: Based on the student's performance, that is, the student's narrative essay, an inference is reached about the level of mastery the student possesses in writing narrative essays.

Your Child and Performance Tests

It is very possible that your child is not currently being assessed with one or more performance tests. You might, therefore, wish to flip this chapter's pages rapidly and scurry on to the next chapter. However, even if your child is not *currently* being assessed with performance tests, I find it difficult to imagine that your child will not encounter performance tests in the future. Actually, performance tests are now being advocated by so many educational measurement specialists, it would be surprising if your child didn't encounter a fair number of performance assessments before the child's education is complete.

Testing Terms:

Performance Test
An assessment of a student's high-level skill by evaluating the student's generated response to a skill-determining task

Educators' Definitional Disagreements

During the 1990s, many educational policymakers became captivated by the allure of performance testing. Theoretically, of course, if a student chooses between *true* and *false* in a True–False test, the student is *performing*. But that performance, of course, is quite a modest one.

The advocates of performance testing have measurement procedures in mind that are meaningfully different from two-choice tests or multiple-choice tests. In fact, it was a dissatisfaction with traditional paper-and-pencil tests that caused many educators to travel down the performance-testing trail.

Most measurement specialists think that what sets performance tests apart is the extent to which the task presented to the student coincides with the teacher's real-life instructional objective. In other words, if the teacher's objective calls for students to achieve a skill they can actually use in subsequent school situations or in postschool life, the task given to the student should approximate that "real life" objective. I have attempted to illustrate this point in Figure 8.1, where there are five different types of assessment options, only some of which would be classified as performance tests by most educators. In Figure 8.1 the teacher's objective is to have students develop the skill of being able to work with other individuals to solve problems. It's a skill that students will often need, in school and beyond.

Suppose that a teacher who had been instructing students in the process of collaborative problem-solving wanted to see whether students had acquired that cooperation-based skill. The *interpretation* at issue centers on the extent to which each student has mastered the skill. The educational decision on the line might be whether students need additional instruction or, instead, whether it's time for the teacher to move on to other instructional objectives.

In Figure 8.1, you will see there are several assessment procedures that could be used to get a fix on a student's collaborative problem-solving skills. Yet, note that the two selected-response assessment options (Numbers 1 and 2) don't really ask students to *construct* anything. For the other three constructed-response assessment options (Numbers 3, 4, and 5), however, there are clear differences in the degree to which the task presented to the student coincides with the class of tasks called for by the teacher's instructional objective. Assessment Option 5, for example, is obviously the closest match to the behavior called for in the objective. Yet, Assessment Option 4 is surely more of a "performance test" than is Assessment Option 1.

What you must realize, then, is that different educators will be using the phrase *performance test* to refer to very different kinds of assessment approaches. Many teachers, for example, are willing to consider short-answer

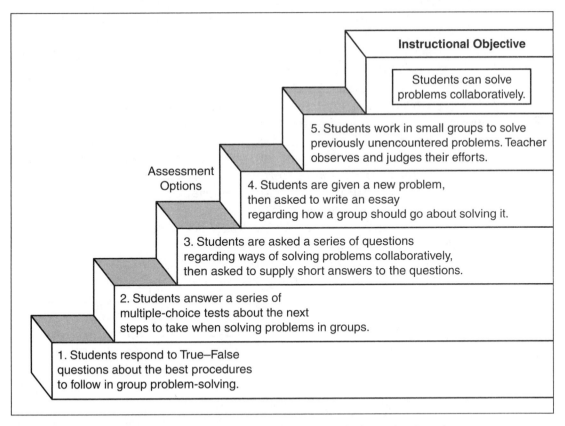

Instructional Objective

Students can solve problems collaboratively.

Assessment Options

5. Students work in small groups to solve previously unencountered problems. Teacher observes and judges their efforts.

4. Students are given a new problem, then asked to write an essay regarding how a group should go about solving it.

3. Students are asked a series of questions regarding ways of solving problems collaboratively, then asked to supply short answers to the questions.

2. Students answer a series of multiple-choice tests about the next steps to take when solving problems in groups.

1. Students respond to True–False questions about the best procedures to follow in group problem-solving.

8.1 A set of assessment options that vary in the degree to which student's task approximates the teacher's real-life instructional objective

tests and essay tests a form of performance testing. In other words, they essentially equate performance testing with any form of constructed-response assessment. Other teachers establish more strict requirements in order for a measurement procedure to be described as a performance test. For example, some educators contend that genuine performance tests must possess at least three features:

- *Multiple Evaluative Criteria:* The student's performance must be judged using more than one evaluative criterion. To illustrate, a student's ability to speak Spanish might be appraised on the basis of the student's accent, syntax, and vocabulary.
- *Prespecified Quality Standards:* Each of the evaluative criteria on which a student's performance is to be judged is clearly described in advance of judging the quality of the student's performance.
- *Judgmental Appraisal:* Unlike the scoring of selected-response tests in which electronic computers and scanning machines can, once programmed, carry on without the need of humankind, genuine performance assessments depend on human judgments to determine how acceptable a student's performance really is.

Looking back to Figure 8.1, it is clear that if the foregoing three requirements were applied to the five assessment options described, Assessment Option 5 would qualify as a performance test, and Assessment Option 4 probably would as well, but the other three assessment options wouldn't qualify under a definition of performance assessment that requires the incorporation of multiple evaluative criteria, prespecified quality standards, and judgmental appraisals.

A good many advocates of performance assessment would prefer that the tasks presented to students represent *real-world* rather than *school-world* kinds of problems. Other proponents of performance assessment would be elated simply if more school-world measurement included more constructed-response rather than selected-response items. Still other advocates of performance testing want the tasks in performance tests to be genuinely *demanding*—that is, way up the ladder of Bloom's Cognitive Taxonomy. In short, proponents of performance assessment often advocate different approaches to the measurement of students.

You'll sometimes encounter educators who use other phrases to describe performance testing. For example, some educators may use the phrase *authentic assessment* (because the assessment tasks in most performance tests more closely coincide with nonschool tasks). Some educators describe performance testing as a form of *alternative assessment* (because such assessments constitute an alternative to traditional paper-and-pencil tests). In the next chapter, you'll be considering *portfolio assessment,* a particular type of performance assessment that should not be considered a synonym for all performance tests.

Why Performance Assessment?

When most of today's parents went to school, performance assessment was rarely seen. Occasionally, of course, some students were asked to write a lengthy essay in response to an essay item, but most of us simply regarded that as an essay item. Why, you might ask, is there so much advocacy of performance testing these days?

Dissatisfaction with Selected-Response Tests

Proponents of performance tests believe that because multiple-choice and two-choice tests call only for *recognition* on the part of the student, those tests fail to tap higher-order thinking skills such as whether students can solve problems, synthesize divergent content, or think independently. Although selected-response tests are sometimes criticized as dealing with unimportant content, the most frequently voiced criticism of selected-response tests is, not surprisingly, that the student need only *select* a response.

The Influence of Cognitive Psychology

Cognitive psychologists are a particular group of psychologists whose members believe that students must acquire both content knowledge and procedural knowledge. Content knowledge deals with the student's memorized information, some of which may be quite important. Procedural knowledge calls for the student's *use* of content knowledge such as when students are called on to use memorized punctuation rules to fix a sentence that has gone "comma-crazy."

Cognitive psychologists argue that all cognitive tasks require both kinds of knowledge, but for certain kinds of tasks, there are different emphases on the two kinds of knowledge. Because particular types of procedural knowledge are simply not testable by selected-response tests, many cognitive psychologists have been calling for increased use of performance testing in education to accompany what they believe should be an increased instructional emphasis on students' acquisition of procedural knowledge.

The Harmful Instructional Impact of Conventional Tests

As the stakes associated with an educational test rise, teachers tend to emphasize instructionally the content embodied in the test. You may recall from Chapter 1 that high stakes function almost like instructional magnets (Figure 1.1, page 6). Consequently, particularly if the instruction coincides too directly with the test, students' scores on the test may rise although their mastery of the domain of skills or knowledge represented by the test does not. Because many educators recognize that high-stakes tests will most likely continue to influence what a teacher teaches, they argue that performance tests will constitute more praiseworthy instructional targets than traditional paper-and-pencil tests. As a consequence of more appropriate high-stakes *assessment* targets, it is believed teachers' *instructional* activities will shift in appropriate directions.

Suppose, for example, that an important statewide multiple-choice achievement test were given to students in your state at your child's grade level. If teachers believe that their *personal* instructional competence was being judged, at least in part, according to how well the teachers' students performed on the test, there would be a meaningful temptation to align the teacher's classroom assessments and classroom instruction with the statewide test's multiple-choice assessment targets. Recognizing that such instructional impacts of high-stakes assessment are likely, proponents of performance testing want to install more appropriate assessment targets.

Identifying Suitable Tasks for Performance Tests

Performance tests typically require students to respond to a small number of more significant tasks rather than respond to a large number of less significant tasks. Thus, instead of answering fifty multiple-choice items on a conventional chemistry examination, students who are being assessed via performance tasks may find themselves asked to perform an actual experiment in their chemistry class, then write an interpretation of the experiment's results and an analytic critique of the procedures they used. From the chemistry teacher's perspective, instead of seeing how students respond to the fifty "mini-tasks" represented in the multiple-choice tests, an estimate of each student's status must be derived from a student's response to a single complex task.

A Parent Puzzle

(Setting: Mr. Wang, a first-year principal, has spent the first four months of the school year getting his elementary school's teachers to develop a series of performance tests, one in each subject area for which a teacher is responsible. Mr. Wang calls this new schoolwide assessment program "Peak Performance in the Classroom." The school's teachers usually refer to it simply as PPC.

Leslie Smith, a fifth-grader, brought home a set of mid-year performance test results. As it turned out, Leslie's father was quite dismayed with the results. Instead of Leslie's results being judged "advanced" or "proficient," all of Leslie's performances on the tests were judged "novice." Mr. Smith, after determining that Leslie didn't know why these performances were evaluated that way, set up a 7 a.m. appointment with Mr. Wang. Here's what was said.)

Mr. Wang: "Thanks for coming in so early, Mr. Smith. Would you like some coffee or a donut?"

Parent: "No thanks, I've already eaten before I left home. I appreciate your taking the time to see me, Mr. Wang. I'm sure that you're really busy, especially because it's your first year here."

Mr. Wang: "Actually, it's my first year as a principal at any school, although I was an assistant principal over at Emerson Elementary for five years. Now, what can I do for you?"

Parent: "Well, it's about the mid-year tests that Leslie just brought home. I think they are part of your PPC program. I very much like the idea of using performance tests, and especially because the skills you've urged your teachers to test are really significant ones. But it's not the tests that bother me."

Teacher: "What is it, then, Mr. Smith?"

Parent: "Did you know that in Leslie's classroom, students are completely unaware of the basis on which their performances are to be evaluated? Mrs. Green, Leslie's teacher, is a tough grader, as Leslie's mid-year PPC results prove. But neither Leslie nor I have even a foggy idea regarding how a 'novice' response is different from an 'advanced' response. To tell you the truth, I'm not sure Mrs. Green knows herself."

Mr. Wang: "Do you mean that Leslie never received the rubrics that Mrs. Green uses to evaluate Leslie's performances?"

Parent: "Leslie asked about scoring guides or, at least, what the basis of the grading was. But Leslie said that Mrs. Green simply responded, and I quote, "I use my best professional judgment.""

Mr. Wang: "But one of the cornerstones of 'Peak Performance in the Classroom' is supposed to be each teacher's careful spelling out of the evaluative criteria by which each student's response to a PPC test was to be judged. Teachers are directed to communicate those criteria to the students as part of the instructional program. I'm astonished that Mrs. Green didn't supply Leslie and the other students with rubrics for her performance tests."

continued

A Parent Puzzle *(continued)*

Parent: If you were the parent, how would you respond?

My Response: As usual, I'd first try to judge the sophistication and the motivation of the educator with whom I'm dealing. Mr. Wang certainly doesn't sound defensive. Unlike some school administrators who seem to believe, "our school's teachers can do no wrong," Mr. Wang senses something is in need of fixing. Moreover, his comments about rubrics make it clear that he is familiar with rubrics and, quite possibly, the instructional benefits they can stimulate.

Given that analysis of Mr. Wang, I'd probably say something mighty mild in the belief that he's likely to follow through with Mrs. Green. I'd respond along these lines: "I understand that a good rubric can not only help teachers as they plan their instruction, but can also help students as they attempt to master a skill. And a parent can also play a useful role in that situation by assisting children as they evaluate their own work using a good rubric. Can you encourage Mrs. Green to create such rubrics? I promise that Leslie's mother and I will use those rubrics at home to help Leslie with her studies."

My Reason: When parents interact with a cooperative school principal, and sense that the principal will follow through in dealing with the teacher concerned, they really don't need to do much more than send a brief signal that says, in essence, "Principal, pay attention to this problem." Overkill might make Mr. Wang defensive, and what you really want is to have Mr. Wang work with Mrs. Green to mend her rubric-less ways. A soft signal is what's needed here. Mr. Wang seems poised to receive it and act.

Given the significance of each task used in a performance-testing approach to classroom assessment, it is apparent that great care must be taken in the selection of such tasks. Generally speaking, classroom teachers will either have to (1) generate their own performance-test tasks or (2) select performance-test tasks from the increasing number of such tasks that are available from educators elsewhere.

Interpretations and Performance-Test Tasks

The chief factors that should determine how teachers assess your child are (1) the interpretation the teacher wants to make about students, and (2) the decision that will be based on that interpretation. For example, imagine you have a child in high school, and the child is scheduled to take a U.S. history class next year. Suppose your child's prospective history teacher

has spent a summer at a lakeside cabin meditating about curricular matters (which, in one lazy setting or another, represents most parents' perception of how teachers spend their vacations).

After three months of heavy curricular thought, the history teacher concludes that what he really wants to teach his students is to be able to apply historical lessons from the past to the solution of current and future problems that, in some meaningful manner, parallel the problems of the past. The history teacher has decided to abandon his week-long, 1,500-item True–False final examination that his stronger students refer to as a "measurement marathon" and his weaker students refer to by using a rich, if earthy, vocabulary. Instead of True–False items, after a lazy lakeside summer, the history teacher is now committed to a performance assessment strategy and wishes to select tasks for his performance tests that will help him infer how well his students can draw on the lessons of the past to illuminate their approach to current and/or future problems.

In Figure 8.2, you will see a graphic depiction of the relationships among (1) a teacher's key educational objective, (2) the interpretation that the teacher wishes to draw about each student, and (3) the task for a performance test intended to secure data to support the interpretation that the teacher wants to make. As you will note, the teacher's instructional objective provides the source for the interpretation, and the assessment tasks yield the evidence needed for the teacher to arrive at defensible interpretations

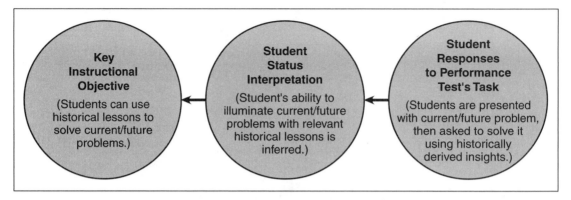

8.2 Relationships among a teacher's key instructional objective, the assessment-based interpretation linked to the objective, and the performance assessment task that will provide evidence for the interpretation

regarding the extent to which students can solve current or future problems using historical lessons. To the degree that your child has mastered the instructional objective, the history teacher will make a decision about how much more instruction, if any, is needed regarding that objective.

The Generalizability Dilemma

One of the most serious difficulties with performance tests is that, because students respond to fewer tasks than would be the case with conventional paper-and-pencil testing, it is often more difficult to generalize accurately about what skills are possessed by the student.

To illustrate, let's say your child's teacher is trying to get a fix on children's ability to multiply pairs of double-digit numbers. If, because of the teacher's instructional priorities, the teacher can devote only a half hour to assessment purposes, the teacher could require the students to respond to twenty such multiplication problems in the thirty minutes available. (That's probably more problems than the teacher would need, but I'm trying to draw a vivid contrast for you.) From a student's responses to twenty multiplication problems, the teacher can get a pretty fair idea about what kind of double-digit multiplier your child is. As a consequence of your child's performance on a *reasonable sample* based on the skill being taught, the teacher can conclude that "These children really know how to multiply those sorts of problems," or "These children couldn't multiply double-digit multiplication problems if their lives depended on it."

It is because the teacher has sampled well the skill (for which the teacher wished to make an interpretation) that the teacher can confidently make inferences about students' abilities to solve similar sorts of multiplication problems. With only a thirty-minute assessment period available, however, if your child's teacher moved to a more elaborate kind of performance test, the teacher might only be able to have students respond to *one* big-bopper item. (*Big Bopper,* incidentally, is not a professionally sanctioned descriptor of classroom assessments.)

For example, if the teacher presented an elaborate multiplication-focused mathematics problem, and wanted students to derive an original solution and then describe it in writing, the teacher would be lucky if students could finish the task in a half hour. Based on this single task, how confident would the teacher be in making interpretations about students' abilities to perform comparable multiplication tasks?

And that, as you now see, is the rub with performance testing. Because students respond to fewer tasks, the teacher is put in a tricky spot when it comes to deriving inferences about students' skills. If your child's teacher uses only one performance test, and your child does well on the test, does this signify that your child *really* possesses the skill that the test was designed to measure, or did the child just get lucky? On the other hand, if your child messes up on a single-performance test, does this signify that the child *really* doesn't possess the assessed skill, or was there a feature in this particular performance test task that misled your child who, given other tasks, might have performed wonderfully?

Classroom teachers are faced with a classic measurement dilemma. Although performance tests often measure the kinds of student abilities that teachers would prefer to assess (because those abilities are in line with really worthwhile instructional aims), the inferences that teachers make about students on the basis of their responses to performance tests must be made with increased caution. As with many dilemmas, there may be no perfect resolution. But there is, at least, a way for teachers to deal with the dilemma as sensibly as they can.

In this instance, the solution strategy is for teachers to devote great care to the selection of the tasks embodied in their performance tests. Among the most important considerations in selecting such tasks is to choose tasks that optimize the likelihood of the teacher's accurately generalizing about students' skills. If teachers really keep generalizability at the forefront when they select/construct performance-test tasks, they will be able to make the strongest possible performance-based inferences about their students' capabilities.

Factors to Consider When Evaluating Performance-Test Tasks

You've now dealt with what many measurement specialists regard as the most important factor that teachers can consider when judging potential tasks for performance assessments: *generalizability*. Let's look at a list of six factors your child's teacher might wish to consider when selecting a performance-test task from existing tasks or, in contrast, creating a new performance-test task from scratch.

Factors to Use in Reviewing Performance-Test Tasks

- *Generalizability.* Is there a high likelihood that the students' performance on the task will generalize to comparable tasks?
- *Authenticity.* Is the task similar to what students might encounter in the real world as opposed to in school?
- *Teachability.* Is the task one that students can become more proficient in as a consequence of a teacher's instructional efforts?
- *Fairness.* Is the task fair to all students—that is, does the task avoid bias based on such personal characteristics as students' gender, ethnicity, or socioeconomic status?
- *Feasibility.* Is the task realistically implementable in relation to its cost, space, time, and equipment requirements?
- *Scorability.* Is the task likely to elicit student responses that can be reliably and accurately evaluated?

If your child is being assessed with performance tests, let's hope the child's teacher is using review factors such as those given above. If you have an opportunity to look over the tasks used with any of your child's performance tests, you might consider whether many of those six factors seem to have been satisfied.

Illustrative Performance-Test Tasks

To give you an idea of the kinds of tasks that might be employed in one of your child's performance tests, I've included Figure 8.3, which describes a performance test in oral communication and supplies examples of the four different types of tasks that students might be called on to tackle. Look over Figure 8.3 and its tasks so you can see what these sorts of performance-test tasks look like.

An Oral Communications Performance Test

Introduction

There are numerous kinds of speaking tasks that students must perform in everyday life, both in school and out of school. This performance assessment focuses on some of these tasks—namely, describing objects, events, and experiences; explaining the steps in a sequence; providing information in an emergency; and persuading someone.

In order to accomplish a speaking task, the speaker must formulate and transmit a message to a listener. This process involves deciding what needs to be said, organizing the message, adapting the message to the listener and situation, choosing language to convey the message and, finally, delivering the message. The effectiveness of the speaker may be rated in terms of how well the speaker meets the requirements of the task.

Sample Tasks

Description Task: Think about your favorite class or extracurricular activity in school. Describe to me everything you can about it so that I will know a lot about it. (How about something like a school subject, a club, or a sports program?)

Emergency Task: Imagine that you are home alone and you smell smoke. You call the fire department and I answer your call. Talk to me as if you were talking on the telephone. Tell me everything I would need to know to get help to you. (Talk directly to me; begin by saying hello.)

Sequence Task: Think about something you know how to cook. Explain to me, step by step, how to make it. (How about something like popcorn, a sandwich, or scrambled eggs?)

Persuasion Task: Think about one change you would like to see made in your school, such as a change in rules or procedures. Imagine I am the principal of your school. Try to convince me that the school should make this change. (How about something like a change in the rules about hall passes or the procedures for enrolling in courses?)

8.3 Task description and sample tasks for a one-on-one oral communication performance assessment

An Illustrative Performance Test and Its Scoring Rubric

A Performance Test in History

You've seen, now, what sorts of tasks constitute a performance test. Now I want you to tangle with a real performance test in U.S. history, plus the rubric that's used to score students' performances. In Figure 8.4 you'll

Performance Test: Using History's Lessons

Skill Description: Students will be able to draw on the lessons of history to predict the likely consequences of current-day proposals. More specifically, students will be presented with a current problem-setting and a proposed solution. The student must then (1) identify one or more historical events that are particularly relevant to the problem-setting and proposed solution, (2) justify those selected, (3) make a history-based prediction regarding the proposed solution's likely consequences, and (4) defend that prediction on the basis of historical parallels.

Nature of Tasks: Students will be given a description of a real or fictitious problem–situation in which a course of action is being proposed as a solution to the problem. Students will be asked to write an essay in which they (1) identify, from a prespecified timeline of major events in U.S. history, one or more historical events that are relevant to the proposed solution; (2) justify the relevance of the identified event(s); (3) make a defensible prediction of the probable consequences of the proposed solution based on the identified historical event(s); and (4) defend the prediction on the basis of parallels between the problem–situation, the proposed solution, and the identified historical event(s).

Sample Task: Read the fictitious situation described in the box below, then follow the directions following the boxed description.

War or Peace?

Nation A is a large industrialized country whose population is almost 100,000,000. Nation A has ample natural resources, and is democratically governed. Nation A also owns two groups of territorial islands that, although quite distant, are rich in iron ore and petroleum.

Nation B is a country with far fewer natural resources and a population of only 40,000,000. Nation B is about one-third as large as Nation A. Although much less industrialized than Nation A, Nation B is as technologically advanced as Nation A. Nation B is governed by a three-member council of generals.

Recently, without any advance warning, Nation A was ruthlessly attacked by Nation B. As a consequence of this attack, more than half of Nation A's military equipment was destroyed.

After its highly successful surprise attack, Nation B's rulers have proposed a "peace agreement" calling for Nation A to turn over its two groups of islands to Nation B.

If the islands are not conceded by Nation A, Nation B's rulers have threatened all-out war.

Nation A's elected leaders are fearful of the consequences of the threatened war because their military equipment is now much weaker than that of Nation B. Nation A's leaders are faced with a choice between (1) peace obtained by giving up the islands or (2) war with a militarily stronger nation.

Nation A's leaders decide to declare that a state of war exists with Nation B. They believe that even though Nation B is now stronger, in the long term Nation A will win the war because of its greater industrial capability and richer natural resources.

Directions: Compose a well-written essay. In that essay, drawing on your knowledge of U.S. history, select one or more important historical events that are especially relevant to the fictitious situation described above. Then justify the relevance of your selection(s). Next, make a reasonable history-based prediction about the likely consequences of the decision by Nation A's leaders to go to war. Finally, defend your prediction on the basis of the historical event(s) you identified.

8.4 Skill and task descriptions plus one sample task for the performance test of *Using History's Lessons*

Source: Based on assessment efforts of the U.S. Department of Defense Dependents' Schools.

find the heart of a performance test in U.S. history. As you can see, the test provides (1) a description of the skill being measured, (2) the nature of the tasks that students will be given, and (3) a sample task for the performance test. If you can remember Figure 8.2 (and, if you can't, look back to page 176), this performance test was depicted graphically in that figure.

Look over the performance test presented in Figure 8.4. I think you'll find it challenging. I worked with the educators who created this particular performance test in U.S. history and I readily admit they put together a genuinely tough skill for students to master. When I was a student in high school and college, I took a hamper-full of history courses. Unfortunately, almost all of those courses centered on "dates and events." Memorization was the heart of my historical studies. None of my history courses even began to approach the teaching of high-level cognitive skills such as that set forth in Figure 8.4's performance test. If I were asked to tackle this performance test today, I would flunk it in the twinkling of an eye.

I don't know how to perform the skill that the performance test in Figure 8.4 is intended to carry out. I never learned to look at historical events on the basis of whether those events offered solid lessons that could be applied thereafter. But if my children had left school with a mastery of the historical skills that the performance test in Figure 8.4 is intended to measure, I would have been overjoyed. It is such a powerful skill for anyone to possess. I wish I did.

The Performance Test's Rubric

In Chapter 7 you learned about rubrics. Rubrics, as you saw, can be used to score students' responses to any sort of constructed-response requiring a fairly extensive response from students. But rubrics really are especially appropriate for scoring students' responses to performance tests because a student's response to a performance-test task usually is scored on the basis of multiple evaluative criteria.

Now consider the rubric for scoring responses to the performance test, *Using History's Lessons*. The rubric is presented in Figure 8.5. If you study Figure 8.5's rubric carefully, you'll see that it has three evaluative criteria, for example, "Prediction Defensibility." And each of those three evaluative criteria is broken down according to two or more key elements. The rubric is intended to be used *analytically*.

Suppose your child were enrolled in a history class in which this rubric was being routinely used. Can you see how your child's familiarity with the three evaluative criteria and their key elements would really clarify for the child what a response to a performance-test task ought to contain?

┌───┐

Scoring Rubric: Using History's Lessons

The quality of students' responses to any task will be evaluated according to three evaluative criteria, namely, (1) the selection and justification of relevant historical events, (2) the quality and defensibility of the history-based prediction regarding the proposed problem–solution's consequences, and (3) the written presentation of the analysis. Each of these criteria will be described in terms of the key elements constituting a criterion. Four levels of quality (Distinguished: 4 points, Proficient: 3 points, Apprentice: 2 points, and Novice: 1 point) will be described for each criterion according to that criterion's key elements. A zero will be given to students who make no response or whose response is illegible or in a foreign language. Although responses will be scored analytically, on a criterion-by-criterion basis, a single overall score will be assigned to a student's response.

Evaluative Criterion One: Historical Event Selection/Justification (identifying relevant historical events, then justifying those events effectively)

Key Elements:

- *Event Selection:* Choosing one or more appropriate events from the *American History Timeline: Major Events,* that is, those events sufficiently parallel to the described problem–situation and the proposed solution to permit a defensible prediction regarding the proposed solution's likely consequences.

American History Timeline Major Events[*] (For 11th-Grade American History)	
Constitution	Depression
Territorial Expansion	New Deal
Civil War	World War II
Reconstruction	Cold War
Industrial Revolution	Civil Rights
Imperialism	Viet Nam
World War	Communication Revolution

[*]A different timeline would be used at lower grade levels.

- *Event Justification:* Supporting the relevance of the historical event(s) selected to the proposed solution by identifying features of the historical event and the proposed solution that are sufficiently similar to warrant a history-based prediction about the proposed solution's consequences.

Quality Levels:

Distinguished (4 points): The selection of historical events is completely accurate, that is, all appropriate historical events are selected while no inappropriate events are selected.[1] The selection of all those events is well justified.

[1] The appropriately relevant historical event(s) for each task will be determined by the examiners.

8.5 A rubric for scoring students' responses to *Using History's Lessons*

Source: Based on assessment efforts of the U.S. Department of Defense Dependents' Schools.

Proficient (3 points): The selection of historical events is satisfactorily accurate, that is, at least one appropriate historical event is selected and any inappropriate historical events selected are justified at least adequately. In addition, all appropriate historical events are justified at least adequately.

Apprentice (2 points): Not all appropriate historical events are selected, but those inappropriate events selected are justified at least adequately.

Novice (1 point): No appropriate historical events are selected, and those inappropriate events selected are inadequately justified.

Evaluative Criterion Two: Prediction Defensibility (making a sound history-based prediction and defending it strongly)

Key Elements:

- *Prediction Quality:* Predicting the consequences of the proposed solution in a manner that is reasonably derivative from the historical event(s) selected.
- *Strength of Defense:* Defending the history-based prediction by identifying those features of any selected historical events that bear on the likelihood of the prediction's accuracy.

Quality Levels:

Distinguished (4 points): The prediction of the proposed solution's consequences is reasonably based on the historical event(s) selected and is strongly defended by the citation of pertinent aspects of the historical event(s) selected.

Proficient (3 points): The prediction of the proposed solution's consequences is adequately based on the historical event(s) selected and is at least adequately defended by pertinent aspects of the historical event(s) selected.

Apprentice (2 points): *Either* the prediction of the proposed solution's consequences is adequately based on the historical event(s) but inadequately defended *or* the prediction is inadequate even though its historically based justification is strong.

Novice (1 point): The prediction of the proposed solution's consequences is inadequate and the defense of the prediction is only adequate or worse.

Evaluative Criterion Three: Written Communication (communicating effectively in writing)

Key Elements:

- *Organization:* Structuring the essay appropriately
- *Mechanics:* Employing suitable spelling, punctuation, and grammar
- *Voice:* Incorporating effective usage and word choice

Quality Levels:

Distinguished (4 points): All three key elements are well developed.
Proficient (3 points): All three key elements are at least adequately developed.
Apprentice (2 points): Only one or two key elements are adequately developed.
Novice (1 point): No key elements are adequately developed.

Overall Score: Derived analytically or holistically, each student should be assigned an overall score of 0–4.

That dividend, of course, is possible because the rubric in Figure 8.5 is a *skill-focused rubric*. You read about such rubrics in the previous chapter. Moreover, the rubric has been fashioned so that it clarifies expectations for teachers (so they can teach the skill), for students (so they can learn the skill), and for parents (so they can help their children learn the skill).

Notice that I said *parents* can help students master the skill in this performance test, even though I've already admitted that the skill is beyond me. I could help my children with this skill, however, and so could you, because of the clarity embodied in the rubric.

I could ask my child about whether the event the child had selected from the U.S. history timeline was parallel to the problem and proposed solution given in the task. I could ask how my child would justify the event selected. In short, I would know enough about the way that my child's responses would finally be evaluated so I could take part in a meaningful dialogue about the child's efforts to acquire this skill. I might be weak on the historical nuances needed to perform the skill, but I would know the framework by which my child's responses would be judged.

I don't have to be able to *perform* a skill in order to help my child master that skill. And I can help with my child's skill-mastery because the rubric lets me know what's really important to skill-mastery.

Performance Tests: A Final Look

Instructional Impact

If you really spent some time with Figures 8.4 and 8.5, you'll have seen a good example of how a high-level cognitive skill can be assessed with a performance test. Moreover, it can be assessed in such a way that the skill can be successfully mastered by children. The quality of the performance test and its rubric make this possible. As I said, I would guess that you and most other parents would be ecstatic if your child could display the historical skill assessed by the performance test we've just been considering.

That's one of the reasons that there has been a dramatic increase in the use of performance tests to measure children's compositional skills. Writing samples are required in almost all school settings these days. And this expanded use of performance tests calling for writing samples is due to two reasons: (1) children's ability to write is a really important skill that's recognized as such by parents, and (2) the performance tests used to assess students' writing skills have been accompanied by well-conceived rubrics that promote students' effective skill-mastery. The quality of children's writing skills in this nation has dramatically improved as a direct consequence of

the prevalent use of solid performance tests and instructionally illuminating rubrics.

Well, if performance tests can make such a contribution to children's mastery of important skills, why don't teachers use performance tests more frequently? Why don't children have "a performance test per week"?

Practical Problems

That's an important question, and I want you to understand why the instructionally judicious use of performance tests suggests that such assessments be limited to only a modest number of highly significant skills. You see, for a teacher to develop an *instructionally illuminating* performance test is not all that easy. The teacher must isolate a significant intellectual skill and identify tasks that will allow judgments about whether students can really master the skill. Then there's the matter of devising a skill-focused rubric. That, too, is difficult.

Finally, assuming the teacher has created a solid performance test, including several tasks for the test, and a rubric to score students' responses, then there's the time-consuming task of scoring students' responses. No, a teacher's use of instructionally helpful performance tests is far from fools' play. It takes loads of time from the teacher.

And that's why you, as a parent, should resist wholesale advocacy of performance tests in your child's class. Well-formed performance tests are remarkably potent in promoting children's mastery of significant cognitive skills. But well-formed performance tests are tough to develop. Sloppy performance tests are easy to develop. (I've seen more weak performance tests than wonderful ones.) And performance tests take hours to score properly (so that each student gets appropriate rubric-based feedback). You must recognize that simply because an educational test is referred to as "a performance test," that test may be powerful and praiseworthy. Or it may not.

As a practical matter, teachers only have so much time to give to the use of performance tests. So, if I were once more a parent of school-age children, I'd urge the teacher to use performance tests judiciously to assess *a modest number of really high-import skills* such as my child's ability to read, to write, to communicate orally, and to solve the kinds of mathematical problems apt to be encountered in later life.

In other words, I'd encourage the teacher to use one or, at most, two performance tests per subject area. I'd urge the teacher to use performance tests to assess only one important skill in science, another one in social studies, and so on. If the teacher ended up using a half-dozen performance tests measuring really significant skills, I'd be more than happy.

If your child is being assessed occasionally by performance tests, and those tests measure truly significant skills, you should be happy too.

What Do You Really Need to Know about This Chapter's Content?

There are only three major points that I hope you'll remember from this chapter:

- Although parents ought to anticipate a fair amount of educational disagreement about the precise definition of a performance test, such tests are usually intended to measure students' high-level cognitive skills by evaluating a student's generated response to a skill-determining task. The closer the assessment approach measures an important real-life instructional objective of the teacher, the more likely the assessment is to be described as a performance test.
- If performance tests are constructed with their instructional implications in mind, such tests can have a powerful and beneficial impact on a child's mastery of a truly significant cognitive skill. However, performance tests vary in their quality. Not all performance tests

warrant being used with children. Some should be sent scurrying to a paper shredder.

- Because teachers are pressed with a variety of time-consuming demands, parents should be realistic in urging teachers to employ performance tests as part of their classroom assessments. If a small number of performance tests assessing truly worthwhile skills are used in children's classes, most parents should be satisfied.

POSSIBLE PARENT ACTION–OPTIONS

If you intend to take any action based on the material covered in Chapter 8, here are a few options for you to consider.

1. You could find out from your child if there are any performance tests used as part of the child's classroom assessments. If not, you might discuss with your child's teacher the role of performance tests and form a judgment about the teacher's familiarity with this form of assessment.
2. If your child's teacher *does* use performance tests, you might review one or more of them according to the content of this chapter. For example, is the skill measured by the performance test truly worthwhile? Are the test's tasks really skill-determining? Is the rubric skill-focused? If there are shortcomings in the teacher's performance tests, you might tactfully raise a few questions about those things with the teacher or, alternatively, with the school's principal.
3. If you think it appropriate, that is, if your child's teacher seems open to such suggestions, you could suggest that the teacher consult one or more of the *Suggested Resources* below.

SUGGESTED RESOURCES FOR YOUR CHILD'S TEACHER OR PRINCIPAL

Printed Materials

Crocker, Linda. "Assessing Content Representativeness of Performance Assessment Exercises." *Applied Measurement in Education, 10,* no. 1 (1997): 83–95. *One of the difficulties using performance tests is that they often fail to satisfactorily represent the content being assessed. In this analysis, one of the nation's leading measurement specialists deals with this significant issue.*

Gronlund, Norman E. *Assessment of Student Achievement.* Boston: Allyn and Bacon, 1998. *"Making Performance Assessments" is the title of Chapter 8, so, because Gronlund believes in truth-in-chapter-titling, he does a solid job in describing the necessary steps in creating performance tests.*

McMillan, James H. *Classroom Assessment: Principles and Practice for Effective Instruction.* Boston: Allyn and Bacon, 1997. *In Chapter 8, the strengths and limitations of performance tests are described along with an analysis of how such tests should be built.*

Videotape Programs

IOX Assessment Associates. *Developing Language Arts Performance: A Conversation with Dr. Roger Farr.* (5301 Beethoven St., Ste. 190, Los Angeles, CA 90066). *Dr. Roger Farr, one of the nation's leading language arts authorities, describes how to connect writing and reading, then how to develop language arts performance tests.*

IOX Assessment Associates. *Performance Assessment: How Authentic Must It Be?* (5301 Beethoven St., Ste. 190, Los Angeles, CA 90066). *From this video, educators learn what performance assessment is—and what it isn't, the various types of performance assessment, and the consequences of using this approach to educational assessment.*

Northwest Regional Educational Laboratory. *Developing Assessments Based on Observation and Judgment.* IOX Assessment Associates (5301 Beethoven St., Ste. 190, Los Angeles, CA 90066). *A step-by-step process for creating performance assessments is set forth in this video. The alignment of assessments with important instructional targets is treated.*

Wiggins, Grant, and Richard Stiggins. *Performance Assessment.* Association for Supervision and Curriculum Development (1250 N. Pitt St., Alexandria, VA 22314). *In this video program, Wiggins and Stiggins describe how performance assessments can stimulate students' synthesizing, evaluating, and reasoning skills.*

9

PORTFOLIO ASSESSMENT

*I*n the previous chapter you considered performance tests—a clear alternative to the traditional paper-and-pencil assessments that most of today's parents recall from their own school days. One of the reasons that performance tests are being strongly advocated these days is that such tests do, in fact, represent a significant departure from same-old, same-old classroom tests. In this chapter you'll learn about another alternative to traditional assessment that some educators are advocating with more than a little zeal. You're going to take a close look at *portfolio assessment.*

What Is Portfolio Assessment?

A *portfolio*, as you already know, is a systematic collection of somebody's work. Portfolios have been used for many years by artists, photographers, models, architects, and so on. An important feature of portfolios is that they can (and should) be updated as a person's skills and achievements grow.

So, if you were trying to select an interior decorator to help you furnish a newly remodeled living room, it is almost certain that prospective decorators would display their previous decorating accomplishments in the form of portfolios containing photos of their prior decorating accomplishments. By reviewing a portfolio, you can often get a good idea of the skills of the person whose work is displayed in the portfolio.

Well, in the last decade or so, portfolios have come to the field of education in the form of *portfolio assessment.* Students collect their schoolwork, or at least samples of that work, in portfolios. Such collections can be assembled in file folders, boxes, paper sacks, or just about any container that will hold a student's *work samples.*

In its most fundamental form, portfolio assessment allows someone, such as a teacher or a parent, to evaluate the quality of a student's academic accomplishments by reviewing a collection of the student's work samples that have been assembled over time.

As you'll see, there are other potential payoffs from portfolio assessment, but its most fundamental appeal is based on the belief that a collection of a student's evolving achievements presents a more accurate picture of the student's skills and knowledge than a student's score on a traditional selected-response or constructed-response test. In a very real sense, then, advocates of portfolio assessment believe that this approach to measuring a student's achievement will yield more *valid* interpretations about what the student can or can't do.

> *Testing Terms:*
> **Portfolio Assessment**
> The evaluation of a student's evolving achievements by appraising a collection of work samples assembled over time

Educators who are caught up with the wonders of portfolio assessment do not necessarily repudiate conventional classroom testing, but they believe portfolio assessment provides a much richer picture *over time* of a student's accomplishments than could be obtained from a *single-snapshot* conventional classroom test.

Your child may not currently be in a class where portfolio assessment is being used. Although portfolio assessment is being pushed with substantial fervor by a good many educators, it is still the exception rather than the rule. So, odds are that your child is not being measured by portfolio assessment—and, indeed, may never be.

But there are pockets of passionate portfolio-assessment educators in many school settings. And portfolio assessment can be used by teachers at all grade levels, K through 12. So, it wouldn't be a bad idea for you to have at least a nodding acquaintance with the nature of portfolio assessment. It's very possible your child may, in the future, be rounding up work samples for a meaningful encounter with portfolio assessment.

As you'll see, if you choose to read this chapter, portfolio assessment has some real dividends and some real deficits. (And, of course, if you don't read the chapter, you'll never know what they are.) If portfolio assessment ever crosses your child's path in the future, it would be a good idea for you to know about the chief features of this assessment approach. If your child is *currently* involved in a portfolio-assessment effort, then you should clearly read this chapter. Moreover, read slowly!

How Portfolio Assessment Works in the Classroom

Teachers who are advocates of portfolio assessment believe that the real payoff for such an assessment approach lies in an individual teacher's classroom, because the relationship between instruction and assessment will typically be strengthened as a consequence of students' continuing assembly of work products in their portfolios. Ideally, teachers who adopt portfolios in their classrooms will make the ongoing collection and appraisal of students' work a central focus of the *instructional* program rather than an assessment-only activity. Portfolio assessment can easily turn into a peripheral activity if students only occasionally gather up their work to convince a teacher's supervisors or the students' parents that good things have been going on in class.

Here's a description of how an elementary teacher might use portfolios to assess students' progress in social studies, language arts, and mathematics. The teacher, let's call him Phil Pholio, asks students to keep three portfolios, one in each of those three subject fields. In each portfolio, the students are to place their early and revised work products. The work products are always dated so that Mr. Pholio, as well as the students themselves, can see what kinds of differences in quality take place over time. For example, if Phil is providing genuinely effective instruction, during the school year there should be discernible improvement in the quality of students' written compositions, solutions to mathematics problems, and analyses of social issues.

Three or four times per semester, Mr. Pholio holds twenty-minute portfolio conferences with each student about the three different portfolios. The nonconferencing students take part in small-group projects and independent learning activities while the portfolio conferences take place. During a conference, the participating student plays an active role

in evaluating his or her own work. When areas of weakness are identified by Phil and a student, they both agree on an instructional activity that addresses the weakness. Toward the close of the school year, students select from their regular portfolio a series of work products that not only represents their best final versions, but also indicates how those final products were created. These selections are placed in a display portfolio that is then featured at a spring open-school session designed for parents. Parents who visit the school are urged to take their children's display portfolios home. Mr. Pholio also sends home portfolios to parents who are unable to attend the open-school event.

There are, of course, many other ways to use portfolios effectively in a classroom. Phil Pholio, our phictitious (sic) teacher, employed a fairly common approach. But a variety of alternative procedures could also work quite nicely. The major consideration is that the teacher uses portfolio *assessment* as an integral aspect of the *instructional* process. Because portfolios can be tailored to a specific student's evolving growth, the diagnostic value of portfolios for classroom teachers is, at least potentially, considerable.

The Significance of Self-Evaluation

Most proponents of portfolio assessment believe the real payoff from proper portfolio assessment is that students' *self-evaluation* capabilities are enhanced. During portfolio conferences, therefore, the teacher encourages students to come up with *personal* appraisals of their own work. The conference, then, becomes far more than merely an opportunity for the teacher to dispense an "oral report card." On the contrary, students' self-evaluation skills are nurtured not only during portfolio conferences but also throughout the entire school year. For that reason, many educators prefer the use of *working* portfolios instead of *showcase* portfolios because they believe that self-evaluation is nurtured more readily in connection with ongoing reviews of work products that aren't intended to impress external viewers.

For self-evaluation purposes, it is particularly useful to be able to compare earlier work with later work. Fortunately, even if a teacher's instruction is downright abysmal, students do grow older and, as a consequence of maturation, tend to get better at what they do in school. So, in most instances, there will be at least some improvement over time in the quality of students' performances.

If a student is required to review three versions of the student's written composition (a first draft, a second draft, and a final draft), self-evaluation can be fostered by encouraging the student to make comparative judgments among the three compositions based on appropriate evaluative criteria. (Well-written rubrics really pay off in portfolio assessment programs.) As anyone who has done much writing knows, written efforts tend to get better with time and revision. Contrasts of later versions with earlier versions can prove illuminating for students because their self-evaluation skills are so critical to their future growth.

Large-Scale Portfolio Assessment

It is one thing to use portfolios for classroom assessment; it is quite another to use portfolios for large-scale assessment programs. Several states and large school districts have attempted to install portfolios as a central component of a large-scale accountability assessment program—that is, a program in which student performances serve as an indicator of an educational system's effectiveness. To date, the results of efforts to employ portfolios for accountability purposes have not been encouraging.

In large-scale applications of portfolio assessments for accountability purposes, students' portfolios are judged either by the student's regular teachers or by a group of specially trained scorers (often teachers) who carry out the scoring of portfolios at a central site. The problem with specially trained scorers and central-site scoring is that it typically costs much more than can be afforded. Some states, therefore, have opted to have all portfolios scored by students' own teachers who then relay such scores to the state department. The problem with having regular teachers score students' portfolios, however, is that such scoring tends to be too unreliable for use in accountability programs. Not only have teachers usually not been provided with adequate training about how to score portfolios, but there is also a tendency for teachers to be biased in favor of their own students. As you can see, the scoring of portfolios in large-scale assessment programs presents a set of difficult problems.

One of the most visible of the statewide efforts to use portfolios for every pupil was a recent performance assessment program in the state of Vermont. Because substantial attention has been focused on the Vermont program, and because it has been evaluated independently, many policymakers in other states have drawn on the experiences encountered in the Vermont Portfolio Assessment Program. Unfortunately, independent evaluators of Vermont's statewide efforts to use portfolios found that there was considerable unreliability in the appraisals given to students' work. And, if you recall my yammering in Chapter 2 about the importance of reliability, you'll realize it's tough to make valid interpretations about students' achievements if the assessments of those achievements are not made with consistency.

It certainly hasn't been shown that portfolios do *not* have a place in large-scale assessment. It's even possible that your child might be required to take part in some sort of large-scale portfolio assessment. What has been shown is that there are significant obstacles, both financial and technical, to be surmounted if portfolio assessment is going to make a meaningful contribution to large-scale educational accountability programs.

Key Features of Portfolio Assessment in the Classroom

If your child is taking part in classroom-level portfolio assessment, you really ought to be familiar with what a high-quality portfolio assessment looks like. The reason that you should familiarize yourself with the key features of a *good* portfolio assessment program is, quite clearly, that some portfolio assessment programs aren't all that wonderful. If the portfolio assessment program your child is experiencing fails to include the following seven significant features, you might want to bring any omissions (tactfully, of course) to the attention of your child's teacher or principal.

Here, then, are seven important elements that are usually found in an instructionally beneficial classroom portfolio assessment program. Your child's teacher might not include all of these elements, but most of them should be there.

1. *Genuine student ownership of their portfolios.* In order for portfolios to represent a student's evolving work accurately, and to foster the kind of self-evaluation that is so crucial if portfolios are to be truly educational, students must perceive portfolios to be collections of their own work and not merely temporary holding-pins for products that teachers ultimately grade. Skillful teachers usually introduce the notion of portfolio assessment to their students by explaining the distinctive functions of portfolios in the classroom—both evaluative and instructional.

2. *Determination of work samples to collect.* Various kinds of work samples can be included in a portfolio. Obviously, such products will vary from subject to subject. In general, a wide variety of work products is preferable to a limited range of work products. Ideally, teachers and students can collaboratively determine what goes in the portfolio.

3. *Collection and storage of work samples.* Students need to collect the designated work samples as they are created, place them in a suitable container (a folder or notebook, for example), then store the container in a file cabinet, storage box, or some suitably safe location. Teachers typically need to work individually with students to help them decide whether particular products should be placed in their portfolios.

4. *Selection of criteria to evaluate work samples.* Working collaboratively with students, a skillful teacher should carve out a set of criteria by which the teacher and students can judge the quality of their portfolio products. Because of the likely variety of products in different students' portfolios, the identification of evaluative criteria is not a simple task. Yet, unless at least basic evaluative criteria are isolated, the students will find it difficult to evaluate their own efforts and, thereafter, to improve. The criteria, once selected, should be described with the same sort of clarity you saw in Chapter 7 regarding how to use rubrics when evaluating students' responses.

5. *Students' continual evaluation of their own portfolio products.* Using the agreed-on evaluative criteria, teachers must be sure that students try to judge the quality of their own work. Students can be directed to evaluate their work products holistically, analytically, or by using a combination of both approaches. Such self-evaluation can be made routine if the teacher requires each student to complete brief 3 × 5-inch evaluation cards on which they identify the major strengths and weaknesses of a given product, then suggest how the product could be improved. Teachers should have their students date such self-evaluation skills. Each completed self-evaluation sheet can then be stapled or paper-clipped to the work product being evaluated.

6. *Portfolio conferences.* Portfolio conferences take time. Yet, these interchange sessions between teachers and students regarding students' work are really pivotal in making sure that portfolio assessment fulfills its potential. The portfolio conference should not only evaluate students' work products but should also help them improve their self-evaluation abilities. Teachers should try to hold as many of these conferences as is practical. In order to make the conferences time-efficient, teachers should be sure to have students prepare for the conferences so that the conference can immediately start on the topics of most concern to the teacher and the student.

7. *Parent involvement in the portfolio assessment process.* Early in the school year, teachers should make sure students' parents understand what the nature of the portfolio assessment process is that has been devised for their children's classroom. Teachers should encourage students' parents/guardians to review periodically their children's work samples as well as their children's self-evaluation of those work samples. The more active that parents become in reviewing their children's work, the stronger the message will be to the child that the portfolio activity is really worthwhile. If teachers wish, they may have students select their best work for a showcase portfolio or, instead, simply use the students' working portfolios. Some teachers try to involve a parent in at least one portfolio conference per year.

A Parent Puzzle

(Setting: Jody Smith is a fourth-grader whose teacher, Mrs. Brown, has installed a portfolio assessment system this year for the first time. At the end of the first semester, in late January, Jody brings home a completed portfolio showing a series of finished projects in science, social studies, and language arts.

Jody's parents, unfamiliar with portfolio assessment, have asked to speak with Mrs. Brown in order to better understand the instructional advantage of portfolio assessment, especially as it applies to their youngster's education.

Here's how an after-school conference involving Mrs. Brown and Jody's parents got underway.)

Mrs. Brown: "I'm delighted that you two could find time to speak with me about Jody's progress. I'm mighty pleased with Jody's performance, and I suspect you are too."

Mr. Smith: "Well, we really are. Jody not only says good things about your class, but seems to be learning a lot."

Mrs. Smith: "I agree with my husband, Mrs. Brown, but we'd like to learn more about this portfolio system that you're using. One of the other parents said that this was the first year you've tried it. How is it supposed to work?"

Mrs. Brown: "Well, you've recently had an opportunity to look at Jody's half-year showcase portfolio. What did you think of it?"

Mr. Smith: "I was very impressed. Jody seems to have turned out some really good things. I think you call them work products. Is that the purpose of portfolio assessment as you're using it—to display students' best work?"

Mrs. Brown: "Actually, it is. I'm still trying to fine-tune my portfolio assessment system, but the most important element is the showcasing of students' best work."

Mrs. Smith: "I'm glad Jody's done well, but what about other students who don't have as many first-rate work products to showcase?"

Mrs. Brown: "Regrettably, they simply end up with very skimpy portfolios."

Parent: If you were Mr. or Mrs. Smith, how would you respond?

- -

My Response: By this point in the conversation, I'd have concluded that Mrs. Brown seems to be missing a major payoff of portfolio assessment, namely, the increase in students' achievement as a consequence of self-evaluation. Ever so meekly, I'd say something such as, "We've been trying to do a bit of reading about portfolios in education, and we both were impressed with the self-evaluation payoffs that students seem to derive from portfolio assessment. I assume that such payoffs are more likely to be seen from students' working portfolios than from their showcase portfolios. Is that how you're approaching this kind of assessment?"

My Reason: If portfolio assessment is, to Mrs. Brown, *only* a collection of work products to impress parents, then it's missing its potential to help children learn how to appraise their own efforts. Maybe Jody's showcase portfolio is loaded with yummy work products, but *every* child's portfolios ought to be chock full of "work products under improvement." I'd try to let Mrs. Brown know that, as parents, we'd like her to consider the virtues of assessment portfolios that are instructional as opposed to those that merely glitter.

Think of the insights that you, as a parent, would gain from sitting in on one of your child's portfolio conferences with the teacher. And think of the message your participation would send to your child about the significance of the portfolio assessment activity.

These seven steps reflect only the most important activities that teachers might engage in when creating assessment programs in their classrooms. There are obviously all sorts of variations that are possible.

Portfolio Assessment Issues

There are a number of choice-points faced by a teacher who intends to implement a portfolio assessment system in the classroom. Let's look, briefly, at several of the more important issues faced by such a teacher. If parents recognize the nature of these issues, then parents can better understand why teachers made certain choices in devising their approach to portfolio assessment.

Portfolios for What Purpose?

There are three major purposes that portfolio assessment can fulfill. Teachers need to be very clear-headed about which of these three purposes their own portfolio assessment program is intended to accomplish.

Documentation of Student Progress.   One function that a portfolio assessment program can fulfill is to provide the student, the teacher, and the student's parents with evidence of the student's growth—or lack of it. Portfolios organized to accomplish this purpose are typically referred to as *working* portfolios. Such portfolios provide meaningful opportunities for students' self-evaluation of their work. The "documentation" of progress is carried out to help determine if suitable progress is taking place. It is not carried out merely to give students a grade.

Showcasing Student Accomplishments.   A second purpose of portfolios can be described as providing an opportunity for students to display their achievements. Portfolios that are aimed at this function are typically referred to as *showcase* portfolios. Showcase portfolios are often advocated for children in the early grades of school when celebrations of students' work can often have a positive impact on the way children view themselves as learners.

One teacher I know always makes sure that students include the following elements in their showcase portfolios:

- A letter of introduction to portfolio reviewers
- A table of contents
- Identification of the skills or knowledge being demonstrated
- A representative sample of the student's best work
- Dates on all entries
- The evaluative criteria (or rubric) being used
- The student's self-reflection on all work samples included

The inclusion of students' self-reflections about ingredients of portfolios is a pivotal ingredient, even in showcase portfolios. Some educators contend that a portfolio's self-evaluation by the student helps the learner to learn better and permits parents who read the portfolio to gain insights about how their children learn.

Student Evaluation.   A final purpose for classroom portfolio assessment is the evaluation of student status, that is, a determination of whether students have met previously determined performance levels. When teachers use portfolios for this purpose, especially for the assignment of significant grades, there must be greater standardization of what's to be included in portfolios and how the portfolio's work products will be appraised.

Typically, teachers select the entries for this kind of portfolio and considerable attention is given to scoring so that the rubrics employed to score the portfolios will yield consistent results even if different scorers were to be involved. For evaluation portfolios, there is usually less need for self-evaluation of entries, unless such self-evaluations are themselves being evaluated by the teacher.

Well, you've peeked at three purposes underlying portfolio assessment. Do you think one portfolio can perform all three functions? My answer is a somewhat shaky *Yes*. But if you were to ask me whether one portfolio can perform all three functions *well*, you'd get a rock-solid *No*. The three functions, though related—somewhat like second cousins—are fundamentally different.

That's why a teacher's very first decision if the teacher is going to install portfolios in the classroom is to determine the *primary purpose* of the portfolios. The teacher can then determine what the portfolios should look like and how students should prepare them.

Scripture tells us that "no man can serve two masters." (The authors of that scriptural advice, clearly insensitive to gender equality, were surely not implying that women are more capable of double-master serving.) Similarly, one kind of portfolio cannot easily satisfy multiple functions. Some classroom teachers rush into portfolio assessment because they've heard about all of the enthralling things that portfolios can do. But one kind of portfolio cannot fulfill all three functions satisfactorily.

If portfolios are being used in your child's classroom, try to find out what the primary purpose of portfolio assessment is. If you're told that the portfolios are accomplishing multiple missions, get worried.

What Work Samples to Select?

For a teacher just entering the portfolio party, another key decision hinges on the identification of the work samples to be put into the portfolios. All too often, teachers who are novices at portfolio assessment will fail to think inventively enough about the kinds of entries that should constitute a portfolio's chief contents. If teachers think creatively, they'll usually identify a considerable range of work samples that might be included.

But inventiveness is not necessarily a virtue when it comes to the determination of a portfolio's contents. Teachers shouldn't search for varied kinds of work samples simply for the sake of variety. What's important is that the particular kinds of work samples to be included in the portfolio will allow teachers to derive valid inferences about the skills and/or knowledge teachers are trying to have their students master. It's far better to include a few kinds of *inference-illuminating* work samples than to include a galaxy of work samples, many of which do not contribute to inferences about students' key knowledge or skills.

In other words, a teacher should try to choose work samples that will help the teacher arrive at accurate inferences about children's skills and knowledge. The fundamental purpose of educational assessment, you'll recall, is to collect evidence that helps teachers and parents arrive at valid inferences about children's levels of skill and knowledge. That's just as true with portfolio assessment as it is if your child were completing a True–False test.

How Should Portfolios Be Appraised?

As indicated earlier in the chapter, students' portfolios are almost always evaluated by the use of a scoring rubric. As you saw in Chapter 7, the most important ingredients in such a rubric are its evaluative criteria—that is, the factors to be used in determining the quality of the work samples in a particular student's portfolio. If there's any sort of student self-evaluation to be done, and such self-evaluation is almost always desirable, then it is imperative that students have access to, and thoroughly understand, the rubric that will be used to evaluate their work products.

If possible, so there will be greater student ownership of any rubric's evaluative criteria, students should have at least some role in determining what the evaluative criteria ought to be. Even more desirably, if your child's teacher is allowing students to have a say in identifying their portfolio rubric's evaluation criteria, wouldn't it be great if your child was directed to get your input about those evaluative criteria before the rubric was cast in final form? Again, the message to your child is simple: "This is important stuff."

Dividends and Deficits of Portfolio Assessment

What you need to keep in mind is that portfolio assessment's greatest strength is that it can be tailored to the individual student's needs, interests, and abilities. Yet, portfolio assessment suffers from the drawback faced by all constructed-response measurement. Students' constructed responses are difficult to evaluate, particularly when those responses vary from student to student.

As you saw with Vermont's Portfolio Assessment Program, it is tough to come up with consistent evaluations of different students' portfolios. Sometimes the rubrics devised for use in evaluating portfolios are so brief and so general as to be almost useless. They're akin to Rorschach inkblots in which different people see in the scoring guide whatever they want to see. In contrast, some rubrics are so detailed and complicated that they simply overwhelm any teacher who tries to use them. It is difficult to devise rubrics that embody just the right level of specificity. Generally speaking, most teachers are so busy that they don't have time to create elaborate rubrics. Accordingly, many teachers (and students) find themselves judging a portfolio's work products using fairly broad evaluative criteria. Such general criteria tend to be interpreted differently by different people.

Another problem with portfolio assessment is that it takes time—loads of time—to carry out properly. Even if teachers are efficient in reviewing their students' portfolios, they'll still have to devote many hours both in class (during portfolio conferences) and outside of class (if teachers also want to routinely review their students' portfolio privately). Proponents of portfolios are convinced that the quality of portfolio assessment is worth the time such assessment takes. Teachers need to be prepared for the required investment of time if they decide to prance down the portfolio assessment path.

And teachers need to receive sufficient training to learn how to do portfolio assessment well. Any teachers who set out to do portfolio assessment by simply stuffing student stuff into folders that are designed for stuff-stuffing will end up wasting their time and their students' time. Meaningful staff development is a must if portfolio assessment is to work well. As a parent, you can lend your support for sufficient staff development so that, if your child's teacher is employing portfolios, those portfolios will yield educational benefits for your child.

On the plus side, however, most teachers who have used portfolios agree that portfolio assessment provides a way of documenting and evaluating student growth in ways that traditional tests simply can't. Portfolios have the potential to create authentic portraits of what students learn. Well-conceived portfolios have a powerful story to tell. Fortunately, that story can be made compatible with improved student learning if portfolio assessment is well conceived.

Most of the teachers I've talked with who use portfolio assessment are primarily enamored with two of its payoffs. They believe that the *self-evaluation* it fosters in students is truly important in guiding students' learning over time. They also think the *personal ownership* that students experience regarding their own work, and the progress they almost always experience, make the benefits of portfolio assessment outweigh its costs.

But to be completely honest, I've also talked to a fair number of teachers who formerly used portfolio assessment, but no longer do so. I suppose we could think of these teachers as "recovering portfolio assessors." Without exception, the complaint of these ex-portfolio-assessors was that "it takes too ____ much time." (Often, an expletive was inserted in place of the blank.)

My own intuition is that portfolio assessment, all by itself, is not a *certain* winner in the classroom. Some teachers' personalities and teaching styles mesh marvelously with the demands of this form of measurement. Some teachers' personalities and teaching styles make portfolio assessment seem, at least to them, an onerous and deflective intrusion on their classroom instruction and assessment.

If teachers don't love portfolio assessment, it's not likely to help children all that much. If teachers love portfolio assessment, and put together a sensible set of procedures for it, then children are likely to benefit from it.

Suppose for a moment, that now, or in the future, your child has a brush with this form of assessment. What I hope you now see is that portfolio assessment is not necessarily a wonderful thing for your child. It *may* be, if it is properly formulated and delivered by a teacher who recognizes its *instructional* dividends for students. But it may not be. You need to do some digging to see if your child's portfolio is a sound assessment strategy or merely a popular fad.

What Do You Really Need to Know about This Chapter's Content?

If you were unfamiliar with the nature of portfolio assessment as it's currently being used by educators, I hope this chapter gave you a general idea about what's involved with this form of assessment. If your child ends up in a class where portfolio assessment is used, here are the key points I think you need to take from this chapter.

■ You need to have a general idea of how portfolio assessment works. In short, you need to know that portfolio assessment is a measurement system designed to appraise a student's evolving achievements by judging a collection of student work samples assembled over time.

■ Most educators who advocate portfolio assessment contend that its chief virtues are the promotion of students' *self-evaluation* capabilities, stimulated by students' *personal ownership* of their portfolios.

■ Although classroom teachers can vary dramatically in the procedures they employ to carry out a portfolio assessment program, seven important features of a portfolio assessment program have been isolated. They are: (1) promotion of students' portfolio ownership, (2) identification of suitable work samples, (3) collection/storage of work samples, (4) selection of suitable evaluative criteria for judging the work samples, (5) insistence on students' continual self-evaluation of their portfolio's contents, (6) use of as many portfolio conferences as possible, and (7) meaningful involvement of parents in the portfolio assessment process.

■ Finally, you must realize that the implementation of a portfolio assessment program in the classroom represents a significant time-consuming commitment for teachers. Accordingly, not all teachers will gleefully embrace it. Nor, for that matter, are all teachers' personalities and instructional styles well suited to this form of classroom testing. If properly designed and delivered by a teacher who is enthusiastic about it, portfolio assessment can help children. If poorly designed, or if delivered by a teacher who views it as a chore, portfolio assessment should be left on the shelf.

POSSIBLE PARENT ACTION–OPTIONS

Whether you take any action based on this chapter's content depends largely on whether your child is currently involved in a portfolio assessment program.

1. If so, then you might determine if most of the seven key features identified on pages 194–195 are present in the program. If they're not, you might discuss with your child's teacher or principal why some of those features are missing. Remember, the purpose of such discussions is to help your child's teacher get the best portfolio assessment system in place so that children profit from it.
2. If your child's teacher is employing portfolio assessment, and you think it could use some *serious* sprucing up, you might refer the teacher to one or more of the entries in this chapter's *Suggested Resources* entries.
3. If you read this chapter carefully, and if your child is not engaged in a portfolio assessment system at the present, and *never* does so in the future, think of all the stuff you now know about portfolio assessment that you'll never be able to use! One action–option for you to consider, then, is *cursing* (not in the presence of your child, of course).

SUGGESTED RESOURCES FOR YOUR CHILD'S TEACHER OR PRINCIPAL

Printed Materials

McMillan, James H. *Classroom Assessment: Principles and Practice for Effective Instruction.* Boston: Allyn and Bacon, 1997. *In an extensive treatment, McMillan devotes Chapter 9 to the creation and use of portfolio assessment systems.*

Stiggins, Richard J. *Student-Centered Classroom Assessment* (2nd ed.). Upper Saddle River, NJ: Prentice-Hall, 1997. *In Chapter 16, Stiggins stresses the role of portfolios in communicating about students' achievement.*

Weber, Ellen. *Student Assessment That Works: A Practical Approach.* Boston: Allyn and Bacon, 1999. *A fan of portfolio assessment, Weber shows in Chapter 5 how to deal with students' individual differences through the teacher's skillful use of portfolios.*

Videotape Programs

IOX Assessment Associates. *Portfolios and Language Arts: A First Look.* (5301 Beethoven St., Ste. 190, Los Angeles, CA 90066). *In this introductory program, educators learn the essential elements of language arts portfolios and how to use them for both assessment and instruction.*

IOX Assessment Associates. *Portfolio Conferences: What They Are and Why They Are Important.* (5301 Beethoven St., Ste. 190, Los Angeles, CA 90066). *Dr. Roger Farr, noted language arts educator, describes a portfolio conference, how teachers should get ready for portfolio conferences, and how to find the time to carry out these conferences in their busy classrooms.*

Northwest Regional Educational Laboratory. *Putting Portfolio Stories to Work.* IOX Assessment Associates (5301 Beethoven St., Ste. 190, Los Angeles, CA 90066). *In this video, four different types of portfolios are described. Student self-evaluation is emphasized. Video footage of classrooms is featured in which students are using portfolios.*

Northwest Regional Educational Laboratory. *Using Portfolios in Assessment and Instruction.* IOX Assessment Associates (5301 Beethoven St., Ste. 190, Los Angeles, CA 90066). *In this video, viewers are taught how to establish criteria for the selection of portfolio materials, how to involve students, and how to create the criteria needed to evaluate students' work products.*

Wiggins, Grant, and Richard Stiggins. *Portfolios.* Association for Supervision and Curriculum Development (1250 N. Pitt St., Alexandria, VA 22314). *This program shows how the use of portfolios can help students revise their work, isolate their skills, and set suitable aims for their own learning.*

10
Assessing Children's Affect

Affect, most educators concede, is important. Student's attitudes toward learning, for example, play a major role in how much learning those students subsequently pursue. The values that students possess regarding truthfulness and integrity shape their daily conduct. And students' self-esteem, of course, influences almost everything they do. There's little doubt that the affective status of students should concern not only educators but parents as well.

In truth, however, few classroom teachers give explicit attention to influencing their students' attitudes and values. Even fewer classroom teachers actually try to assess the affective status of their students. Certainly, a teacher may observe a student's sour demeanor and conclude that he's "out of sorts" or she's "a mite depressed," but how many times have you heard about a teacher who tried to gather *systematic* evidence regarding students' attitudes and values? Unfortunately, systematic assessment of affect is uncommon.

This chapter will address the issue of affective assessment by providing you with general insights regarding the assessment of students' attitudes and values. As you'll discover, although it will be impossible for teachers to get an accurate fix on *your* child's affect, it is still important for you to advocate that teachers routinely measure students' attitudes. This sounds contradictory, but by the time you finish the chapter, you'll understand why it's not.

Why Assess Affect?

One question parents might be asking themselves is, why assess attitudes at all? Many teachers, particularly those who teach older students, believe that their only educational mission is to increase students' knowledge and skills. Affect, such teachers believe, simply doesn't fall into their proper sphere of influence. However, students who learn to do mathematics like magicians yet detest mathematics certainly aren't apt to apply the mathematics they've learned. Students who can compose outstanding essays but believe they are "really rotten writers" won't whip out many essays in their free time—just for the fun of it.

The Impact of Affect

I'd like to get my own bias regarding this issue out on the table so you don't think I'm trying to sneakily influence you. I personally think that affective outcomes are as significant, if not more significant, than cognitive outcomes. How many times, for example, have you seen people who weren't all that "gifted" intellectually, yet still succeed because they were highly motivated and hardworking? Conversely, how many times have you seen truly able people simply veer away from challenges because they did not consider themselves worthy? Day in and day out, we see the enormous impact that people's affective status has on them. Affect is every bit as important as cognitive ability.

Have you ever seen kindergarten children troop off to school loaded with enthusiasm and gumption, only to encounter those same children a few years later and see that a fair number are disenchanted with school and, in some cases, negative about themselves? Well, I have. And what's going on with such children is surely taking place in the affective realm.

When most kindergartners start school, they are enthused about school and about themselves. However, after *failing to measure up* for a year or two, many of those formerly upbeat children carry around decisively lowered self-concepts. They've tried and they've been found wanting. Negative attitudes about self and school will typically influence all of a child's subsequent education. Yet, because few teachers try to assess their students' affective status, most teachers don't know what their students' attitudes and values really are. That situation, I believe, needs to change.

Stimulating Affectively Focused Instruction

Even if there were no such thing as externally imposed "educational accountability" whereby students' performances on high-stakes tests serve as indicators of educational effectiveness, what's on achievement tests would still influence what teachers teach.

For example, when I was a high school teacher, I knew what kinds of items I had on my final exams. (That is, I knew during my second year of teaching, after I'd whipped out my first-year exams only minutes before my students needed to take those exams.) Because in subsequent years I wanted my students to do well on my final exams, I made reasonably sure that I spent at least some instructional time on the content covered by those examinations. I knew what was on my end-of-instruction tests, and I wanted my students to learn what was being tested. Most teachers behave in the same way.

It's the same with affective assessment. Let's say a teacher has installed a fairly straightforward pretest–posttest evaluation plan to assess any meaningful changes in students' responses to an attitude inventory regarding how much those students are interested in the subject(s) the teacher is teaching. The teacher's recognition that there will be a formal pretest–posttest assessment of students' subject-matter interest will, as surely as school buses run late, incline the teacher to provide instruction so that students will, in fact, become more positive about the subject(s) being taught.

In other words, the presence of affective postinstruction measurement will influence teachers to include affectively focused activities in their instruction. In a sense, teachers who engage in affective assessment are telling the world that affective outcomes are important enough to be formally assessed. You can be assured that what's important enough to be assessed, even if it's measured in one teacher's classroom and nowhere else in the world, is likely to influence that teacher's instruction.

I would not only like to see teachers routinely measure students' affect, I'd like to see teachers spend at least some classroom instructional time in promoting worthwhile affective changes in children. I wouldn't want teachers to go overboard on their affective instructional efforts. The promotion of children's skills and knowledge should always predominate. But an hour or so per month on affect wouldn't offend me one bit.

Monitoring Students' Status

In addition to serving as an end-of-instruction goal, if affective assessment devices are administered regularly, they can help teachers determine if modifications in the instructional program are warranted. For example, imagine that you are the parent of a high school student who is taking a physics class taught by Mr. Hill. Let's say that Mr. Hill wants to get a fix on how enthused his students are about continuing their study of physics in college. Ideally, Mr. Hill would like a reasonable number of his students to get fairly ecstatic over the raptures of future physics coursework. Suppose that each month Mr. Hill employed a brief self-report attitude inventory focused on the likelihood of students' pursuing future physics instruction. For illustrative purposes, let's assume that in September, 60 percent of Mr. Hill's students registered an interest in taking college physics courses and that in October, 65 percent indicated interest. In November, however, interest in future physics courses nose-dived so that only 25 percent of Mr. Hill's students signified any interest in college physics. This is a clear message to Mr. Hill that something went on in late October or early November to really turn off his budding Nobel Laureates. A review of Mr. Hill's instructional program during that period, and some serious effort on his part to generate more interest in postsecondary physics, would seem to be warranted. As you can see, periodic monitoring of students' affective status can assist teachers in seeing what sorts of shifts in their instructional program might be needed.

In review, there are a number of reasons that classroom teachers should devote at least a segment of their assessment program to the measurement of students' affect. If, as a parent, you don't believe that your child's attitudes and values are important, of course, you'll not agree with the views I've expressed. But if you do think student affect is significant, I suspect you'll want to learn about the kinds of affective variables that should be assessed and how to assess them. That's coming up shortly.

The Other Side of the Argument

Before turning to the innards of affective assessment, I need to point out that a good many citizens do not share my view regarding the importance of affective assessment and instruction. Particularly in the past few years, we have seen the emergence of a vocal group of individuals who have taken strong positions against schools' offering anything other than traditional academic (cognitive) education. Usually representing religious or conservative constituencies, these critics have argued that it is the job of the family and church to promote values in children, and that any attempt by the schools to modify students' attitudes or values should cease.

In several states there have been heated attacks on outcomes-based education (an approach to education in which heightened attention is given to the outcomes of an educational program rather than the procedures employed to deliver the program). A major argument voiced by those who argue against outcomes-based education is that it may foster attitudes and values that are unacceptable to certain religious or political groups.

I agree with these critics that if any attention to affective outcomes is to be given, it must be focused *only* on those affective consequences that would be almost *universally approved.* For example, I regard the promotion of students' positive attitudes toward learning as an affective aspiration that just about everyone would support. Similarly, I can't really imagine that there are too many people who wouldn't want the schools to nurture students' self-esteem. Clearly, we don't want teachers to spend so much time promoting affective objectives that a teacher's pursuit of knowledge and skills objectives is neglected.

However, I would hate to see educators dabbling with any controversial attitudes or values—that is, those that a meaningful number of parents wouldn't want their children to possess. If teachers decide to devote some of their classroom assessment/instruction time to affective targets, those teachers clearly need to consider carefully the legitimacy of the targets they select.

If you find that your child's teacher is assessing an affective outcome that you consider inappropriate for your child, then you have every right to register your strong disapproval. But I hope that you'll not consider it inappropriate if the teacher is spending a modest amount of time promoting (and assessing) really worthwhile sorts of affective consequences.

Which Affective Variables to Assess

A Closer Look at Affect

Before discussing the sorts of variables that a classroom teacher might want to assess, let's spend just a moment looking at the nature of *affect* itself. The reason that such affective outcomes as students' attitudes and values are important to educators is that those variables typically influence students' future behaviors. If you think about that point for a bit, you'll realize educators don't really care much, in the abstract, whether students' attitudes toward learning are positive. The reason that educators want to promote positive attitudes toward learning is because students who have positive attitudes toward learning *today* will be disposed to pursue learning *in the future.*

The current affective status of students lets educators foresee how students are predisposed to behave subsequently. If teachers find that students believe healthy bodies are important, those students will be predisposed to maintain their own bodily health in the future. If teachers find that students have positive attitudes toward people from other ethnic groups, then in the future such students will be predisposed to behave appropriately toward people from other ethnic groups. As you can see in Figure 10.1, people's current affective status predicts their future behavior.

Do attitudes predict future behavior *perfectly?* Of course not. But suppose there are 100 third-graders who display very negative attitudes

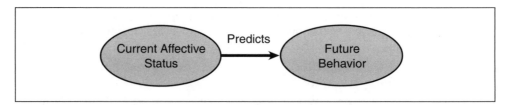

10.1 The predictive relationship between current affect and future behavior

toward violence as a way of settling disputes, and that there are 100 third-graders who believe that violence is a suitable way of resolving disputes. On probability grounds, in the future there are likely to be fewer violent dispute-resolution behaviors from the first 100 third-graders than from the second. Affective assessment, therefore, allows teachers to get a far-better-than-chance fix on the behavioral dispositions of their students. Affective assessment helps educators make probability-based forecasts regarding children's future behaviors. That's why affective assessment is so important.

As you know, schools have historically focused on cognitive variables. And that's probably the way it's always going to be. Thus, if teachers are interested in giving some modest attention to affect in their own classrooms, they'll need to select affective targets judiciously. That's what I'd like you to consider next. You'll look at attitudes first, then values.

Possible Attitudinal Targets

There are all sorts of possible attitudinal targets for a teacher's instruction. Here are a few of the attitudes that are most commonly endorsed by teachers as reasonable affective targets:

- *Attitudes toward subjects.* Students should regard the subject matter taught (for example, mathematics) more positively at the end of instruction than they did when instruction began. At the very least, students should be no more negative toward the subject being taught as a consequence of instruction.
- *Positive attitudes toward learning.* Students should regard the act of learning positively. Students who are positive today about learning will tend to be tomorrow's learners.
- *Positive attitudes toward self.* Self-esteem is the attitude on which most people's personal worlds turn. Although children's self-esteem is probably influenced more by parents and nonschool events than by teachers, what happens in the classroom can have a significant impact on children's self-esteem.

- *Positive attitudes toward self as a learner.* Self-esteem as a learner is an affective variable over which educators have substantial influence. If students believe they are capable of learning, they will tend to learn.

There are numerous other subject-specific kinds of attitudes that teachers will want to foster. For example, many teachers who deal with language arts will want to enhance students' heightened confidence as writers—that is, students' more positive attitudes toward their own composition capabilities. Science teachers will want to promote students' curiosity. Health education teachers will wish to foster students' accurate perceptions of their vulnerability to health risks such as sexually transmitted diseases. Depending on a particular teacher's instructional responsibilities, most teachers will discover that there are usually several attitudinal assessment contenders that they'll want to consider.

Possible Value Targets

There are all sorts of values to which people subscribe that the schools should have nothing to do with. Most educators agree that political values and religious values, for example, should not be dealt with instructionally in the schools. Whether students turn out to be liberals or conservatives is really none of a teacher's business. And, historically, there's been a long tradition of separating church and state. Teachers, therefore, certainly shouldn't be advocating the acceptance of particular religions or the rejection of others. Well, then, what sorts of values are sufficiently *meritorious and noncontroversial* so that they could serve as the targets for classroom attention? Here are a few to consider:

- *Honesty.* Students should learn to value honesty in their dealing with others.
- *Integrity.* Students should firmly adhere to their own code of values, for example, moral or artistic values.
- *Justice.* Students should subscribe to the view that all citizens should be the recipients of equal justice from governmental law-enforcement agencies.
- *Freedom.* Students should believe that democratic nations must provide the maximum level of permissible freedom to its citizens.

Although these kinds of values may seem to be little more than lofty, flag-waving endorsements of goodness, teachers may still wish to consider them and similar values for potential effective assessment in their classrooms. If there really are significant values that teachers would like students to embrace, and those values fall properly in the sphere of what schools should be about, then the possibility of including such values in a classroom assessment program may have real appeal.

How to Assess Affect

The assessment of affect can be carried out at varying levels of complexity and sophistication. To illustrate, in psychological experiments designed to get a fix on children's honesty, researchers have utilized trained accomplices who create elaborate situations where a child can or cannot cheat, then the researchers observe the child's behavior through one-way mirrors in order to draw inferences about the child's tendencies to be honest or dishonest in situations where the attractiveness of the temptations vary.

I know few teachers who have the time or inclination to engage in very elaborate assessment of their students' affective status, although I suspect that those teachers would know how to use one-way mirrors advantageously.

Some teachers believe that they can get an accurate reading of students' affect by attending to certain physical evidence that students provide. For example, if students have been encouraged to adopt attitudes focused on "keeping our classroom tidy," the teacher might simply study the amount of wastepaper that, because it wasn't deposited in wastebaskets, is left on the floor each night.

But it is often difficult to come up with valid interpretations about students' affect based on physical evidence that children provide. Remember, just like all students' knowledge and skills, affect is unseen. For instance, if certain children provide daily apples for the teacher, especially before grading time, does this really mean that those students get truly turned on by school?

As a practical matter, the classroom assessment of student affect must be relatively easy to pull off, or it simply isn't going to happen. Teachers are too busy carrying out the galaxy of responsibilities that they face each day to take on many additional tasks. Accordingly, in this chapter I'm going to set out only a simple, easily accomplishable procedure to assess students' attitudes and values.

Self-Report Assessment

A teacher can get a decent fix on students' affective status by asking them to complete self-report assessment devices. If teachers set up the assessment situation so that students can respond in a truly anonymous fashion, the data derived from self-report instruments can really be useful. Just as importantly, the use of straightforward self-report devices won't be so aversive that teachers become disenchanted with such measurement.

Because of its applicability to a variety of affective assessment targets, the approach to attitudinal measurement introduced in the early 1930s by Likert is the most widely used. Likert inventories will handle almost all of a teacher's affective assessment requirements. It is, by all odds, the most serviceable affective measurement strategy teachers will encounter. (Some educators pronounce the name of these inventories as "Lick-ert." Some pronounce them as "Like-ert." As a parent, and supposedly not a specialist in measurement, you should probably adopt the teacher's pronunciation preference. Or, if you wish to drive your child's teacher wild, you could change your pronunciation every other time.)

Testing Terms:

Self-Report Inventories

Assessment instruments, typically measuring students' affect or behavior, to which students supply answers reflecting their preferred responses

You've probably responded to Likert inventories many times in your own life. They consist of a series of statements to which you register your agreement or disagreement. For example, you are given a statement such as "Reading this book about school testing represents one of the finest educational experiences of my life." You then choose from a set of options to decide whether you agree or disagree with the statement. The usual options, at least for adults, are *strongly agree, agree, uncertain, disagree,* and *strongly disagree.* (I am altogether confident that you would have opted for the *strongly agree* response regarding the previous illustrative statement about this book's educational impact.)

Clearly, depending on the age of the students, teachers need to make adjustments in the statements used and in the number and/or phrasing of the response options. With very young children, for example, teachers might need to use brief statements containing simple words. Teachers might even have to read the statements aloud. Older students might be able to handle the five-choice agreement scale just described, but for younger students a teacher will most likely want to drop down to three response options (for instance, *agree, don't know,* and *disagree*) or even two response options (perhaps *yes* or *no*). Teachers are usually good judges of the language level that should be used with their students. In general, teachers should err in the direction of less-demanding rather than more-demanding language.

If teachers want to use at least some affective assessment in their classrooms, and want to use Likert inventories in that effort, they'll find that such assessment instruments are really quite simple to build. As an appendix to this chapter, I've included a simple eight-step model that teachers can follow if they wish to whip up a Likert inventory. If you wish to,

you could copy the appendix and give it to your child's teacher. If you're interested in the details of how to build a Likert inventory, feel free to look over those eight steps. (After all, this is *your* book.)

I'm not trying to suggest that Likert-type inventories are the only way of getting an estimate of students' affect. There are other fairly straightforward self-report assessment schemes that teachers may want to consider. For example, if a fifth-grade teacher were interested in improving her students' attitudes toward mathematics, the teacher might simply give students a list of a number of subjects, one of which was mathematics, then ask students to rank-order the subjects on the basis of which subject they most preferred to study. What the teacher would hope for, of course, is a pre-instruction to postinstruction shift showing that students rank-ordered mathematics more positively after instruction. This rank-the-subject approach, of course, is also a self-report affective measurement strategy.

Importance of Anonymity

In order for teachers to draw accurate inferences about their students' affective state based on their responses to self-report inventories, it is clearly necessary for students to *respond truthfully* to the affective inventories. Unfortunately, many students tend to provide what are referred to as *socially desirable* responses to affective self-report devices. In other words, many students are inclined to respond in the way that they think the teacher wants them to respond. Students are particularly apt to provide socially desirable responses if they believe there's any way the teacher can trace their responses back to them. Consequently, to increase the likelihood that students will respond honestly to affective inventories, it is imperative that teachers not only make all students' responses anonymous, but that a teacher also employ as many procedures as possible so that most students regard their responses as truly untraceable.

Among the more simple but effective anonymity-promotion procedures teachers might want to consider are these:

1. *Directions.* Teachers should make sure the directions for affective inventories stress the importance of honest answers and that students are not to put their names on the inventories.

2. *Response restrictions.* The inventories should be set up so that the *only* form of student response is to be check marks, circling of preferred answers, and so on. Students should be prohibited from writing any words whatsoever on their inventories. Because students believe that the teacher may figure out who completed which inventory by recognizing students' handwriting, teachers must not permit any handwriting whatsoever on affective inventories.

3. *Collection.* Teachers should install a procedure so that students personally deposit their completed inventories in a collection box, or have a student (not one thought to be a teacher's "pet") collect the completed inventories. The teacher should announce *before* students start to fill out the inventories that one of these collection methods will be employed.

As a parent, you can see that teachers must try to make sure their students really don't think there's any way to trace their responses back to them. Even under those circumstances, this doesn't ensure that students will respond truthfully. However, well-conceived anonymity-promotion techniques definitely increase the odds that students will respond honestly.

When to Assess Affect

When should classroom teachers assess their students' affective status? Well, for openers, it seems important that teachers set up at least a pre-instruction and a postinstruction measure of students' attitudes and/or values. Thus, for elementary teachers teaching students in self-contained classrooms, an affective assessment at the start of the school year and,

again, at its close will allow teachers to detect any meaningful changes in students' affect.

Ideally teachers can also engage in occasional "affective dip-sticking" to monitor students' affect. For example, every couple of months, a teacher might measure students' self-esteem as learners as well as their attitudes regarding learning. If these occasional assessments suggest that inappropriate affective changes are occurring, the teacher may wish to modify affect-related aspects of the instructional program. For teachers at the secondary level, a pre-instruction and postinstruction assessment of affect would be required at the beginning and end of each semester or term.

What Sorts of Interpretations Are Possible with Affective Assessment Instruments?

Group-Based Interpretations

When teachers use cognitively oriented tests, they typically make interpretations about individual students based on how well the student performs. If, for instance, Harvey Haley earns a high score on a mathematics test, the teacher makes an inference about Harvey's solid possession of the mathematics knowledge and skills that were assessed. Teachers need to make inferences about individual students in order to make decisions about how to provide suitable instruction for those students.

Teachers also sum together students' individual scores on achievement tests to arrive at group-focused interpretations. For instance, if most students in a history class performed poorly on a start-of-the-term achievement pretest, yet most students earned high scores on a comparable posttest administered near the term's conclusion, the teacher would conclude that the students, as a group, had learned substantially more about history.

Testing Terms:

Group-Focused Inferences

Interpretations about the average status of a group of students

It's different with the measurement affect. Whereas cognitive tests are measures of students' *optimum performance*, affective inventories strive to measure students' *typical performance*. Remember that when students complete affective devices, those results don't count toward students' grades. In addition, self-report assessment offers students a wonderful opportunity to distort their responses, so there's a strong likelihood that at least some students won't respond honestly. As a consequence, interpretations about the affective status of *individual* students (based on a student's responses to an affective inventory) are likely to be invalid.

Besides, instructional decisions about individual students based on affective assessment devices are fairly rare. If a student knows history well, but happens to hate it, few teachers would give the student a low grade in history based on the student's dislike for "ancient folks' activities."

In contrast, however, teachers often make instructional decisions about what goes on in class based on summed-together affective data. Assuming that there will be a small number of students who supply inaccurate responses, it is still reasonable to believe that the total *collection* of students' responses will permit meaningful *group-focused interpretations*. And that's the kind of interpretations teachers should be making when they use affective assessment instruments. These assessment devices are simply too crude to yield accurate individual-focused interpretations. As a group, however, students' affective responses can enable teachers to make some very solid judgments about how students, as a collective group, are affectively disposed. That is why teachers can, in some cases, collect affective data from only half a class, yet arrive at reasonably accurate interpretations about the whole group's affective status.

Affective Interpretations about Your Child

Here's how all this boils down as far as you are concerned regarding your child's attitudes, values, and interests. If you believe, as I hope you do, that

A Parent Puzzle

(Setting: Chris is a high school sophomore enrolled in a chemistry class with Mr. Green who has been teaching high school chemistry for nearly twenty-five years. Mr. Green has been trying something new in class this year. He's been collecting monthly affective inventories from students about how much they like certain aspects of the chemistry content they encounter.

Mr. Green sends students off each month, on a Friday, with an affective inventory and a responsibility to think about their "Chemistry Attitudes." Students are to return the completed inventories on the following Monday. Chris's mother, Mrs. Smith, looked over one of these affective inventories and decided to talk with the school's principal, Ms. Hollins. At an after-school session, here's what was said.)

Ms. Hollins: "I'm pleased you could stop by, Mrs. Smith. How can I help you?"

Mrs. Smith: "Well, Ms. Hollins, I'm a bit concerned about the attitude surveys that Chris has been receiving in Mr. Green's chemistry class. Are you familiar with them?"

Ms. Hollins: "Actually, I'm not. I know that some of our teachers use attitude inventories, but I haven't seen the particular ones Mr. Green uses. If I'm not mistaken, this is the first year he's used such inventories."

Mrs. Smith: "Well, here's a copy I had made of an inventory that Chris brought home last weekend. It's the third one that Chris has had to complete this term. And, frankly, I'm not sure these inventories are educationally sound."

Ms. Hollins: "Why is that?"

Mrs. Smith: "For one thing, the inventories are not anonymous. Notice that Mr. Green wants students to actually supply their names. I really don't think most students will be honest if Mr. Green can tell which students said what. Besides that, Mr. Green is using students' responses, in part, to determine students' grades. The better the student's attitudes, the higher the grades. It's obvious to me that many students will simply respond with attitudes about chemistry that they think Mr. Green will want."

Ms. Hollins: "These are serious concerns that you have, Mrs. Smith, and I'm going to look into it immediately. At this school we do consider students' attitudes important, but we don't want to measure them in a way that is either misleading or coercive. I'll set up a meeting with Mr. Green tomorrow to explore this issue, and I'll not say that you, in paticular, were the cause of my concern."

Parent: If you were Mrs. Smith, how would you respond?

- -

My Response: Ms. Hollins seems to sense the impropriety of Mr. Green's affective assessment and appears willing to get right on it. I'd say something like, "I appreciate your willingness to look into the problem. I'll look forward to hearing how it's resolved. Is there any chance you could let me know, by telephone or in person, what happens?"

My Reason: Given Ms. Hollins' immediate recognition of the problem and her plan to institute a speedy inquiry, I would be delighted with the situation. I'd applaud her effort and be obviously appreciative. There's no need to push the point. Ms. Hollins gets it.

your child's affective dispositions are very important, then it's only natural that you'd like to know something about your child's important attitudes, values, and interests.

Unfortunately, there are no assessment instruments on hand that will provide you with that kind of information about your child. Because assessors of children's unseen affective dispositions are forced to rely on *self-reports,* and because most human beings tend to shade self-reports in their own best interests, a self-report strategy for assessing an *individual* child's affect just doesn't work.

Indeed, as was stressed earlier in the chapter, unless affective instruments are given to students *anonymously,* there's little likelihood a teacher could have any confidence in the interpretations the teacher is trying to make even for *groups* of students. However, the use of genuine anonymity, of course, eliminates any opportunity teachers have to get a fix on an individual child's affective status. Remember, if the child's responses are not anonymous, there's little reason to believe those responses accurately reflect the child's affect.

Testing Terms:

Individual-Focused Inferences

Interpretations about the status of a particular child

You'll simply have to observe your child's behavior in settings where the child is free to do anything the child wants to do, then make your best observation-based interpretations about the child's affect. For example, if your child really does pick up a book to read instead of watching TV, then that's powerful evidence that your child grooves on reading. (Unfortunately, it could also be a function of really lousy programs on television.) And that, of course, is why it is so devilishly difficult to arrive at sound inferences about children's affect. We simply don't know what's going on inside those adorable little heads.

Does the school's inability to provide you with ironclad affective interpretations about your child mean that you should discourage your child's teacher from measuring affect for all the teacher's students? I hope not. If you regard children's affective status as important, then if your child's teacher both assesses and promotes worthwhile kinds of affective outcomes, odds are that your child will benefit from such an assessment/instruction intervention.

To illustrate, suppose you wish your child to really be interested in science and to want to learn about scientific things. Then it is decisively in your child's best interest if the child's teacher routinely collects affective information about all students' interest in science. As you saw earlier in the chapter, affective assessment (1) *stimulates affectively oriented instruction,* that is, the things the teacher could do to make all students interested in science, and (2) *monitors students' affective status* so that, if interest in science is waning, the teacher can un-wane that interest. Your own kids' interest in science is likely to be increased because of the teacher's assessment of all students' interest in science.

What Do You Really Need to Know about This Chapter's Content?

It is unlikely that your child will ever take part in much affective assessment, especially in the classroom. Nevertheless, there are a number of important points about affect that you really should keep in mind.

- Many educators (and your friendly, unassuming author) believe that students' affective status, that is, their attitudes, interests, and values, are remarkably important. This belief is based on the power of affective attributes to influence one's future behavior.

- Affective assessment in the classroom can stimulate affectively oriented instruction and can help teachers monitor students' affective status so that appropriate affectively focused instructional decisions can be made.

- Because many parents are, quite properly, reluctant to have teachers meddle in attitudes or values that should be the province of the family, any affective outcomes pursued in school should be universally (or almost universally) approved by citizens. The "almost universally approved" option allows the views of a few cranks to be discounted.

- The most reasonable approach to the assessment of affect in schools is through the use of student-completed, self-report affective inventories.

- It is imperative that, for any affective self-report instruments, all student responses be anonymous, and that students believe their responses are untraceable to them.

- Although it is appropriate to make valid group-focused interpretations about the affect of a collection of students, it is not appropriate to make valid inferences about an individual student's affective status.

POSSIBLE PARENT ACTION–OPTIONS

Here are several things you might do with respect to the assessment of affect in your child's classroom. Obviously, whether you take any action will depend on how much importance you place on a teacher's promotion of affective objectives.

1. The most obvious action–option for you to consider stems from whether or not your child's teacher is assessing children's affective

status. If not, then it is possible to have an exploratory discussion between you and the teacher about the appropriateness of the teacher's engaging in such assessment, and, by implication, affectively focused instruction.

2. If there is some affective assessment going on in your child's class, then it would be useful for you to make certain that sufficient anonymity-enhancement procedures are in place. You'd be surprised, and saddened, to learn that tons of teachers ask students to sign their names on inventories getting at such affective attributes as students' attitudes toward school, interest in certain subjects, and even attitudes toward the teacher. Even more teachers encourage students to write comments on their "anonymous" affective inventories, thus blowing anonymity altogether.

3. You might encourage your child's teacher or principal to do a bit of honing up regarding affective assessment. The *Suggested Resources* contains several useful items that educators might find illuminating.

SUGGESTED RESOURCES FOR YOUR CHILD'S TEACHER OR PRINCIPAL

Printed Materials

Anderson, Lorin W. *Assessing Affective Characteristics in the Schools.* Boston: Allyn and Bacon, 1981. *In this classic volume, educators learn how to measure students' attitudes, interests, and values. The author recommends heavy reliance on Likert self-report measures.*

McMillan, James H. *Classroom Assessment: Principles and Practice for Effective Instruction.* Boston: Allyn and Bacon, 1997. *"Assessing Affective Traits and Learning Targets" is the title of Chapter 10 in this volume. The author describes the strengths and weaknesses of four methods to assess students' affect, namely, observation, constructed-response self-report, selected-response self-report, and peer ratings.*

Stiggins, Richard J. *Student-Centered Classroom Assessment* (2nd ed.). Upper Saddle River, NJ: Prentice-Hall, 1997. *In Chapter 12, "Assessing Student Dispositions," Stiggins shows teachers how to consider varied approaches to the assessment of affect, then how to match method to target.*

Webb, Eugene J., Donald T. Campbell, Richard D. Schwartz, Lee Sechreat, and Janet Belew Grove. *Nonreactive Measure in the Social Sciences* (2nd ed.). Boston: Houghton Mifflin, 1981. *Here's another classic assessment book for educators who are inclined to think inventively about the assessment of students' affect. A galaxy of ingenious assessment techniques is described.*

Videotape Programs

IOX Assessment Associates. *Assessing Student Attitudes: A Key to Increasing Achievement.* (5301 Beethoven St., Ste. 190, Los Angeles, CA 90066). *From this video, educators learn how to assess student affect and why such assessment is important. Illustrative student attitude inventories are provided.*

IOX Assessment Associates. *Improving Instruction: Start with Student Attitudes.* (5301 Beethoven St., Ste. 190, Los Angeles, CA 90066). *Because many teachers, during their teacher-training experiences, were not taught how to promote affective objectives for students, this video describes four instructional tactics for doing so.*

AN APPENDIX FOR YOUR CHILD'S TEACHER

Building a Likert Inventory

Presented here, you'll find eight steps teachers can carry out to create Likert inventories for assessing students' affect:

1. *Choose the affective attribute to be assessed.* Teachers should decide what attitude or value they want to assess, then try to be as clearheaded as possible about what the affective attribute really means.

2. *Generate a series of favorable and unfavorable statements regarding the affective attribute.* For example, if a teacher were interested in students' attitudes regarding reading, the teacher might construct a positive statement such as "I like to read on my own when I have free time" or a negative statement such as "People who read for fun are stupid." A teacher should try to generate a few more statements than the teacher ultimately plans to use. For students in secondary schools, a ten-item Likert inventory takes little time to complete. For students at lower grades, teachers will probably want to use fewer items, perhaps five or six. Teachers should attempt to construct an approximately equal number of positive and negative statements.

3. *Get several people to classify each statement as positive or negative.* Teachers should snare a few colleagues or family members to look at the generated statements and classify each statement as positive or negative. A teacher should toss out any statement that isn't unanimously classified as positive or negative.

4. *Decide on the number and phrasing of the response options for each statement.* The original Likert inventory had the following five options: SD = Strongly Disagree, D = Disagree, NS = Not Sure, A = Agree, and SA = Strongly Agree. Likert inventories for younger children should employ fewer and, possibly, simpler options.

5. *Prepare the self-report inventory, giving students directions regarding how to respond and stipulating that the inventory must be completed anonymously.* If students haven't previously completed such inventories, they'll need good, clear directions. It is helpful to include an illustration or two of how students might respond. Sample statements about generally known topics, such as foods or movies, work well for such illustrations.

6. *Administer the inventory either to the teacher's own students or, if possible (as a tryout), to other students.* If a colleague is willing, the teacher should try out the inventory with students similar to the ones in the teacher's class. Based on the responses of those other students, the teacher can then improve the inventory before giving it to the teacher's own students. If teachers must use their own students, they can still improve the inventory for use later in the year with the same students or, perhaps, next year with another set of students.

7. *Score the inventories.* Teachers should assign points for each student's response to every item based on the *direction* of the statement. For instance, if the inventory used five response options, the teacher would give five points to *strongly agree* responses to positive statements and also five points to *strongly disagree* responses to negative statements. Thus, for a ten-item inventory the scores could range from ten to fifty. Generally speaking, the higher the score, the more appropriate students' affective status appears to be.

8. *Identify and eliminate statements that fail to function in accord with other statements.* If the teacher knows how to compute correlation coefficients, simply compute the correlation between students' responses to each item (1, 2, 3, 4, or 5, for example) and their total scores on the inventory (10 to 50). Teachers should eliminate those statements whose correlations to the total score are not statistically significant. (This is referred to as "Likert's criterion of internal consistency.")

If teachers don't know how to compute correlation coefficients, they should simply "eyeball" students' responses and try to identify statements to which students are responding differently than to the rest of the statements. Those statements should be dumped. (This is referred to as "Likert's criterion of internal consistency for teachers who don't know squat about computing correlations.") Then the teacher should rescore the inventories without the rejected items.

It's really just that simple to bang out a Likert inventory for the teacher's own assessment purposes. For each affective attribute of interest, the teacher will need a different inventory (or at least a different set of items). A teacher can certainly measure several affective attributes with different sets of items on the same inventory. The more experience a teacher accumulates in creating Likert inventories, the easier it gets. After a short while, most teachers really become quite skilled in whipping out such affective assessment devices.

If a teacher is really under time pressure, and few teachers aren't, the teacher can even skip some of the eight steps just listed. For instance, teachers don't really need to get other people to classify statements as positive or negative (Step 3) if they don't have the time to do so. And although teachers might like to have a formal tryout of the inventory (Step 6), the teacher may not have time to do it. What is being suggested is that if teachers are faced with a choice between (a) skipping some desirable procedural steps and *using* an affective inventory or (b) *not using* an affective inventory because the teachers don't have time to carry out all the recommended procedural steps, teachers should do some step-skipping!

11

THE PRESSURE TO IMPROVE TEST SCORES— AND ITS CONSEQUENCES

*T*oday's teachers are under enormous pressure to raise students' test scores. As you've read earlier in this book, the public demand for improved test scores stems most directly from an "accountability movement" in which educators are held responsible for boosting children's *measured* achievement.

Design for Deception?

Teachers, unfortunately, are being required to play an accountability game that, *if they play by the rules,* they will most certainly lose. That's like forcing someone to play *Monopoly,* but never allowing them to pass GO (and, therefore, pick up those $200 dividends for doing so). Educational policies should be set up to benefit children, not to intimidate teachers.

The reason teachers are trapped in a no-win game is that, with few exceptions, teachers are being asked to improve students' scores on *standardized achievement tests.* As you've already learned in Chapter 3, standardized achievement tests were created for a different assessment mission, namely, comparing an individual student's test performance with the test performances of other students in the test's norm group.

Students' scores on standardized achievement tests do *not* provide an accurate reflection of how well an educator has taught. There are too many items in standardized achievement tests that primarily assess a student's socioeconomic status or inherited academic capabilities. There are too few items on standardized achievement tests that really measure what teachers ought to be teaching.

But many citizens, and especially educational policymakers, believe standardized achievement tests constitute a suitable measuring-stick by which to judge educational quality. As a consequence, most educators are experiencing immense pressure to "get those test scores up!" And until there is a greater understanding of the limitations of standardized achievement tests as indicators of educational quality, we can safely predict continued pressure on educators to have their students earn high scores on these sorts of tests.

Teacher Trap

It is important for you, a parent, to understand just what kinds of stress teachers experience to elevate a school's or district's test scores. You should try to "get inside the teacher's head" on this issue so you'll be better able to understand why it is some teachers may engage in test-preparation activities that might, indeed, boost test scores, but might, as a consequence, do educational harm to your child.

Because so many people are clamoring for high standardized test scores these days, that kind of clamor readily finds its way into the teacher's perception. When a school district's standardized achievement test scores hit the local newspapers, usually in late spring or mid-summer, members of the district's school board invariably see how their district's kids stack up against kids elsewhere.

If the district seems to be doing wonderfully, based on these comparisons, then there's usually a fair amount of crowing, but little more action. If the district does not fare too well based on national or state comparisons, then it's likely that the local school board will inform the district superintendent that "our test scores must rise."

Superintendents, typically possessing the gift of delegation, quickly notify all principals of their district's schools that higher test scores are expected. And principals, most of whom are still honing their delegative skills, quickly let their school's teachers know that "Scores should soar!" The message to the teacher is eminently clear: "Get your students' scores up!"

So far, nothing seems out of whack. Educational policymakers, believing that children's scores on standardized achievement tests reflect what children have learned, demand higher test scores. So, from top administrator to classroom teacher, the word gets out to "boost those test scores." But it is at that precise point, when teachers get ready to engage in a bit of score-boosting, that this test-based accountability system falls flat on its backside.

Tests as Representatives.   If you'll recall Chapter 2's short course in the basics of educational measurement, you'll remember that an educational test *represents* a body of knowledge and/or skills that we'd like students to possess. The test *samples* from the domain of knowledge and/or skills it represents. Then, when students complete that test, educators make an interpretation of the student's mastery of the body of knowledge and/or skills *represented* by the test.

If a teacher were to directly teach children the correct answers to the items on a standardized achievement test, *and only those correct answers,* do you think a student's test score would permit a valid interpretation regarding that student's mastery of the knowledge and/or skills *represented* by the test? Of course not.

Teaching toward Taffy.   So, if a teacher wants to play the *instructional* game with integrity, the teacher's instruction should be directed not toward a specific set of test items but, instead, toward the knowledge and/or skills that the test items represent. This is illustrated in Figure 11.1 where you can see that, in order to permit valid test-based interpretations about children's mastery levels, instruction ought to be aimed at the knowledge and/or skills represented by a test, not aimed at the test itself.

So, a well-intentioned teacher will typically consult one or more of the descriptive booklets for teachers that always accompany standardized achievement tests. These booklets are supposed to spell out for teachers

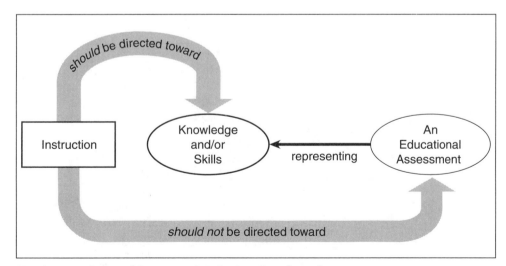

11.1 Appropriate and inappropriate instructional emphases

what (1) the bodies of knowledge are that are being assessed or (2) what the cognitive skills are that are being assessed. If the descriptions of the to-be-assessed skills and knowledge are sufficiently clear so that teachers could design effective instruction aimed at the measured skills and knowledge, all would be terrific.

But the descriptions provided for the teacher are *not* adequate for purposes of instructional planning. The descriptions of what's supposedly being tested are far too general and much too fragmentary for the teacher to really design and deliver effective, well-targeted instruction.

I doubt if you've ever looked at the kinds of booklets I'm talking about, that is, the booklets for teachers accompanying standardized achievement tests. They're usually called "Teacher's Guides," "Content Descriptions," or something similar. The purpose of these booklets is to supply guidance to teachers regarding how they can organize their instruction. And, if you were to look at any of these guides quickly, you'd probably conclude that the descriptions were adequate for purposes of teachers' instructional planning. You'd be wrong.

If you were a classroom teacher, and you really wanted to aim your instruction at the skills and knowledge, represented in the test, and not at particular test items, you'd find the level of clarity provided by a standardized achievement test's descriptive materials altogether inadequate.

As an example, several years ago I was teaching a UCLA course to experienced teachers about testing. The class of about twenty-five students

had just examined the curriculum guide for one of the nation's most popular standardized achievement tests. I had asked the students if, based on the curriculum guide's descriptions of what instructional objectives the test was supposed to measure, they could match the test's items to the guide's instructional objectives. Being fairly cocky, as graduate students often are, they responded, "You bet we can!"

Well, I gave them ninety minutes to match seventy-five items from that standardized test with the instructional objectives (from the curriculum guide) the teachers thought were being measured. After the teachers finished, I distributed copies of the test's technical manual that, according to the test's publishers, indicated which test items were supposed to measure which instructional objectives. Not one of the experienced teachers in my class scored better than 50 percent correct. Some of those teachers misclassified more than sixty of the seventy-five items.

What was going on was quite simple. The adequacy of the content-description booklets accompanying standardized achievement tests is altogether inadequate for purposes of a teacher's day-to-day instructional planning. A teacher who really wants to teach toward the knowledge and skills measured by a test is up against it. Those skills and bodies of knowledge are not sufficiently well staked out.

And the reason that the content-description guidebooks accompanying standardized achievement tests do not crisply spell out what's being measured is really quite straightforward. The *specific* knowledge and/or skills being measured are not systematically measured with enough items (that is, enough items per skill or enough items per body of knowledge) to permit clear descriptions. Rather, standardized achievement tests, because they must be limited in length, include only a smattering of items dealing with different skills or bodies of knowledge—too few items to permit descriptions suitable for teachers' instructional planning. So, it's not that the distributors of standardized achievement tests don't describe what's being measured because they don't want to, they don't provide such descriptions *because they can't!*

And what, then, does a teacher do who is under such pressure to boost children's test scores? You guessed it. They often end up *teaching to the test's items.* And that approach, though altogether understandable, can instructionally shortchange students. It should not be permitted.

Parent Patrol

There's so much pressure these days to see students' test scores rise, that parents have to be vigilant regarding the kinds of test-preparation activities taking place in their child's classroom. Certain kinds of test-preparation are appropriate. Certain kinds are inappropriate. Certain kinds are borderline. As a parent, you have to know which is which.

If you do find that there is inappropriate test preparation taking place in your child's school, or in your child's classroom, then you need to bring this to the attention of the school's principal. In the remainder of this chapter you'll learn about two test-preparation guidelines that, if followed by teachers, will lead to the sort of appropriate test-preparation efforts that should be going on in school.

Test-Preparation Practices

If your child's teacher is behaving in accord with the two guidelines I'm about to describe, you can be reasonably sure that inappropriate ("boost the scores at all costs") test preparation is not taking place.

Professional Ethics

The first test-preparation guideline that teachers should adhere to deals with *professional ethics.*

Test-Preparation Guideline No. 1: Professional Ethics

No test-preparation practice should violate the ethical norms of the education profession.

This first guideline obliges teachers to avoid any test-preparation practice that is unethical. Ethical behaviors, of course, are rooted not only in fundamental morality, but also in the nature of a particular profession. For example, physicians should be governed not only by general ethical principles dealing with honesty and respect for other people's property, but also by ethical principles that have evolved specifically for the medical profession. Similarly, teachers should not engage in test-preparation practices that involve violations of general ethical canons dealing with theft, cheating, lying, and so on. In addition, however, teachers must take seriously the ethical obligations that they undertake because they have agreed to serve *in loco parentis.* Teachers who serve "in place of the parent" take on an ethical responsibility to serve as models of ethical behaviors for children.

I can recall visiting a high school driver-education class several years ago. The teacher was getting students ready to take their written driver's exam on the coming weekend at the local Department of Motor Vehicles (DMV). The class I was observing took place on a Friday afternoon. A few minutes before the class was over, the driver-education teacher distributed a copy of a written driver's exam form to the class and said, "As you know, at the DMV they have a half-dozen different forms of the written test. I've found out that this is the form they'll be using on Saturday. If you look up the answers in your DMV booklets, and make sure you remember them, I think you'll do well on Saturday!"

I had to agree that students who have access to a test in advance of the test's administration are somewhat more likely to do "well" than students who don't know what items are coming at them. The teacher's message to students was accurate. But the teacher was sending another message to students—a message just as powerful, namely, "Students, I think it's okay if you cheat on tests." The teacher I observed that Friday afternoon was clearly violating Test-Preparation Guideline No. 1.

When teachers engage in any kind of test-preparation practices that, if brought to the public's attention, would discredit the education profession, such practices should be considered professionally unethical. This is because, in the long term, such practices erode public confidence in our schools and, as a result, diminish financial support for those schools. Consequently, this erosion of public support renders the education profession less potent.

Thus, according to the professional ethics guideline, teachers should not engage in test-preparation practices that involve such behaviors as violating state-imposed security procedures regarding high-stakes tests. A growing number of states have enacted regulations so that teachers who breach the state test-security procedures can have their teaching credentials revoked.

Teachers should not engage in test-preparation practices that are unethical merely because there are potential personal repercussions (for example, loss of credentials) or professional repercussions (for example, reduced citizen confidence in public schooling). Most importantly, teachers should avoid unethical test-preparation practices because such practices are *wrong*.

Educational Defensibility

The second test-preparation guideline deals with *educational defensibility*. But before dealing specifically with this guideline, I need to clarify the way that a test functions as a representation of a student's level of knowledge or skill mastery.

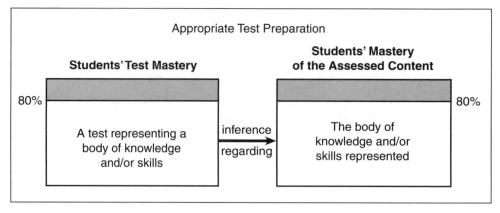

11.2 How a test permits inferences regarding student mastery of the content represented by the test

An educational achievement test is employed in order for educators to make a valid interpretation about a student's status with respect to the knowledge and/or skills it represents. Ideally, of course, an achievement test will sample such knowledge and/or skills representatively so that the level of a student's performance on the achievement test will serve as a reasonably accurate reflection of the student's status with respect to the knowledge and/or skills assessed. The nature of this relationship is illustrated in Figure 11.2 where it is indicated that a student who answered correctly 80 percent of the items in an achievement test (on the left) would be expected to have mastered about 80 percent of the knowledge and/or skills that the test was measuring (on the right). The relationship between a student's test performance and that student's mastery of the content represented by the achievement test, as will be seen later, is a key factor in the second test-preparation guideline.

With that relationship in mind, let's look at the second of the two test-preparation guidelines.

Test-Preparation Guideline No. 2: Educational Defensibility

No test-preparation practice should increase students' test scores without simultaneously increasing students' mastery of the content represented by the test.

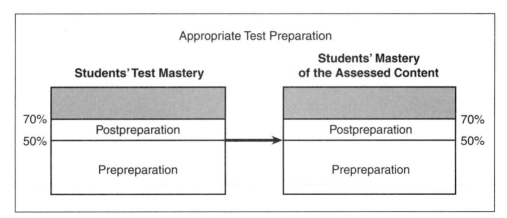

11.3 Appropriate test preparation based on the guideline of educational defensibility

This second guideline emphasizes the importance of engaging in instructional practices that are in the educational best interests of students. Teachers should not, for example, artificially increase students' scores on a test while neglecting to increase students' mastery of the knowledge and/or skills being tested. This situation, that is, *appropriate* test preparation, is illustrated in Figure 11.3 where you can see that a 20 percent prepreparation-to-postpreparation jump in students' mastery was present both on the test and on the content it represents.

Conversely, an *inappropriate* test-preparation practice raises students' prepreparation-to-postpreparation performance on the test, but not students' mastery of the content being assessed. This situation, that is, inappropriate test preparation, is illustrated in Figure 11.4 where students' test performances increase, but their content mastery doesn't.

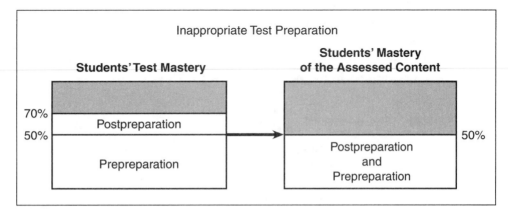

11.4 Inappropriate test preparation based on the guideline of educational defensibility

The result of such inappropriate test-preparation practices is that a deceptive picture of students' achievement is created. The test results no longer serve as an accurate indicator of students' status with respect to the knowledge and skill being assessed. As a consequence, students who in reality have not mastered a body of content may fail to receive appropriate instruction regarding such content. The students will have been instructionally overlooked because inappropriate test-preparation practices led to an inflated estimate of their content mastery. Such test-preparation practices, because they often rob students of needed instruction, are educationally indefensible.

So if your child's teacher adheres to both of these powerful test-preparation guidelines, you can be reasonably confident that appropriate instruction is taking place. Let's see, however, the ways in which students' test-scoring can be raised.

How Test Scores Get Raised

There are a number of ways that standardized achievement test scores can be raised. Few, if any, are appropriate. Most of these score-boosting procedures violate one or both of the two guidelines just described.

Suppose at your child's school there has been a dramatic increase in children's standardized achievement test scores from one year to the next. How could that happen? Well, here are a few possibilities:

General Test-Taking Preparation

In some schools, children are given formal instruction about how to take tests most effectively. Teachers describe how students should allocate their test-taking time. Students are also made aware that certain standardized tests employ "correction-for-guessing" scoring procedures that penalize students who make wild guesses for many items. Such correction-per-guessing scoring schemes simply subtract a proportion of the students' wrong answers from the number of correct answers a student gets. So, depending on the test, it may or may not make sense for students to guess about an answer when they are not sure.

Test-taking preparation also addresses the differences between the way students should respond to selected-response items versus constructed-response items. Because, in most standardized achievement tests, the bulk of a test's items continue to be of the multiple-choice variety, students are typically given help in narrowing the options, that is, eliminating clearly incorrect distractors from the response options.

Students can also be familiarized with the different ways that test items might be formatted. In that way, students will not be perplexed by an unanticipated form of test item.

These sorts of general test-taking preparation sessions, *if they are not too time-consuming,* are quite appropriate. To devote several hours to readying students for different kinds of standardized achievement tests makes sense. If students are familiarized in a general way with what they might encounter in an upcoming test, then there will be fewer "surprises" at testing time. As a result, students' test performances should yield more valid interpretations about students' actual levels of achievement.

But care should be taken that these sessions not be more than a few hours in duration. I've encountered test-taking preparation sessions that literally went on for a full month! Such "get-them-ready" activities typically take away instructional time from other important things that children ought to be learning.

Finally, although brief test-preparation sessions of the type just described are sensible, they will rarely raise scores dramatically. A number of students are likely to improve their performances somewhat, but not gigantically.

So, returning to our fictitious example, if the test scores in your child's school took a sizable jump, it's unlikely that such a jump could be accounted for solely by short-duration, general test-taking preparation activities.

Increased Teacher Attention to Tested Content

In almost all educational settings, standardized achievement tests are administered by classroom teachers. Because standardized achievement tests are typically reused for a number of years in the same school district, teachers naturally become familiar with the content of many items on the test. Indeed, some publishers of standardized tests require teachers to go through the test's items themselves, so teachers can better help students who might become confused during the test's administration.

Thus, teachers become familiar with the content of test items that, in subsequent years, are supposed to reflect improvements in students' scores. Is it surprising that sometime during the next school year—prior to next year's students' taking the test—such content finds its way into the teacher's instructional activities?

Let's give most teachers the benefit of the doubt regarding motives. Suppose there's an item on a fifth-grade science test regarding the origins of steam engines. Now, if a fifth-grade teacher notes the "steam-engine item" one year, then during the next year the teacher might give some time in class to a steam-engine's origins. The teacher may do so not because the teacher was trying to coach children to answer the test item correctly, but merely because the teacher concluded that, "because there's an item in a *national* test about the origins of steam engines, then that content must be important, and I should probably already have been teaching it."

In other words, the teacher's estimate of certain content's importance has been influenced because that content appears on a nationally standardized achievement test. As a consequence, the teacher stresses that content in future years. That's both understandable, and should not *necessarily* be regarded as improper test-preparation on the part of teachers. But, perhaps without realizing it, teachers who infuse such tested content into their future lessons are violating the Educational Defensibility Guideline. Students' test scores are apt to go up, but their mastery of the knowledge and/or skills the test is supposed to represent most likely did not go up as well.

In other cases, however, some teachers are far more direct in their quest for improved test scores. They may systematically identify the content of the items that they are not dealing with in class, then make certain that in subsequent years their students deal with those topics in sufficient depth to make sure students answer the test items correctly. This constitutes a blatant form of "teaching to test items." It is a clear violation of the Educational Defensibility Guideline and, in my mind, violates the Professional Ethics Guideline as well.

So, back to our fictitious example, if test scores in your child's school rise dramatically because teachers were teaching to test items, should you be elated? Of course not; there's clear deception afoot. Students' scores are rising not because students possess increased knowledge and/or skill in the subject area tested, but simply because they are being taught how to answer a particular set of items that appear on the test.

Let me pause for just a moment to draw a distinction that might arise if you ever find yourself talking to an educator about this topic. You've surely heard the expression, "teaching to the test." Usually, that expression carries with it a negative flavor. Well, if "teaching to the test" means *teaching students to answer actual test items correctly,* then that form of "teaching to the test" is clearly wrong. Teachers shouldn't do it. That form of "teaching to the test" violates both of the two guidelines given earlier in the chapter.

But if "teaching to the test" means *teaching students to master the knowledge and/or skills represented by the test,* then that kind of teaching is altogether appropriate. And different people use the expression, "teaching to the test," in different ways. So, if a teacher or school principal uses that expression, gently inquire about what is meant by it. You'll often avoid some unproductive discussions by tying down what educators mean when they advocate or denigrate "teaching to the test."

Testing Terms:

Teaching to the Test

Can mean either instruction aimed at specific test items **or** instruction aimed at the knowledge and skills represented by the test

All right, you've seen that increased attention to tested content will, from year to year, artificially increase students' test scores. In fairness to many teachers who are completely well-intentioned about their teaching, some teachers will engage in such preparation efforts with only the students' best interests in mind. They really want their students to learn what's important, and what's tested on a national examination would seem to be important. Other teachers, hopefully a decisive minority, will bang away at tested content simply to get students' scores up. The motives of those teachers are clearly suspect.

We can empathize with those teachers because they're caught up in a no-win game where increased scores on standardized achievement tests are the grand prize. But such inappropriate test-preparation, however understandable, is almost certain to reduce the quality of children's education, perhaps reduce the quality of your child's education. School is there to help children learn, not make educators look good.

Commercial Test-Preparation Materials

With educators under so much pressure to raise students' test scores, it is hardly surprising that a number of commercial firms have scurried to provide score-boosting services. To illustrate, extensive (and expensive) test-preparation booklets are available for the nation's major standardized achievement tests. Such test-preparation materials are directly designed to increase students' test scores. Officials in school districts, or particular schools, often buy copies of these materials for their students. The booklets then become part of a concerted effort to increase students' test scores.

What those commercial test-preparation booklets often contain are practice tests that are *remarkably* close to the actual version of the standardized achievement test then in use. The practice materials may not use an exact item (because that would constitute a copyright violation), but the cognitive task presented to the student in a practice item and in an item on the actual test are astonishingly similar. There are even serious content similarities between practice items and actual test items.

From the perspective of the folks who publish these test-preparation booklets, there is good sense in building practice tests that are as parallel to the real tests as possible. After all, if a practice test were off-target, how would that help a student score high on the actual standardized test? But by using practice tests that are near-replicas of actual tests, the practice materials run afoul of the Educational Defensibility Guideline. Students' test scores may go up, but their mastery of the content represented by the test probably won't.

You'd be surprised at the number of educational entrepreneurs who are getting into the score-boosting business. Only last month I was reading a newspaper for educational administrators who were being invited to sign up for workshops that can "raise your test scores 20 to 200 percent." I think you'll agree that a 200 percent hike in test scores is a pretty substantial increase. For those of you who are mathematically inclined, it's ten times as big as a 20 percent hike in test scores.

But some school administrators, buffeted by pressures to boost test scores, are likely to succumb to such blatant hustling. The problem with these commercial score-boosting extravaganzas is that, while they may raise students' test scores, they often do so by eroding the validity of any score-based inference about a student's achievement levels. Test scores go up, but the meaningfulness of those test scores evaporates.

It seems that every few weeks I receive either (1) an announcement of another book about how school administrators can increase test scores or (2) a description of a conference or workshop dealing with how to increase scores on standardized achievement tests. In your child's school, be assured that administrators are receiving the same sorts of commercial materials. And, because those administrators are being asked to improve scores on standardized achievement tests—tests constructed in such a way that legitimate score-improvement is unlikely—it's possible your district administrators or school administrators may succumb to the lure of these quick-fix score-boosting approaches.

Departures from Test-Administration Requirements

There's yet another way that students' scores on standardized achievement tests may rise. And that is by educators' not following test-administration procedures properly. Remember, standardized achievement tests are supposed to be administered in a predetermined *standardized* fashion, that is, with a specified time allowed for students to respond, no on-the-spot item-coaching by teachers during the test, and so on. Yet, because of the unjust requirement that teachers raise scores on tests that do not measure legitimate instructional improvement efforts, some teachers will "make allowances" during the actual test-administration itself.

For instance, they may give students "a few extra minutes" to finish a subsection of the test that most students haven't completed yet. Or teachers may walk around the class during an actual test-administration session and, if they see that a student has made a mistake, say something such as, "you might want to think about that item again." There are, indeed, all sorts of subtle adjustments in test-administration procedures that will give students a better chance to score well. Some teachers, understandably but not acceptably, will engage in a raft of these subtle score-boosting adjustments during the test's administration.

Then there are self-serving decisions made at the school or district level to raise the scores that are reported to the public. One of the most common examples is to exclude certain students from the testing itself. For instance, even if *all* students are supposed to take a standardized achievement test, district officials find ways to circumvent this requirement. Perhaps the district's learning-disabled students are hastily scheduled to take part in an off-campus field-trip on the day of the test. Such practices are often described as "Don't test; don't tell." Such policies may make a district's test performances look better. They do so *dishonestly*, however, so such student-exclusion practices clearly violate the Professional Ethics Guideline.

Score-Boosting and Your Child

Before looking at how efforts such as those just described might impact the education your child receives, let me briefly review the key points considered so far. First, educators are under considerable pressure to raise scores on standardized achievement tests because many people, although mistakenly, believe such tests can be used to measure instructional effectiveness. Second, standardized achievement tests, insensitive to detecting the effects of even first-rate instruction, do not provide teachers with content descriptions sufficient for on-target instructional planning. Third, pressured educators sometimes employ procedures to raise test scores that violate one or both of the two guidelines presented earlier in the chapter, namely, *professional ethics* or *educational defensibility*.

If it turns out that in your child's school, or in your child's classroom, there are score-boosting efforts that violate either of these guidelines, then there's a strong likelihood that your child's education will suffer. If teachers violate the Professional Ethics Guideline, they may be serving as an inappropriate model for your child. You don't want your child observing a teacher whose message is that "the quest for higher test scores justifies questionable test-preparation practices." If teachers violate the Educational Defensibility Guideline, your child's strengths and weakness may be masked (and as a result, not addressed instructionally) because the test-boosting procedures distort the test's assessment accuracy.

In either of these cases, you need to bring to the attention of an appropriate educator or official what's going on so that it can be stopped. I say an appropriate educator or official, because the nature of the inappropriate practice will dictate whom you should be contacting. For instance, if a teacher is engaging in inappropriate test-preparation activities in that teacher's classroom, then the school principal is the person you should contact. If the school principal has devised an inappropriate test-preparation program, then you should see the district's superintendent. If a district superintendent, however, has installed a district-wide score-boosting effort that you think violates either of our two test-preparation guidelines, then you may need to communicate with members of the district's school board. And if the school board itself has established an inappropriate test-preparation policy, you may need to register your complaint in the opinion pages of your local newspaper. In short, you need to identify the culprit who provides inappropriate test preparation, then go gleefully over that person's head.

In the Appendix of this book, on pages 283–289, you'll find some draft letters regarding educational assessment. You are welcome to use any of these letters as is or modify them to suit your local situation better. One draft letter deals directly with inappropriate test-preparation practices.

Sham Detection

In recognition of the relentless pressure that's exerted on educators to raise students' scores on standardized achievement tests, parents need to be suspicious about substantial year-to-year improvements on those tests. If, in your child's school, there has been a big gain in scores, then you'd better start asking yourself, "How come?" Because students' performances on standardized achievement tests are not that readily changed from one year to the next, parents should typically view with a decent amount of doubt any *major* jumps in student's test scores.

Small year-to-year gains, or small year-to-year losses, are nothing to get excited about. Contrary to most people's belief that these standardized tests produce remarkably precise results, there's a considerable degree of wobble in children's test performances, even from one week to the next. Just because there are numbers involved, and even numbers with decimals, this doesn't signify that the scores yielded by standardized achievement tests are all that accurate.

So, if the principal of your child's school starts taking some credit for relatively teensy year-to-year gains, these gains could probably take place by chance alone. Remember Chapter 2's description of the standard error of measurement? That index of the consistency of an individual child's test performance should remind you that there's a good deal of imprecision associated with standardized test scores. Tiny year-to-year increases should not be considered all that significant.

The first thing you need to do when considering a school's year-to-year changes in standardized achievement test scores is view any dramatic gains with considerable caution. Be on guard against counterfeit score-boosting.

A Parent Puzzle

(Setting: Kelly Smith's parents have been informed, as have all other parents at Kelly's school, that "this year will be the year of giant increases in our students' standardized test scores." This message has been transmitted in the school's Parent Newsletter and was announced at the school's opening PTA meeting by Mr. Grimshaw, the school's principal.

During the first three months of the school year, Kelly has reported that as much as a third of available class time will be devoted to students' doing practice exercises similar to the items on standardized tests.

Kelly's parents are concerned with what seems to be an overemphasis on test preparation. Kelly's father sets up an early morning meeting with Mr. Grimshaw to discuss the situation. Here's what was said.)

Mr. Smith: "Thanks for seeing me so early, Mr. Grimshaw. I hope it didn't inconvenience you."

Mr. Grimshaw: "On the contrary, Mr. Smith, I'm delighted to meet with you. This early session meshes with my schedule perfectly. Now, what was it you wanted to talk about?"

Mr. Smith: "To be candid, Mr. Grimshaw, Kelly's mother and I are both troubled by the amount of time that is being given in Kelly's class to test-preparation, more specifically, to preparation for this coming spring's standardized achievement test."

Mr. Grimshaw: "But as you know, Mr. Smith, all of the district's schools are doing their best not only to teach students what they should learn, but to raise our district's test scores to where they should be. The more time we spend time boosting those test scores, the more that students like Kelly will learn."

Parent: If you were Mr. Smith, how would you respond?

- -

My Response: Based on what I'd just heard Mr. Grimshaw say, I'd continue the conversation for as brief a period as possible. What I'd do is ease out of the office because I'd sense that I need to be heading off to the district superintendent, Mr. Grimshaw's boss. I might say something such as, "I see. Do you think there's this same kind of preoccupation with test scores at all of the district's schools? Is it a board policy? I'm just curious."

My Reason: As always when dealing with educators, parents have to make a quick determination of the kind of person with whom they're dealing. This principal displays an immediate insensitivity to the difference between educating children and improving scores on standardized tests. This principal, I would conclude, will be of little or no help in clearing up the situation at Kelly's school. I'd politely scurry out of Mr. Grimshaw's office and set up an appointment with the district superintendent as quickly as possible. And if I received a similar response from the district superintendent, because that's quite possible, I'd be prepared to race to the district school board with my concerns.

Appraising Score-Boosting Procedures

If score-improvement procedures have been used in your child's school, you really need to find out more regarding the nature of those procedures. Your child is a good initial source of information regarding test-preparation activities. Just ask whether the child's teacher has had students do anything special to get ready for major tests.

The next stop would be the child's teacher. A simple, nonthreatening question could be posed about what sorts of test-preparation activities, if any, take place in the teacher's class. If there are no special test-focused preparation activities the teacher uses, then that's the end of it. If, however, there are formal test-preparation activities, then you need to know what they are so you can see whether those activities are consonant with the Professional Ethics and Educational Defensibility Guidelines.

If what the teacher describes to you seems to violate either of those two test-preparation guidelines, then you need to register some concern with the school's principal. Remember, activities that violate either of the two test-preparation guidelines are apt to be educationally harmful to your child. Such activities should cease.

Should Teachers Be Held Accountable for Promoting Measured Student Improvement?

I've been trying to get you to appreciate the intolerable situation in which many teachers today, possibly including your own child's teacher, find themselves. They are being pressured to increase scores on tests that, by their very nature, are insensitive to the detection of high-quality instruction. Does this mean, therefore, that teachers have no responsibility for promoting increased student achievement?

The answer to this question is a decisive *No.* Teachers *do* have a responsibility to increase the knowledge and/or skills their students possess. But those increases need to be measured by assessment instruments other than standardized achievement tests. In Chapter 13, I'll describe the kinds of assessments that are needed. I'll also show you how teachers can collect evidence of instructional effectiveness using those assessments. If you want to hold teachers accountable for the promotion of your child's increased knowledge and/or skills, it is possible to do so. In Chapter 13, you'll see how.

What Do You Really Need to Know about this Chapter's Content?

This chapter is, in a very real sense, closely linked to Chapter 3's dismissal of standardized achievement tests as measures of instructional quality. It is because teachers are forced to improve their students' scores on such tests that you may find some shoddy test-preparation practices taking place in your child's classroom. Here are the chapter's most important points.

- The pressure that educators are under these days to improve students' test performances is enormous. The tests that most people want used to display these improvements are standardized achievement tests.

- Because educational tests are only supposed to *represent* the knowledge and/or skills that children should learn, teachers should be directing their instruction toward promotion of the knowledge and/or skills represented, not toward the test itself.

- Yet, because the content-description materials accompanying standardized achievement tests do not provide sufficient clarity for teachers to plan their instruction, some teachers succumb to inappropriate test-preparation practices.

- One guideline by which to judge the appropriateness of a teacher's test-preparation practices is *professional ethics.* This guideline dictates that no test-preparation practice should violate the ethical norms of the educational profession.

- A second test-preparation guideline is *educational defensibility.* This guideline points out that no test-preparation practice should increase students' test scores without simultaneously increasing students' mastery of the content represented by the test.

- Several ways that some educators raise scores on standardized achievement tests were discussed, namely, (1) general test-taking preparation, (2) increased teacher attention to tested content, (3) use of commercial test-preparation materials, and (4) departures from test-administration requirements.

- Parents of children in a school where a dramatic year-to-year gain has been seen on standardized achievement tests should be suspicious regarding the legitimacy of those gains. It is appropriate for parents to discover what kinds of score-boosting activities have been carried out in the school. These activities can then be judged by the test-preparation guidelines of *professional ethics* and *educational defensibility.*

POSSIBLE PARENT ACTION–OPTIONS

You'll first need to decide whether you want to look into this test-preparation area at all. In some schools, the pressure on teachers to raise test scores is easy to sense. Every third sentence outlined by the principal, or so it seems, will somehow refer to the need for score-boosting.

1. By asking your child's teacher, or an administrator in your child's school, you ought to be able to find out whether there are any specific activities intended to help students perform well on standardized achievement tests or any other significant tests used in your school (such as a high-stakes state-developed test).

2. If there are any test-preparation activities geared toward boosting children's scores on standardized achievement tests, you might then judge their appropriateness according to the chapter's two test-preparation guidelines. If one or both guidelines have been violated, then this should be brought to the attention of your child's teacher or an appropriate official. As always, the spirit of your interaction with educators about this issue should be decisively constructive, not accusatory. The aim here is to help your child, and your child's classmates, get a better education.

3. You can, of course, bring educators' attention to the *Suggested Resources* cited at this chapter's conclusion.

SUGGESTED RESOURCES FOR YOUR CHILD'S TEACHER OR PRINCIPAL

Printed Materials

Mehrens, W. A., W. James Popham, and Joseph M. Ryan. "How to Prepare Students for Performance Assessments." *Educational Measurement: Issues and Practice, 17,* no. 1 (1998): 18–22. *In this essay, the authors set forth a series of guidelines to help teachers arrive at defensible preparation procedures aimed at the skills assessed by performance tests.*

Mehrens, W. A., and J. Kaminski. "Methods for Improving Standardized Test Scores: Fruitful, Fruitless, or Fraudulent." *Educational Measurement: Issues and Practice, 8,* no. 1 (1989): 14–22. *This essay was one of the first thoughtful analyses of the potential dangers associated with the preparation of students for standardized tests. It is still a thought-provoking piece.*

Taylor, Kathe, and Sherry Walton. *Children at the Center.* Portsmouth: NH: Heinemann, 1998. *This is a workshop approach to the preparation of students for standardized tests in grades K–8. The authors attempt to "coopt" standardized tests in the service of learning.*

Videotape Program

IOX Assessment Associates. *Test Preparation Practices: What's Appropriate and What's Not.* (5301 Beethoven St., Ste. 190, Los Angeles, CA 90066). *From this video program, educators can learn about two guidelines for evaluating test-preparation procedures. Four varieties of test preparation are then analyzed according to the two guidelines.*

12

HOW STUDENTS ARE GRADED

*I*n this chapter, you're going to be looking at an activity that, though not specifically focused on educational testing, is closely linked to it. You're going to learn about how students are graded.

You have, after reading this book's first eleven chapters, become an unusual parent. You know a good deal about educational testing. And because of that knowledge, it's really quite likely that you'll find yourself involved in education-related discussions both with educators and other parents. During those conversations, it would be surprising if one activity closely associated with educational testing didn't come up. I'm referring to *student grading*. Student grading, of course, is closely linked to student testing. If you are familiar with the ways that teachers grade students, you'll be able to be a better advocate for your child. That's why this brief chapter is intended to familiarize you with the nitty-gritty of how teachers grade their students.

Two Words—Two Meanings

Let's make certain that you and I are employing the same meaning when we use two terms around which this and the final chapter are fashioned. In casual conversation, you'll sometimes find educators using the terms *evaluation* and *grading* interchangeably. But these two words really stand for distinctively different education-related activities.

There was a time when educators didn't distinguish between *evaluation* of students and *grading* of students, but those days have passed. Because the evaluation of instructional programs has become such a prominent part of educational practice, when most educators encounter the term *evaluation* these days, they think about the evaluation of an educational program such as a newly installed parent–tutor program for students who are in need of remedial help.

When classroom teachers engage in *evaluation*, those teachers are typically arriving at conclusions about the quality of their own instructional efforts. In that sense, therefore, you should use the term *evaluation* to refer to "program evaluation." And because the program under consideration in most classrooms consists of the instructional activities provided to students by the teacher, *evaluation* is typically used to signify an attempt on the part of teachers to determine how well they're doing instructionally.

Testing Terms:
Grading
The assignment of quality-level designators to students

In contrast, the focus of *grading* is on *students*. When a teacher grades a student, the teacher is assigning some kind of symbol (we'll discuss several options later), such as a letter grade of *A, B, C, D,* or *F,* that signifies "how well the student has done." Although in most classrooms there's surely a relationship between the quality of the teacher's instructional program and the grades that students receive, those two notions are really independent. For example, Mrs. Bevins, a third-grade teacher, could evaluate her own language arts program very negatively because her instruction seemed to confuse many students. Nevertheless, Mrs. Bevins would still award grades of *A* to several students who, despite the confusing instruction, nevertheless seemed to grasp the language arts concepts being taught.

Testing Terms:
Evaluation
Judging the quality of instructional activities or the teachers who provide them

Ordinarily, teachers' judgments about their own instructional effectiveness, as well as their decisions about what grades to assign individual students, are greatly influenced by assessment results. Both grading and evaluation, as you'll see, can be illuminated by other sources of information. Neither of those two activities should be *ruled* by test results.

Student Grading

Teachers give grades. Indeed, one supposes that when the original blueprints for "teacher" were drawn, there must have been a mandatory grade-giving component included somewhere. Other than tradition, however, why is it that teachers dispense grades to students so regularly?

The answer is fairly simple. A teacher needs to let students know (1) how well they're doing, as when a teacher assigns interim grades based on how students complete various assignments during the school year, and (2) how well they've done, as when a teacher dishes out end-of-year grades to students. In general, both of these activities lean heavily on the assessment of student's learning.

Although there are other factors to be considered in grading students than simply how well the students have performed on classroom assessments, there's little argument that a *major* consideration in the grade a student receives should be the quality of the student's assessment performances.

Deciding on Grading Factors and Weighting the Factors

It is all too common, unfortunately, for teachers to give little serious thought to grading until they are confronted, face-to-face, with the need to give grades. (When I was a beginning high school teacher, I decided how to give my initial set of first-semester grades approximately thirty seconds before I had to assign those grades.) A more appropriate approach to grade-giving would be to think out—well in advance of the press of imminent grade-giving demands—just what factors should be used in awarding grades to students and, beyond that, just how much weight should be assigned to each of those factors.

It's likely that several of the grading factors a teacher uses will be based on students' assessment performances, but often on different types of tests. For instance, students' final examination results are apt to be weighted more heavily than students' midterm examination results which, in turn, are likely to be weighted more heavily than results on weekly quizzes. If a portfolio system is employed in the class, it is likely that substantial weight would be given to the evidence of students' capabilities reflected by the contents of their portfolios. In a similar vein, if students are required to respond to fairly elaborate performance tests, then surely the resulting student performances would be thought more important by the teacher than other, less demanding assessment activities. In short, teachers weight differently the importance of students' performances on various kinds of assessments based on teachers' judgments about the significance of the particular assessments.

Beyond assessment-based evidence, however, there are other factors that teachers typically employ when dispensing grades. For example, class participation, homework-completion rates, and classroom cooperation are used by some teachers as factors to be employed in the grading process. What is being suggested here is simple. Before teachers are faced with time-induced pressures to award grades, they should give serious thought to (1) identifying the factors to consider when grading, and (2) deciding how much each of those factors will count.

TABLE 12.1   An Illustrative Set of Grading Factors for a High School Government Class

---

Grading Factors	*Contribution to Final Grade*
1. Final examination	30%
2. Midterm examination	20%
3. One-month performance test	25%
4. Periodic weekly quizzes	5%
5. Homework-completion rate	10%
6. Classroom participation	10%

In Table 12.1, you'll find an illustrative grading scheme devised along the lines being recommended here. The fictitious illustration in Table 12.1 indicates what might have been decided on by a high school government teacher. Note that there are six factors, the first four of which are based on students' assessment performances. In the opinion of the fictitious teacher whose grading system is set forth in Table 12.1, a full 80 percent of students' grades should be based on the results of classroom assessments. You can see in the table that students' results on the one-week performance test actually count more than their results on the midterm examinations. That kind of weighting would reflect the teacher's decision. Remember, this is a fictitious example for illustrative purposes only. Teachers must decide what grading factors to use and how much to weight each of those factors. Hopefully, your child's teacher will tackle those two tasks thoughtfully.

Grade Designators

When teachers award grades, there are several options available to them. For final, end-of-term or end-of-year grades, it is necessary to adhere to whatever grade-designator system has been adopted by the district. Thus, if a district's policy is to use grades of *A, B, C, D,* or *F,* then the district's teachers must use those grades even if, during the course of the year, the teachers employed different grade-designator schemes in class. Although many school districts, or schools within those districts, have grading policies that are quite general, some grading policies are remarkably restrictive, even setting forth specific limits on the percentages of particular grades that can be awarded by teachers. Generally speaking, there are three major options available to teachers when they describe how well a student has performed. Teachers can use (1) letter grades, (2) numerical grades, or (3) verbal descriptors.

"Mr. Rath really does dispense his final grades with a flourish."

Most parents are familiar with *letter grades* because such grades have been widely used for a long, long time. A grade of *A* is admirable and a grade of *F* is foul. In some districts, teachers are also allowed to add plusses or minuses to letter grades, thus transforming a grading scale that has only five points (*A, B, C, D,* or *F*) to a grading scale with 15 points. A grade of *F-*, we assume, reflects genuinely wretched, rock-bottom performance.

A *numerical grading system* is usually organized around some chosen number of points such as 100, 50, or 10. Students are then given a number of points on each classroom assessment so that when they see their grade for the assessment, they realize they have earned, for example, "7 points out of a possible 10." Teachers must be careful not to get their numerical grading scales confused because a student who received 89 points "out of 10" would be undeservedly jubilant.

Verbal descriptors are used instead of numerical or letter grades when teachers rely exclusively on phrases such as "excellent," "satisfactory," and "needs improvement." The number of such phrases used—that is, the number of possible verbal-descriptor grades that might be employed—is up to the teacher. If verbal-descriptor grades are used throughout an entire district, the choice of verbal descriptors is typically decided by district officials.

Counting Scores versus Giving Grades

It's delightfully easy for teachers to score a twenty-item True–False test. All they have to do is count up the number of correct answers that a student supplied, then divide that sum by twenty. What the teacher gets as a consequence of such fairly low-level arithmetic is a "percent correct." And when teachers pass back students' test papers with a percent correct on each paper, most students have a pretty good idea of what that means. Those students who earned percent-correct scores of 95 or 100 are elated; those who earned scores of 55 or 60 are less enthused. (They would be particularly dismayed if they realized that on a True–False test they should get 50 percent correct by chance alone.)

However, when a teacher calculates students' percent-correct scores for any type of selected-response test, the teacher is not giving students grades. Rather, the teacher is simply calculating the proportion of correct answers selected by the student. To give a student a *grade,* the teacher needs to take another step by indicating *how good* a given percent correct is. Remember, a teacher grades students to let them know how well they're doing. And even though most students realize that if they scored at or near 100 percent correct on a test, they've done pretty well, it's also possible that, on a particularly tough test, a 75 percent correct score would be a very fine performance. That's why teachers need to assign grades.

Although teachers who use selected-response tests can delay the necessity to make grading decisions by giving students a series of percent-correct scores throughout the school year, teachers who use constructed-response tests are usually faced with the need to make grading decisions somewhat earlier.

For example, if an English teacher's students have churned out an original sonnet as part of their midterm examination, it's pretty tough to assign such sonnets a percent-correct score. But it is possible. Some teachers go through a complex series of grade-avoidance procedures even for constructed-response tests, by establishing a maximum number of points attainable, then giving students feedback in such forms as "27 points earned out of 40." As with teachers who rely on percent-correct scores for selected-response tests, this simply delays the moment of truth when grades will, indeed, have to be determined.

I am not suggesting that teachers who provide along-the-way feedback to their students in the form of percent-correct or proportion of points earned, are displaying evaluative cowardice. As a high school teacher and a college professor, I've used such systems many times. I'm only trying to point out that score-counting is not grade-giving, and that teachers ultimately have to give their students grades.

Grade-Giving Options

Let me describe the three most common grade-giving approaches used in our schools. Each of these approaches can be employed not only for end-of-term or end-of-year grades, but also for grading the performances of students during the school year. In other words, these three grading approaches can be applied whether a teacher is assigning Johnny an end-of-term grade in science class or a grade for Johnny's two-week experiment dealing with "Psychological Depression in Earthworms." You're probably already familiar with the three grading approaches to be described because, when you were a student, you most likely encountered them all.

Absolute Grading

When grading *absolutely,* a grade is given based on a teacher's idea of what level of student performances is truly necessary to earn a particular grade, for instance, an *A.* So, if an English teacher has established an absolute level of proficiency needed for an *A* grade, and in a given class one year no student performs at that level of proficiency, then no student would get an *A* that year. Conversely, if the teacher's absolute grading standards were such that *all* students had performed beyond the necessary level, then the teacher would shower all students with *A* grades. An absolute system of grading has much in common with a criterion-referenced approach to testing.

The major argument in favor of an absolute approach to grading is that there are legitimate levels of expectation for students which, although judgmentally determined by teachers, must be satisfied in order for specific grades to be awarded. And, of course, teachers actually form their absolute expectations based on seeing how students *usually* perform in their classes. Absolute expectations, therefore, flow from one's normative experiences.

Relative Grading

When teachers grade *relatively,* a grade is given based on how students perform in relation to another. Thus, for any group of students, there will always be the *best* and the *worst* performances. Those students who outperform their classmates will get high grades irrespective of the absolute caliber of the students' performances. Conversely, because some students will always score relatively worse than their classmates, such low scorers will receive low grades no matter what. This system of grading is similar to a norm-referenced approach to testing.

As I suggested earlier, there is a sense in which even a teacher's *absolute* expectations regarding the level of performance needed to achieve an *A, B, C, D,* or *F* are derived from years of working with students and discerning how well students are capable of performing. But a relative grading system uses the students *in a given class* as the normative group, not all the students whom the teacher has taught in the past.

The chief argument for a relative system of grading is that because the quality of the teacher's instructional efforts may vary, and the composition of a given group of students may vary, some type of class-specific grading is warranted. Teachers who use a relative-grading approach tend to appreciate its flexibility because grading expectations change from class to class.

Aptitude-Based Grading

When grading on *aptitude,* a grade is given to each student based on how well the student performs in relation to that student's academic potential. To illustrate, if a particularly bright student outperformed all other students in the class, but still performed well below what the teacher believed were the student's capabilities, the student might be given a *B,* not an *A.* In order to grade on the basis of children's aptitude, of course, the teacher needs to have an idea of what children's academic potentials really are. To gain an estimate of each student's academic aptitude, teachers either need to rely on the student's prior performance on some sort of academic aptitude test or, instead, must form their own judgments about the student's academic potential. Because academic aptitude tests are being administered far less frequently these days, in order to use an aptitude-based grading approach teachers will generally need to arrive at their own estimate of a student's cognitive potential.

The main argument in favor of aptitude-based grading is that it tends to "level the playing field" by grading students according to their innate gifts. Thereby, aptitude-based grading is thought to encourage students to fulfill their potential. A problem with this grading approach, as you might guess, is the difficulty of deciding on just what each student's academic potential really is.

As indicated earlier, any of these three grading approaches can be used to assign grades for individual efforts of students, such as their performances on a short essay examination, or for arriving at a student's total-year grade. For instance, thinking back to Chapter 9's treatment of portfolio assessment, it would be possible for teachers to use any of the three grading approaches in order to arrive at students' portfolio grades, grades that might be dispensed in letter, numerical, or verbal form. (Musically inclined teachers might distribute grades lyrically against a background of gentle guitar chords.)

Hodgepodge Grading

Given the substantial grading options available to teachers, how do teachers end up grading students? Well, several researchers have recently concluded that most teachers assign *hodgepodge grades.* A hodgepodge grade is one based on the teacher's loosely combined judgment of students' (1) assessed achievement, (2) effort, (3) attitude, (4) in-class conduct, and (5) growth.

Teachers who employ hodgepodge grading typically hope for uniformly high performance in all five areas, and recognize that really poor student performances in any one area might lead to lower grades. Students' achievement, effort, attitude, conduct, and growth, however, are all combined subjectively by the teacher. In hodgepodge grading, there are no scientific-looking quantitative models that, based on students' performances in a variety of areas, obligingly pump out clear-cut grades. Hodgepodge grading is much more mushy.

In one recent study of more than 300 teachers and over 7,000 students, hodgepodge grading was reported by teachers to be the most common approach they used when dispensing grades. Students confirmed that most of their teachers did, indeed, use a hodgepodge approach to grading. Interestingly, by and large the students supported their teachers' hodgepodge grading practices. It appears that students are willing to risk teachers' subjectivity in combining assessed achievement and other nonachievement factors. Or, perhaps more accurately, students are more willing to run *that* risk than to see teachers consider *only* a student's assessed achievement.

Do not be surprised, therefore, if your child is typically given grades on the basis of some hodgepodge of achievement, effort, attitude, conduct, and growth. At least for the time being, hodgepodge grading appears to be the most appealing grade-determination approach for many teachers and students.

Typical Grade-Communication Mechanisms

When teachers give in-class grades to students, those grades are usually written directly on the students' completed examinations, term projects, or whatever work products have been given grades. When teachers communicate to students' parents, on the other hand, there are three fairly standard grade-communication mechanisms employed.

Report Cards

First, there is the time-honored and oft-maligned *report card*. Report cards are intended to relay to the student's parents an estimate of how well a student is performing. Some report cards can be relatively terse documents with room for only a grade-per-subject and nothing else. In contrast, others can be elaborate documents with all sorts of information provided to parents. The more elaborate versions of report cards, of course, take far more time for teachers to complete and for parents to read. (I recall vividly being asked to review several of these voluminous report cards for several of my children. Frankly, after spending what seemed like an eternity reading those super-detailed reports, I concluded they told me far more than I ever wanted to know about my kids.) The nature of report cards typically depends on the preferences of district officials. Individual teachers usually don't have all that much to say in the composition of a district-wide report card.

Interim Reports

A second form of grade reporting to parents consists of *interim reports:* brief written communications to parents regarding their children's progress in school. In some instances, interim reports are little more than short notes indicating such things as a student's areas of strength and weakness as well as what the child should be working on at home. Interim reports can be much lengthier, especially if the teacher has recently completed a staff-development workshop on the joys of compulsivity. District policy may or may not govern the form and frequency of interim reports.

Conferences

The third form of grade reporting to parents relies on *parent/teacher conferences.* Such conferences, used more frequently with parents of younger children, allow the teacher to communicate more fully to parents regarding a child's progress and to give parents an opportunity to raise questions about the quality of their child's performances. Again, district policy may or may not prescribe the number and nature of such grade-focused conferences. Many elementary teachers, although they realize that parent/teacher conferences consume much time, appreciate the opportunity that such conferences provide, so they can offer parents a richer descrip-

A Parent Puzzle

(Setting: Last night your child, Pat, brought home a report card showing grades of C in several subjects that Pat had thought would be As or Bs. You've decided to visit Mrs. Havers, Pat's teacher, so you can see whether Pat's perceptions or Mrs. Havers' grades are out of whack.)

Mrs. Havers: "It's nice to see you again. I always enjoy visiting with you about Pat. What can I do for you today?"

Parent: "Well, frankly, it's about Pat's report card. You may remember giving Pat grades of C in social studies, science, and math. Pat had expected higher grades in all three areas. I was hoping you could help me understand what's going on in those three subjects."

Mrs. Havers: "It's interesting that you ask about those three subjects. Actually, if you only looked at Pat's test scores, then it would appear that a *B*, or even an *A*, is warranted in all three content areas. But that's if you *only* looked at test scores."

Parent: "What else do you look at?"

Mrs. Havers: "Actually, I look at a whole series of factors when I assign grades to my students. There's the children's classroom conduct as well as their test scores. But I pay particular attention to a student's growth over time and to the student's effort. In a sense, I try to see if students are achieving at their potential.

In the case of those three subjects, Pat's growth has been minimal. Moreover, Pat could be doing so much better in all three subjects. Pat's progress is way below potential. Does this make sense to you?"

Parent: If you were Pat's parent, how would you respond?

My Response: I'd reach an immediate judgment that Mrs. Havers is trying to play the grading game properly, so I'd most likely respond, "Your grading system makes a lot of sense to me. I see why Pat was looking forward to higher grades—based on test scores alone. But let's talk about that unachieved potential. What can I do to help?"

My Reason: After reading this chapter, you've hopefully concluded that teachers' grading practices vary widely not only in how they work, but in the expectations teachers have of their students. Mrs. Havers seems to be employing a hodgepodge grading system. Such systems really defy parental assault because they're based on many different loosely linked factors. It sounds like Mrs. Havers is trying to do a good job in grading her students. Therefore, I'd try to pitch in and help Pat make progress regarding growth and unachieved potential.

tion of their children's progress than would be possible with other grade-reporting systems. With the increasing popularity of e-mail communication, it's likely that we'll soon see teachers and parents holding electronic grade-reporting conferences.

Grading's Inherent Imprecision

Wouldn't it be nice if teachers never made mistakes when they grade students? But, as you probably know all too well from having been the personal recipient of school grades that were too low or too high during your own years as a student, teachers make grading errors. Certainly, teachers don't want to make mistakes in the grades they give to their students. However, grading is a judgment-based enterprise in which flawed decisions will surely be made.

Fortunately, in the long haul, such errors tend to balance each other out. Over the years, a given student will probably be on the receiving end of several undeserved high grades and several unwarranted low grades. What you need to remember is that if teachers do the best job they can in dispensing grades to their students—that is, if they assign grades carefully and with the kind of deliberateness suggested in this chapter—teachers will have done their grading as well as they can. Human judgment, as potent as it is, is not error-free. And it certainly isn't error-free when it comes to grading students.

Standard Setting in High-Stakes Tests

You should be aware that the same kind of judgmentally based choices about quality levels that individual teachers have to wrestle with must also be faced by those who must set the "cut-score" or "passing standard" for high-stakes tests. To illustrate, on all of the statewide graduation tests that must be passed before students receive state-sanctioned diplomas, a cut-score must be established to distinguish between those students who should receive diplomas and those who shouldn't. Because of the substantial attention received by those diploma-sanction tests, and their important consequences for individual students, considerable attention is invariably given to the establishment of such a test's passing standard.

Testing Terms:
Passing Standards

The cut-score determined necessary for a student to attain in order to pass a high-stakes test

The most common method of setting a passing standard for high-stakes tests was devised a number of years ago by a measurement specialist named William Angoff. Angoff's procedure calls for a standard-setting committee of educators to be established, then have its members render individual judgments about the difficulty level of every item in the test. Committee members did so by deciding on the proportion of qualified students who would answer each item correctly. For example, committee members might be asked, "How many students out of a 100 who are *just barely qualified* to receive a high school diploma would answer this item correctly?" Committee members' per-item difficulty estimates were then summed and discussed by committee members after they had been given data showing how difficult each item actually was (in a specially arranged tryout of the test) for a group of students similar to those for whom the test is ultimately to be used. The committee then learns of the consequences of setting various passing standards. In other words, committee members are told how many students (total students as well as different ethnic groups) would fail if the passing standard were set at particular points. Finally, after one or more days of item judging and group deliberation, a passing standard is consensually established by the committee for the high-stakes test involved.

Having moderated a good many of these standard-setting sessions, I want you to realize that even with all the whistles and bells of the high-stakes standard-setting process, most members of the standard-setting committee walk out the door at the end of the process every bit as uncertain they made a good decision as teachers do when they're deciding whether to give Hortense an "excellent" or a "satisfactory." Grading is a gunky, gunky game. If your child is an occasional recipient of a less-than-accurate grade, that's regrettable. But it should come as no surprise. Even when passing standards are set for high-stakes tests, there's a strong likelihood that mistakes will be made even by the most systematic and well-intentioned standard-setters. Grades given by teachers are apt to be much less precise.

You're always free to discuss your child's grades with the teacher who dispensed the grades. But don't be argumentative in such situations. It's possible that a grading error has been made, and that it will be recognized by the teacher. More often than not, however, you'll be running into hodge-podge grading. And a hodgepodge, as the dictionary says, is a *jumble*. It's definitely tough for parents to deal with a grading jumble if the teacher is in a jumble-defending mood. Don't be distressed if the grade that your child initially received ends up unchanged.

What Do You Really Need to Know about This Chapter's Content?

There are very few "truths" to be shared about grading. Here are a few that were treated in the chapter.

- Teachers' grading practices vary substantially. Although it may be desirable for teachers to systematically determine the factors on which grades are to be assigned, then weight those factors according to their importance, most teachers are far less systematic.
- The three chief grade-giving options are absolute grading, relative grading, and aptitude-based grading. Recent research suggests that many teachers employ a form of hodgepodge grading in which they consider a student's achievement, effort, attitude, conduct, and growth. Students both recognize hodgepodge grading and, in general, approve it.
- Grading is far less precise than is often thought. Even though many teachers try their best to make the awarding of student grades both accurate and fair, there is still substantial imprecision associated with the grading of students.

POSSIBLE PARENT ACTION-OPTIONS

If your child never ends up with grades that seem inappropriate, then you'll probably have no interest in undertaking any action linked to this chapter's content. But you might.

1. It's never a bad idea for parents to become more familiar with a teacher's grading approach. So, if the occasion ever arises when you can inquire about the factors your child's teacher uses when grading, that's not bad information to have. You'll need to make it clear to the

teacher that you're not attacking the grading system, only trying to understand it better.

2. If you do run into a substantial grading disagreement, then setting up a formal conference with your child's teacher makes sense. Now that you realize grading is such a judgmental enterprise, it's very difficult to dispute a teacher's grading scheme. However, by your *mild* inquiry regarding the teacher's grading rationale, you're likely to get the teacher thinking more seriously about the teacher's grading procedures.

3. There are some items in the *Suggested Resources,* of course, that you might wish to identify for the educators who work with your child.

SUGGESTED RESOURCES FOR YOUR CHILD'S TEACHER OR PRINCIPAL

Printed Materials

Association for Supervision and Curriculum Development. *ASCD Yearbook 1996: Communicating Student Learning.* Alexandria, VA: Author, 1996. *This collection of essays by thoughtful educational scholars provides a series of keen insights into the currently available options for describing students' progress—or lack of it. Thomas Guskey, the Yearbook's editor, has assembled a first-rate collection of essays relevant to the grading of students.*

Krumboltz, John D., and Christine J. Yeh. "Competitive Grading Sabotages Good Teaching." *Phi Delta Kappan, 78,* no. 4 (December 1996): 324–326. *This brief essay describes the dangers of a grading system that fosters competition among students.*

Linn, Robert L., and Gronlund, Norman E. *Measurement and Assessment in Teaching* (7th ed.). Upper Saddle River, NJ: Prentice-Hall, 1995. *In Chapter 13, "Marking and Reporting," the authors describe how teachers can most appropriately evaluate students' work, then report those evaluations to students and to parents.*

Stiggins, Richard J. *Student-Centered Classroom Assessment* (2nd ed.). Upper Saddle River, NJ: Prentice-Hall, 1997. *In the final chapter of his popular book about classroom assessment, Stiggins focuses on how educators can most effectively communicate students' achievement to parents and to students.*

Videotape Programs

Assessment Training Institute, Inc. *Student Involved Conferences.* (50 SW Second Ave., Ste. 300, Portland, OR 97204). *Two experienced assessment experts show how to successfully involve students as partners in parent conferences. They describe the importance of quality assessment, explain how to prepare for conferences, and present keys to making conferencing and follow-up useful and practical.*

Association for Supervision and Curriculum Development. *Reporting Student Progress.* (1250 N. Pitt St., Alexandria, VA 22314). *Viewers learn how to make reporting a pivotal part of the learning process, not simply an end-of-course evaluative exercise. A variety of novel grading schemes are described.*

IOX Assessment Associates. *Making the Grade: Helping Parents Understand What's Important.* (5301 Beethoven St., Ste. 190, Los Angeles, CA 90066). *Although this video was created especially for parents, it provides educators with a framework for reviewing their own grading practices.*

Northwest Regional Educational Laboratory. *Developing Sound Grading Practices.* IOX Assessment Associates (5301 Beethoven St., Ste. 190, Los Angeles, CA 90066). *This video explores the purposes of report-card grades, student characteristics that should be factored into grades, suitable sources of evidence for grading, and how to combine such evidence over time for grading purposes.*

13

How to Evaluate Teachers

*I*n this chapter, I want to direct your thinking to the issue of how a parent can tell whether a child's teacher is effective. There may be some years when you become genuinely concerned about the quality of your child's teacher. Clearly, you'd like every teacher encountered on your child's educational journey to be simply dazzling. There may be occasions, however, when your child draws a dud. Can the quality of teachers be judged? If so, how? The final chapter of this book will try to answer those questions.

Less Than Wonderful Teacher-Evaluation Systems

You would think that, because teachers have been teaching for hundreds of years, there would have been some first-rate procedures developed by now to determine a teacher's competence. In the United States, for example, researchers have been wrestling with the problem of how to evaluate a teacher's quality for almost a century. In that wrestling match, however, the problem is way ahead of the researchers.

There is, at this time, no widely accepted procedure for evaluating a teacher's instructional competence. In different localities, educational administrators have installed different kinds of teacher-evaluation mechanisms. But, to be candid, other than the parental pride often displayed by the architects of these local teacher-evaluation systems, there's little to commend most of these approaches to appraising the quality of teaching.

So, if you were hoping that you'd find a handy, time-tested method of telling whether your child's teacher is a winner or a loser, get ready to be disappointed. It's not that educational researchers and school administrators have not been *trying* to come up with defensible teacher-appraisal systems. Every sensible educational administrator knows that teachers differ in their quality. But the trick is to devise a teacher-evaluation system that is both fair and accurate. That's far easier said than done.

Obstacles

There are a number of serious obstacles confronting those who wish to establish sensible teacher-evaluation systems. Without going into elaborate detail, let me just highlight a few of those difficulties.

Unsatisfactory Outcome Measures

Most people would agree that the ultimate criterion by which a teacher ought to be judged is the growth made by the students being taught. But, as you saw in Chapter 3, standardized achievement tests don't provide satisfactory evidence of what students have learned in school.

And even if there are district-developed or state-developed tests of students' achievements, these tests are rarely administered more than once a year. So, if a fourth-grade teacher's students are tested in the spring of each year, it is silly to judge a teacher on the basis of changes in performances of the teacher's fourth-grade students. This year's fourth-graders are *different* children than last year's fourth-graders. Last year's fourth-graders are now fifth-graders. The teacher's new fourth-graders may be decisively different in their abilities than the teacher's previous crop of fourth-graders. Perhaps this year's fourth-graders were taught by an ineffective third-grade teacher, but last year's fourth-graders were taught by a super third-grade teacher who's since retired. What sense is there in comparing the test performances of two different groups of students?

Later in the chapter, I'll describe a way that teachers can collect meaningful test evidence about students' achievement levels before and after the teacher's instruction. If teachers follow the approach I'll recommend, you'll see that parents can place more confidence in whether the teacher has, in fact, promoted worthwhile growth in students. But it is silly to compare the test performances of two different sets of children, then try to infer anything about a teacher's instructional skills.

If students' performances on classroom tests are going to play a role in a teacher's evaluation, then it is all too possible that any teacher-made classroom tests may be too soft. It's only human nature. If teachers are going to be evaluated on the basis of how well their students perform on classroom tests, then some teachers will create classroom tests on which students have a better than middling chance of succeeding. There have been many instances when teachers, if they were to be evaluated on the basis of students' test performances, created inordinately easy tests. Parents should be aware of this possibility. So, the first obstacle in evaluating teachers is that there often aren't suitable outcome measures by which to determine changes in students' knowledge, skills, or affect.

Different Students

No matter on what basis a teacher is evaluated, so much of the success of what goes on in a teacher's class is determined by the students who walk through the classroom door. Suppose Teacher *A* gets a group of goody-goody, learn-a-lot children, but Teacher *B* gets a collection of disinterested future felons. There is likely to be a genuine difference in the instructional results produced in the two teachers' classrooms. Because the usual way that students are assigned to teachers makes it unlikely that the composition of different teachers' classes will be similar, it is difficult to contrast the effectiveness of teachers when so much of their success is dependent on the caliber of the specific students they are assigned.

And if you hear that statisticians have developed procedures so that the differences in students' ability levels can be compensated for by statistical procedures, be doubtful. Statisticians who make such claims are promising more than they can deliver.

Research-Based Instructional Procedures

A great deal of research has been devoted to the identification of the "principles of effective teaching." There's research, for example, showing that if teachers inform students about what a lesson's instructional objective is, the students will tend to achieve that objective more successfully. Then there's research indicating that if teachers give students a chance to practice a sought-for skill during the instructional process, students will tend to learn that skill better. There are, in fact, a substantial collection of such research-established principles about how teachers should teach, if they want students to learn well.

Therefore, you might think, all an observer (such as a principal) would have to do is watch teachers to see whether they employ these research-proven procedures. Those teachers who do so should be regarded as effective teachers. Those who don't should be regarded as ineffective. Yes, you might think that. But you'd be wrong.

The problem is that the research underlying the "principles of effective teaching" is *tendency* research. If a teacher uses these research-based principles, the teacher's students *tend* to learn more. But they might not. You see, research-based teaching guidelines are far from definitive. Teachers can violate a pile of research-proven principles, yet still get marvelous

results from children. There may be something in the teacher's personality, or the special style of working with students, that allows the teacher to depart from proven principles, yet still accomplish wonders with children. In short, you can't tell just by looking. At least you can't tell how effective a teacher is merely by seeing if the teacher uses research-established principles of teaching.

If a principal observes a teacher and finds that the teacher sleeps during class or that the teacher physically abuses children, then such a teacher should be dismissed without any hesitation. I'm not referring to such obvious instances of incompetence. More often than not, principals need to judge a teacher's effectiveness on the basis of evidence that's much less clear-cut. Seeing if a teacher fits a preestablished pattern of using "effective teaching principles" doesn't work. A teacher can adhere to a galaxy of research-based instructional principles, yet still be ineffectual. A teacher can violate a pile of research-based principles, yet still get great results with kids. Unfortunately, you can't tell just by watching teachers as they teach.

The Need for Professional Judgment

Because almost any source of evidence regarding a teacher's skill must be considered in the particular setting that the evidence is gathered, the best approach currently available for judging teachers is to have qualified professional educators consider *all* of the relevant evidence regarding a teacher, then render their best professional judgment about the teacher's competence.

By "qualified" professional educators, I mean that those educators have received specific training in how to judge a teacher's skill using diverse kinds of evidence. Ideally, those educators carrying out teacher evaluation would have to demonstrate, by some sort of performance test, that they really were "qualified."

The evidence about a teacher's skill must be considered *in context*, that is, the quality of the evidence must be judged so that sensible decisions can be made about how much to weigh each source of evidence. For example, suppose Mr. Billings were being evaluated by a team of three educators, namely, a teacher from Mr. Billings' school and two instructional supervisors from the district office. The evidence that the three-person review team had available for Mr. Billings was the following:

1. Ratings of Mr. Billings by the school's principal, Mrs. Wren, based on six 40-minute preannounced classroom visits. Mrs. Wren rates Mr. Billings only "so-so" in his teaching skills.

2. Mr. Billings' self-rating of his own instructional skill, assembled by Mr. Billings at the end of each month of school. Mr. Billings believes he is "well above average" in his teaching skills.

3. Scores of Mr. Billings' sixth-grade students on a spring administration of a nationally standardized achievement test. Mr. Billings' students score at about the 20th percentile based on national norms.

4. A summary judgment of Mr. Billings' instructional skills based on four 45-minute, unannounced observations of his teaching techniques by a district instructional supervisor. Mr. Billings is described as a "talented teacher who knows his instructional tactics quite well."

5. Anonymous evaluations of Mr. Billings' instructional practices by his students, collected from Mr. Billings' students near the end of the school year by another teacher. The average ratings of the students indicate that they think he is an "excellent" teacher.

6. Pretest versus posttest scores on three examinations constructed by Mr. Billings, administered in the fall and again in the spring. The school's principal, Mrs. Wren, has reviewed all three exams and regards them as "tough." All pretest-to-posttest gains are quite impressive. Students appear to have learned a good deal from Mr. Billings during the course of the school year.

Now, if the three-member review team considers all six sources of evidence, they might choose to discount the principal's ratings because they know Mrs. Wren's reputation for "saying something negative even about the most talented teachers." Mrs. Wren, the review team realizes, tends to be too stringent in her evaluation of teachers. Some of the school's teachers have said that "Mrs. Wren would find instructional deficits if she were evaluating Socrates!"

The review team might place little importance on the low standardized achievement test scores because Mrs. Billings is dealing with a largely low-income group of students whose backgrounds are apt to penalize them when they take standardized achievement tests. But the review team, *in this instance,* might consider each of the other four sources of evidence not only credible, but very convincing. The review team would surely reach a positive professional judgment about Mr. Billings' teaching competence.

What I've been illustrating is the considerable difficulty of coming up with defensible evaluations of a teacher's skills. Most parents, quite understandably, assume that there's a well-honed teacher-evaluation technology just sitting on the shelf, waiting to be used. Some district-level teacher evaluation programs are better than others. None is flawless.

Moreover, given the absence of accurate teacher evaluation systems, teachers' unions have quite often negotiated contracts for their members that make it unbelievably difficult to get a teacher discharged for lack of instructional skill. So, when school administrators identify a weak teacher who can't seem to improve, it is no small undertaking to fight through the legal battles necessary to get the teacher discharged. If the teacher has been teaching for several years, and has been granted *tenure* by the district, then it is next to impossible to terminate the teacher's employment.

Two Grounds for Dismissal

I have personally been carrying out research regarding teacher evaluation for over forty years. I've tried out just about any conceivable approach to teacher evaluation during that period, and most of those approaches have fallen flat. I know how tough teacher evaluation is because I've seriously tried to evaluate teachers.

Back in the early sixties, I even kept track of the legal grounds in each state that could be used to get rid of poor teachers. With few exceptions, the two grounds that I encountered were always *incompetence* and *immorality.*

As I've tried to point out, the problems of assembling evidence to show that a particular teacher is incompetent, in the particular setting where that teacher functions, are substantial. That's because almost all of the evidence regarding the teacher's skill is debatable, that is, mighty slippery. *Incompetence*, therefore, is tough to establish.

Regarding *immorality*, it's pretty clear what's involved there. I remember fondly in the sixties when I was collecting all the rules and regulations from states regarding grounds for dismissal, one western state (that I'll identify only by saying it has lots of mountains) indicated that "a public school teacher could be discharged either for incompetence or gross immorality." Apparently, in that state, mere run-of-the-mill immorality wasn't sufficient to bounce a teacher. No, in that state the immorality had to be *gross*, that is, genuinely rocko-socko!

The Role of Students' Test Results in Teacher Evaluation

As you saw earlier, evidence regarding a teacher's ability to promote student growth is only one factor to consider in judging a teacher. But it is an important factor. If a teacher employs all sorts of research-supported instructional tactics, but the teacher's students don't learn, it's hard for parents to be very happy about that result. Yet, as you've already seen, standardized achievement tests are, by their very nature, not suitable for detecting a teacher's impact on students' achievement levels. Moreover, because standardized achievement tests are administered only once per

year, the changes in a teacher's students makes it impossible to see if a teacher is really contributing to meaningful student growth.

The Need for Pretest-to-Posttest Changes

If you want evidence regarding whether your child's teacher is promoting worthwhile growth on the part of the teacher's students, you really need to see (1) how the teacher's students were performing at the start of the school year, and (2) how they were performing at the end of the school year. You need to see, in other words, some sort of *pretest–posttest* evidence of student growth.

With young children, of course, the simple act of growing older can make a major difference in the way students respond to tests over the period of a nine-month school year. What a parent of a third-grader would like to see, therefore, is pretest–posttest evidence that a teacher's students had made *striking* pretest–posttest gains well beyond what might arise from increased maturity alone.

For teachers in elementary schools, the pretest–posttest period involved would typically be a full school year so that the pretesting of students would take place in the fall and the posttesting of students would occur in the spring. For secondary teachers, a pretest–posttest period might extend only over the course of a semester because teachers are often assigned new students at that time.

Teacher-Made Tests as a Likely Source of Evidence

In a few school districts, assessment instruments have been developed at district expense and made available for teachers to use in pretest–posttest data-gathering. More often than not, however, if teachers want to collect evidence showing that they are promoting worthwhile growth in students, the teachers are going to have to rely on classroom tests they construct themselves. And if the evidence from teacher-made classroom tests is going to provide compelling pretest–posttest evidence of the teacher's effectiveness, then it's pretty obvious that those tests should be measuring really worthwhile kinds of student outcomes.

To use a silly example, suppose a teacher constructed a test based on a student's ability to memorize an arbitrary sequence of three-letter nonsense syllables such as *nen, gup, lit, jad.* Well, even if there were a striking pretest-to-posttest gain in students' abilities to memorize such nonsense-syllable sequences, who cares?

If evidence of a teacher's instructional effectiveness is going to be collected via student tests on a pretest–posttest basis, the tests should deal with *important* knowledge, *significant* cognitive skills, or *worthwhile* affective outcomes. Pretest–posttest evidence of students' trivial accomplishments is not what's being sought.

The more important the outcomes being measured, the more compelling will be a teacher's collection of evidence showing that meaningful growth has occurred. For example, suppose a fifth-grade teacher can show parents that, over the course of a school year, the teacher's students have become markedly more skilled in being able to write descriptive essays (that is, essays describing an event, person, or place). Not only are students' posttest essays far more free of mechanical errors (in spelling, grammar, and punctuation), but the posttest essays also provide richer and more perceptive descriptions of whatever students have chosen to write about.

Parents who see evidence that their children have improved dramatically in their essay-writing skills ought to be genuinely pleased. And they ought to think that, at least with respect to promoting worthwhile student changes, the teacher who fosters that improvement should be given high marks.

Problems with a Simple Pretest–Posttest Model

One of the most intuitively appealing ways of determining how much students have learned is to pretest them prior to instruction, then provide instruction, and then posttest the students when instruction is over. Such a model is displayed in Figure 13.1.

A problem with the pretest–posttest model is that if the *same* test is used prior to and following instruction, the pretest may *sensitize* students to what's important so that the students devote unusual attention (during instruction) to whatever was covered on the pretest. This is referred to as the "reactive" effect of pretesting. Reactive pretesting tends to cloud any estimate of how much students have learned because excellent posttest performances may have occurred simply because students knew "what was coming."

Sometimes, the problem of reactivity is dealt with when teachers use a different pretest and posttest. But, as a practical matter, it is almost

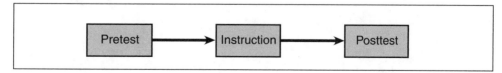

13.1 A simple pretest–posttest design

impossible for teachers to create two equally difficult test forms. Unfortunately, therefore, if the posttest is easier than the pretest, the students' "growth" may have occurred simply because of the difference in the two tests' difficulty levels. Or, conversely, a tougher posttest may lead to the erroneous conclusion that a skilled teacher has had no pretest–posttest impact on students.

A Parent Puzzle

(Setting: Mr. & Mrs. Smith believe their second-grade child, Robin, has a weak teacher this year. Robin almost always comes home from school unhappy about what's gone on that day. When Mr. & Mrs. Smith question Robin about what goes on at school, they get a response such as, "All we do is a bunch of drills on dumb stuff. I hate it!"

Because these parents recognize that the quality of a teacher's instruction falls within the responsibility of school administration, they set up a late October appointment with Mr. Mager, the school's principal. Here's what went on.)

Mrs. Smith: "Thanks for seeing us today, Mr. Mager. We're really troubled about the quality of instruction that Robin is getting, and we hope you can help."

Mr. Mager: "What is it that's troubling you, Mr. & Mrs. Smith? As you know, Robin's teacher is Mrs. Higgins. She's an experienced primary-grade teacher. In fact, this year marks her twentieth year of teaching children in grades K–3."

Mr. Smith: "She may have been teaching for a long time, Mr. Mager. In fact, maybe that's the problem. But we'll leave that to you. What my wife and I can tell you is that every day Robin comes home from school genuinely discouraged and feeling that she hates school."

Mrs. Smith: "And that's a complete turnaround from Robin regarding school. In kindergarten, with Ms. Rice, Robin loved school and, as far as we could tell, did very well. And Robin's first-grade experiences with Mr. Jergins were a delight. But now, Robin is becoming *so* negative about school. My husband and I are sure it's what's going on in Mrs. Higgins' class."

Mr. Mager: "I have to admit, a turnaround like that is troubling. As you probably recognize, Mrs. Higgins is a tenured teacher in this district, and she's long since demonstrated that she's capable of being a competent teacher."

Mrs. Smith: "But even tenured teachers can fall off in their effectiveness, can't they?"

Mr. Mager: "Yes, it's surely possible that even experienced teachers can fall into a rut. I'm not sure that this is the case in Mrs. Higgins' situation, but I will look into it. My autumn round of unannounced classroom observations is scheduled to take place in two weeks. Why don't I put in some extra time in Mrs. Higgins' class?

"I'll not say anything to her about your visit and the cause for it. But I will get back to you regarding what I see in Robin's class. If there are some problems, I'll

continued

A Parent Puzzle *(continued)*

work with Mrs. Higgins to correct them. Even tenured teachers, according to the district's collective bargaining agreement, must take part in evaluation-based improvement activities."

Parent: If you were Mr. or Mrs. Smith, how would you respond?

My Response: I'd probably say something like, "Great. That sounds fine. We'll look forward to your getting back to us."

My Reason: Mr. Mager, it seems to me, is adopting a sensible plan of attack on one of the toughest problems that a principal can face, namely, an incompetent tenured teacher. If Mrs. Higgins is as weak as Mr. & Mrs. Smith have reason to suspect, then Mr. Mager will doubtlessly need to carry out a series of improvement-focused, formal evaluation activities with her. If a systematic improvement effort fails to produce the necessary increase in instructional competence, only then will Mr. Mager be able to initiate formal evaluative activities that, in time, could result in Mrs. Higgins' termination.

Getting a tenured teacher dismissed is a major, major undertaking. If Mr. Mager can employ evaluation procedures to help Mrs. Higgins renew her zest for teaching, and Robin's class can receive better education, then that's clearly a desirable outcome.

Mr. Mager appears to be on the ball, but I'd stay in close touch. Squeaky wheels do, in fact, get more than their share of grease.

The Split-and-Switch Model

To avoid these problems, teachers can use the *split-and-switch* variation of the pretest–posttest model. This data-gathering design is portrayed graphically in Figure 13.2. The split-and-switch pretest–posttest model requires teachers to use two test forms of approximately equal difficulties, not identical difficulties. For example, a teacher might use two thirty-item multiple-choice tests of similar difficulties. Or the teacher could use two similar performance-test tasks calling for students to write persuasive essays about (1) the *pro* side of an issue or (2) the *con* side of the same issue.

As you can see in Figure 13.2, a teacher subdivides the class randomly into two half-classes (Half-Class 1 and Half-Class 2), then gives each half-class, as a pretest, one of the two test forms (Test Form A or Test Form B). Instruction then takes place, for example, during a three-month period, after which the test forms given to the two half-classes are switched so that Half-Class 1 that received Test Form A at pretest time now takes Test Form B as a posttest. Half-Class 2's posttest is also reversed from the pretest form.

Ideally, the pretests and posttests for each *test form* are coded (so that, later, they can be identified as pretests or posttests), mixed together, and *then*

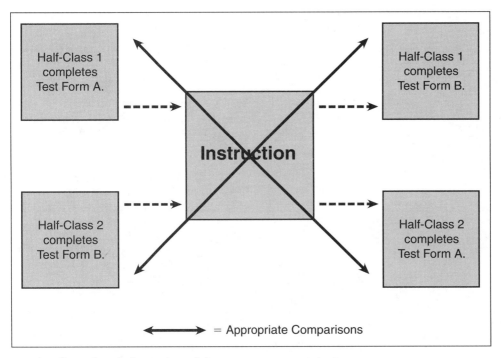

13.2 A split-and-switch version of the pretest–posttest design

scored without the scorer's knowing whether a given test was completed at pretest time or at posttest time. After having been scored, the codes are employed to redivide the test forms into their respective pretest and posttest piles. Then it can be seen if significant pretest–posttest growth occurred. In other words, the average performance of the tests completed by Half-Class 1 at pretest time is compared with the average performance of the tests completed by Half-Class 2 at posttest time. (The appropriate pretest-to-posttest comparisons are signified by the solid arrows in Figure 13.2.)

The split-and-switch data-gathering design rests on the assumption that a sample of roughly half the teacher's students will provide a reasonable approximation of how well the whole class would have scored on a test. Because pretest and posttest responses are to be compared on the same test form, but different students are completing the tests, the forms are obviously identical in difficulty. Yet, there is no pretest reactivity (because the students taking Test Form A as a posttest, for example, have never seen that test form previously). The teacher, in essence, has two opportunities (the Test Form A contrast and the Test Form B contrast) to see how much students have learned.

The split-and-switch data-gathering model can be used with affective assessments as well as with cognitive ones. Because affective pretests are especially likely to be reactive, the split-and-switch model works quite well with such assessments to see if desirable changes in students' affect have occurred.

If a teacher really wanted to assemble persuasive evidence of the teacher's effectiveness, then the teacher might enlist the assistance of non-partisan scorers such as other teachers or even parent volunteers. Because those scorers are *blindscoring* a set of intermixed pretests and posttests, that is, judging all student responses without knowing at which time (pretest or posttest) the responses were provided, any evidence seen of pretest-to-posttest growth won't be regarded as simply the partisan appraisal of a self-interested teacher who "sees student growth even when none exists." When students' results are blindscored by nonpartisans, inferences about a teacher's skill are clearly more compelling than if teachers score their own students' pretests and posttests.

One of the attractive features of the split-and-switch data-gathering design is that teachers don't need to have test-scorers who bring identical scoring standards to the enterprise. To illustrate, suppose Mother Martin and Father Firth are two parent-volunteer scorers. Mother M. is a "tough" scorer, while Father F. is a "softy." Because Mother M. will be stringent as she scores *both* the mixed-together pretests and posttests, her stringency will come crashing down on students in an even-handed manner. The

same is true for Father F.'s marshmallow standards. He'll score the pretests as softly as he'll score the posttests. Consequently, when the pretests and posttests have been sorted out, irrespective of who supplied the scores, the same scoring standards will have been applied to both. Observed pretest–posttest *gains* will be real gains.

One Indication of a Teacher's Instructional Skill

Use of the split-and-switch pretest–posttest design can supply one important type of evidence regarding a teacher's instructional skill. If you wish to bring the attention of your child's teacher to this data-gathering design, a step-by-step approach to its implementation is supplied as an appendix to this chapter. If you want to learn more about this data-gathering design yourself, you'll find that the step-by-step description in the chapter appendix supplies additional details.

Testing Terms:

Formative Teacher Evaluation

Improvement-focused appraisals of teachers' instructional activities

Testing Terms:

Summative Teacher Evaluation

Appraisals of teachers' instructional activities designed to support permanent decisions about the teacher such as dismissal or the granting of tenure

Two Types of Teacher Evaluation

There are two sorts of evaluation that bear on the appraisals of teachers' instructional efforts. *Formative evaluation* refers to the appraisal of the teacher's instructional activities for purposes of improving those activities. For example, suppose Mr. Coe is teaching a three-week social studies unit on International Cooperation to a class of fifth-graders for the first time. Suppose further, while you're supposing, that Mr. Coe wants to improve the social studies unit so that the next time he offers it, the unit will be more effective. That's a task for formative evaluation, and students' assessment results will surely help Mr. Coe.

Summative evaluation, in contrast, is not improvement-focused. Summative evaluation refers to appraisals of teachers' competencies in order to make more permanent decisions about those teachers such as (1) continuation of employment or (2) awarding of tenure. When teachers are evaluated summatively, they're almost always evaluated by some type of external evaluator, for example, an administrator, an instructional supervisor, or a specially trained teacher evaluator.

Classroom teachers, therefore, usually do their own formative evaluations because they often wish to spruce up their instruction. For summative evaluation, classroom teachers may be called on to supply evidence (such as students' test results) to other educators who will then use that evidence for evaluative purposes.

What Do You Really Need to Know about This Chapter's Content?

You've now had a quick peek into the workings of teacher evaluation. As a parent, you surely hoped that the news about our skill in evaluating teachers would be more positive. I'm sorry it wasn't. However, here are those things I hope you concluded from the chapter.

- At present, despite almost a century of serious research activity, the procedures available to evaluate teachers are not all that wonderful. Serious practical and technical problems have prevented the creation of first-rate systems of evaluating teachers.
- Because no single source of evidence provides a definitive indication of a teacher's instructional skill, and because so much of a teacher's accomplishments are influenced by the particulars of the teacher's setting (particular students, a particular principal, a particular school building, particular textbooks, and so on), a professional judgment approach to teacher evaluation was recommended. In such an approach, qualified educational professionals would evaluate a teacher in context by judging the quality of various indicators of the teacher's effectiveness.
- Because one important type of evidence regarding a teacher's skill is the extent to which a teacher can promote students' growth, a split-and-switch pretest–posttest design was recommended for the collection of evidence regarding the growth of a teacher's students.

POSSIBLE PARENT ACTION–OPTIONS

I'd advise you to move very cautiously if you think your child has been dealt a weak teacher. The removal of incompetent teachers is much tougher than you'd think. It makes more sense for administrators to devise a formative evaluation plan in which the focus is on improving a teacher's instructional efforts.

1. One of the most productive things a parent can do if there's doubt about a teacher's competence is to raise a concern with the teacher's principal. That's one of the major responsibilities of school administrators—to help teachers improve their instructional quality. If you visit a principal with an improvement focus in mind, you'll often find a principal who'll be willing to help the teacher in question initiate a meaningful improvement program.

2. You might suggest to a principal that the collection of preinstruction and postinstruction test results could shed light on the teacher's ability to promote measurable growth in students. The step-by-step implementation of the split-and-switch design presented on pages 273–275 could be placed in the principal's hands with the suggestion that such evidence be collected by the teacher in question. Ideally, both cognitive and affective assessment would help illuminate the principal's estimate of the teacher's competence.

3. An item or two from the chapter's *Suggested Resources,* of course, might be brought to the attention of your child's principal.

SUGGESTED RESOURCES FOR YOUR CHILD'S TEACHER OR PRINCIPAL

Printed Materials

Journal of Personnel Evaluation in Education. This entire journal is devoted to the appraisal of educational personnel. Educators who have access to this journal will encounter a continuing series of analyses and research studies bearing on the evaluation of teachers and administrators.

Popham, W. James. *Educational Evaluation.* Los Angeles: IOX Assessment Associates, 1993. *Chapter 15 of this text about educational evaluation is entitled, "Teacher Evaluation—A Special Challenge." The role of professional judgment is endorsed for the appraisal of teachers.*

Stanley, Sarah J., and W. James Popham (Eds.). *Teacher Evaluation: Six Prescriptions for Success.* Alexandria, VA: Association for Supervision and Curriculum Development, 1988. *In this edited volume, six approaches to the evaluation of teachers are described by different authors. Educational practitioners then comment on each evaluative approach.*

Videotape Program

Hunter, Madeline. *Teaching and Testing: A Conversation with Dr. Madeline Hunter.* IOX Assessment Associates (5301 Beethoven St., Ste. 190, Los Angeles, CA 90066). *Madeline Hunter was one of the most influential staff developers in the United States. This video, recorded a few years before her death, reveals how Dr. Hunter conceived of the linkage between testing and teaching.*

Educational Testing Final Confidence Inventory

Directions: This inventory is designed to measure the confidence you would have in carrying out certain activities related to educational testing. There are no right or wrong answers, so please answer honestly. Below, at the left, are 10 things a parent might be called on to do. If *you* were required to carry out each activity, indicate how confident you would be by circling the appropriate response for that activity using the following scheme:

VC =	FC =	LC =	NC =
Very Confident	Fairly Confident	A Little Confident	Not Confident at All

If *you* were asked to:	How confident could you be?			
1. explain to a friend why standardized achievement tests shouldn't be used to evaluate instruction.	VC	FC	LC	NC
2. discuss with a friend the most common ways that teachers give grades to students.	VC	FC	LC	NC
3. help other parents to draft a set of guidelines about "how *not* to prepare students for major tests."	VC	FC	LC	NC
4. describe to a friend the chief strengths and weaknesses of two-choice test items.	VC	FC	LC	NC
5. lead a parent study group's discussion of "Portfolio Assessment: Should Our School Use It?"	VC	FC	LC	NC
6. explain to another parent what is meant by the expression "assessment validity."	VC	FC	LC	NC
7. describe to a friend how teachers could collect convincing test-based evidence of their instructional effectiveness.	VC	FC	LC	NC
8. explain to a parent–teacher meeting what is meant by a performance test and how such tests can guide instruction.	VC	FC	LC	NC
9. tell a school principal what kinds of affective assessment instruments should be used in your child's school.	VC	FC	LC	NC
10. show parents what a rubric is and how it should be built if it is going to help instructional decision making.	VC	FC	LC	NC

Scoring Guide: Score each item using the following key: VC = 4, FC = 3, LC = 2, NC = 1; then add the scores for all 10 items. Scores of 30–40 = substantial confidence; 20–29 = moderate confidence; 10–19 = weak confidence.

AN APPENDIX FOR YOUR CHILD'S TEACHER

Collecting Evidence of Instructional Effectiveness

For teachers who wish to use the split-and-switch data-gathering approach, the following steps should be taken:

1. Teachers will need two forms (A and B) of a test. The test can be a traditional selected-response test or a more elaborate constructed-response performance test (complete with a rubric). Ideally, the two test forms should both be measuring a student's mastery of an important skill or knowledge domain and should be at least *approximately* equivalent in difficulty. Label one form as Form A and another as Form B. The test can also assess students' affect.

2. For the pretest, half of a class should receive one test form and the other half of a class should receive the other test form. It is suggested that the teacher simply count the number of students, for example, thirty, then go down the alphabetical class list so that the first-listed fifteen students receive one test form and the other students receive the second test form.

3. The teacher should be sure to use the same kind of paper on test forms for both the pretest and posttest so that either the teacher (or, if the teacher prefers, colleagues or parents) can subsequently "blind-score" the tests without knowing which responses were made as pretests or posttests. The teacher should direct all students, at both pretest and posttest, to put their names on their responses but *not* to put a date on their responses. Ideally, the teacher should ask students to put their names on the *back* of the last page of the test form.

4. Next, using a code that only the teacher knows, the teacher should mark each pretest response unobtrusively (for instance, on the back of the last page) so that, *after* the papers have been scored, they can be identified as pretests. (The teacher might use a group of numbers that appear to be random, but the teacher knows that the next-to-the-last number is always even.) Posttests, of course, would have a different coding scheme so that, for instance, the second number in the sequence was always odd. Any coding scheme will work as long as the teacher can tell how to separate pretest and posttest responses after they have been scored.

5. The teacher must encourage students to do well on both the pretest and the posttest by stressing, in the teacher's own words, the significance of the tests. For the pretest, the teacher may want to provide some small grade or similar incentive for students' participation. Ideally, the students' motivation levels should be the same for both the pretest and the posttest.

6. The teacher should then teach as effectively as possible toward the skill, body of knowledge, or affect being assessed by the test forms. *The teacher must not teach toward the particular items being used for pre-posttests.* Teachers want to promote increases in students' skill, knowledge, or affect, not students' familiarity with a given test's particulars. If teachers instruct toward the items on the test forms, an inaccurate picture of students' growth will be present.

7. At posttest time, teachers should reverse the test forms taken at pretest so that all students will be responding to different test forms. For instance, using Form A and Form B, a teacher must make sure the students who completed Form A at pretest time get Form B at posttest time (and vice versa).

8. When the posttests have been collected, the teacher should split them into Form A and Form B. Then the teacher must code the posttests so they can be distinguished from the pretests.

9. Next, the teacher must mix the Form A pretests and posttests together and, thereafter, do the same for Form B. When the tests are scored, the scorer must not know whether a pretest or posttest is being scored.

10. Teachers may wish to score each set of tests (Form A, then Form B) themselves, or the teacher may wish to call on a colleague or parent to supply truly nonpartisan scoring.

11. After the student responses to a form have all been scored, using the preestablished coding system, the teacher should separate students' responses into pretests and posttests. Then, for number-correct tests, or affective inventories, the teacher should compute the average pretest and posttest scores for the pretests and for the posttests. For skill-determining performance tests, a teacher should calculate the percentage of papers assigned to different rubric-defined quality categories. This process should be repeated for the other form. The teacher should then compare students' pretest and posttest performances.

12. If the teacher intends to use the students' responses to posttests (for any cognitive tests) for grading purposes, the teacher should make certain that the two test forms are approximately equal in difficulty. If not, the teacher must take any difficulty differences into consideration when grading.

AN APPENDIX OF DRAFT LETTERS FROM PARENTS

Draft Letters Regarding Assessment-Related Issues

The following collection of draft letters is intended to help you communicate with various individuals about issues you might have related to educational assessment. Please feel free to use any of these draft letters, with or without modification. You'll note that each draft letter is written to a specific individual (such as the principal of your child's school). With minor changes, most of the draft letters can easily be directed to another individual (such as your child's teacher or the superintendent of your child's school district).

The basic message contained in each draft letter would always be made more effective if the letter is particularized. In other words, while the draft letter might say, "our school," it would be better to use the actual name of your child's school, for example, "Rhoda Street Elementary School." It would also be helpful if you named your child and pointed out how the issue you're writing about might have an impact on your child.

For an actual letter to accomplish its mission, I hope you'll try to maintain a positive tone in the letter. Most letter recipients are more responsive to constructive suggestions than negative castigations.

So, please look over the following draft letters. If any of them seem to address your concerns, now or in the future, simply mix, match, and modify the drafts as you wish. Then affix a stamp and let the postal service take over from there.

Your Concern: Excessive Test Preparation

If you think there's been an overemphasis on getting students ready for standardized achievement tests or any comparable high-stakes test, here's a draft letter to the principal of your child's school.

Inside Address Information   Date: _____

_____

_____

Dear _____:

    I want to register my concern that there seems to be an excessive emphasis in our school on getting students ready for the standardized achievement tests scheduled for administration during _____ *(give the month of the upcoming test-administration)*. The reason I'm concerned is that I'm fearful the teaching staff's preoccupation with raising scores on those tests may be preventing the teachers from covering other important skills and knowledge that the school's students need.

    I realize that you and your teaching staff are under considerable pressure to "raise test scores" because it is widely believed that students' scores on standardized achievement tests reflect the quality of a teaching staff and, by implication, the quality of the school's principal. I've been doing some reading on that topic, and I understand why it is that students' standardized test scores do *not* provide an appropriate indication of a teaching staff's competence. Scores on those tests are more a reflection of the student population served by a school than an indication of the skill of the school's educators.

    I hope that you and your staff will address this test-preparation issue in the near future. Parents want the school's children to get the very best education possible. I'm sure you do too. That will not happen, however, if our school's heavy emphasis on test-preparation deflects the school's teachers from dealing with the curricular content our children need.

                  Sincerely,

                  _____

Your Concern: Quality Rankings Based on Standardized Achievement Test Scores

If you find that your local newspaper is ranking schools based on students' scores on standardized achievement tests, here's a draft letter to the editor of your local newspaper.

Inside Address Information   Date: _____

_____

_____

Dear Editor:

Once again this year, the _____ *(give name of the newspaper)* has released a set of school rankings based on students' scores on standardized achievement tests. The implication of these rankings is clear. Schools with high test scores are considered effective; schools with low test scores are considered ineffective.

These sorts of quality rankings represent a misuse of standardized achievement tests. Many of the items on these tests measure students' socioeconomic status and their inherited academic abilities. Many of the items on those tests, therefore, do not measure what teachers are supposed to be teaching. It is grossly unfair to judge teachers' instructional effectiveness based on tests that really don't assess what teachers teach.

I am a parent, not an educator, but I think teachers in low-scoring schools are unfairly labeled as inadequate simply because of their students' performances on standardized tests. Conversely, teachers in high-scoring schools may become complacent because they're regarded as effective based on standardized test scores, even though this may not be true.

Educators definitely need to supply the public with solid evidence that our children are attaining worthwhile skills and knowledge in school. But standardized achievement tests won't supply such evidence. Standardized achievement tests measure what students bring to school, not what they're taught there.

Sincerely,

_____

Your Concern: Inadequate Staff Competence in Educational Assessment

If you find that the teachers and administrators of your child's school appear to possess little knowledge about educational assessment, you might wish to stimulate some interest in getting an assessment-focused staff-development program underway. Here's a draft letter to the superintendent of your local school district.

Inside Address Information   Date: _____

_____

_____

Dear Superintendent _____ :

    As a parent of a child in our school district, I'd like to call your attention to a problem that I hope you and your colleagues can address, namely, insufficient staff expertise in the area of educational assessment.

    Because you are our district's superintendent, you know better than most educators how important educational measurement has become during recent years. And I'm sure that many of our district's educators have a first-rate understanding of educational assessment. But, unfortunately, many do not.

    I realize that, during their graduate programs or teacher-training programs, many educators only have a casual brush with educational assessment. But there have been a number of significant advances in educational assessment during recent years that, frankly, I simply don't see practiced in our district's schools.

    I've just finished reading a book for parents about educational testing. The author contends that well-constructed educational assessments can make a major contribution to instructional quality. I'd like to see our district's students picking up those instructional dividends from well-devised assessments.

    Is there any way that you and your colleagues at the district office can provide staff-development in educational assessment for our district's teachers and administrators? If properly developed classroom tests can really improve educational quality in a district, we need to help district educators create the very best tests they can.

                           Sincerely,

                           _____

Your Concern: No Instructional or Assessment Attention to Student Affect

If your child's teacher never assesses students' attitudes, interests, or values, it's a pretty safe bet that the teacher devotes little instructional attention to the promotion of worthwhile instructional objectives dealing with the affective domain. If you'd like to see some classroom attention to affect, here's a draft letter to your child's teacher.

Inside Address Information   Date: _____

_____

_____

Dear _____ :

     I'm writing this letter to offer a suggestion. I hope you don't think I'm being presumptuous, but I've just finished reading a book for parents about educational assessment. In that book, there's a strong recommendation for teachers to use classroom assessments that deal with student affect, especially students' attitudes and interests. During conversations with _____ *(give your child's name)* about school, there's never been any mention of affective measurement. Perhaps it's going on and simply is not recognized by my child. However, if you're not currently measuring such things as students' interest in learning or their confidence in using the skills you promote, I wonder if you'd consider doing so. I think it's very important that _____ *(your child's name once more, please)* develop and maintain a positive affect toward education.

     I've run across some materials designed to help teachers assess student affect, and I'd be happy to share them with you if you're interested. (You can supply a copy of the eight-step procedure for developing Likert affective inventories found at the close of Chapter 10, as well as the *Suggested Resources* for that chapter, if the teacher is interested.)

     I hope you'll consider this only as a constructive suggestion. I found myself struck with the potential importance of affective assessment and instruction. I hope you'll agree.

                  Sincerely,

                  _____

Your Concern: Rubric-Less Evaluation of Your Child's Constructed Responses

If your child's teacher uses exams containing constructed-response items, but fails to supply students or parents with the evaluative criteria used in judging the quality of students' performances, here is a draft letter to your child's teacher.

Inside Address Information   Date: _____

_____

_____

Dear _____:

    I've been following with interest the performances of _____ *(give your child's name)* on the constructed-response items you often use on your tests. I'd like to help my child improve on those tests, and it's in that regard I write to you.

    I've been reading recently about the increased use of rubrics by educators. The heart of those rubrics, as I understand it, is the set of evaluative criteria by which the quality of a student's performance is judged. If students know in advance what a rubric's evaluative criteria are, then students can engage in self-evaluation as they provide their answers to a test's questions.

    Is it possible that you could supply advance rubrics for at least some of your test's items? As a concerned parent, I'd like to work with my child in using a rubric's evaluative criteria so that a higher quality of student performance is possible. I'd try to support your efforts at home if I could better understand how to do so. Rubrics would help.

    Thanks for considering this suggestion.

                         Sincerely,

                         _____

Your Concern: Too Much Pressure on Teachers to Boost Students' Scores on Standardized Achievement Tests

If it appears that educators in your district are being pushed to increase students' scores on standardized achievement tests, you might wish to tackle a draft letter to your district's school board.

Inside Address Information   Date: _____

_____

_____

Dear Board Member:

As a parent in the district, I'd like to bring what I regard as a serious problem to your attention. I regard the substantial pressure our district's teachers are now experiencing to raise standardized test scores as altogether unsound. Teachers and school administrators seem to talk about few other things whenever I attend any kind of parent–educator functions at my child's school. This tunnel-vision focus on higher test scores, I am convinced, cannot be in the best interests of the district's students. Teachers who are caught up in a score-boosting frenzy will simply be unable to devote their attention to the full range of our children's educational needs.

I've only recently finished reading a book written for parents about educational testing. In that volume, examples are given of the kinds of test items found in standardized achievement tests. What surprised me is that a good many of the items in standardized tests simply do not measure the things our district's teachers are supposed to be teaching.

District teachers are really the victims in this unfortunate situation. They're being forced to focus on raising standardized test scores, but the nature of those tests really precludes appropriate test-preparation efforts by teachers. I fear that many of the district's teachers, operating under intense score-boosting stress, may employ test-preparation activities with their students that are educationally unsound.

As our district's educational policymakers, you can change this situation. Wouldn't you at least investigate the extent to which the district's educators are being required to take part in a score-boosting game in which, unfortunately, they are destined to lose?

Sincerely,

_____